**Approaches to Teaching
Cabeza de Vaca's *Account*
and Other Texts**

Approaches to Teaching Cabeza de Vaca's *Account* and Other Texts

Edited by

Luis Fernando Restrepo

and

Carlos A. Jáuregui

The Modern Language Association of America
New York   2025

© 2025 by The Modern Language Association of America
85 Broad Street, New York, New York 10004
www.mla.org

All rights reserved. MLA and the MODERN LANGUAGE ASSOCIATION are trademarks owned by the Modern Language Association of America. To request permission to reprint material from MLA book publications, please inquire at permissions@mla.org.

To order MLA publications, visit www.mla.org/books. For wholesale and international orders, see www.mla.org/bookstore-orders. The EU-based Responsible Person for MLA products is the Mare Nostrum Group, which can be reached at gpsr@mare-nostrum.co.uk or the Mare Nostrum Group BV, Mauritskade 21D, 1091 GC Amsterdam, Netherlands. For a copy of the MLA's risk assessment document, write to scholcomm@mla.org.

The MLA office is located on the island known as Mannahatta (Manhattan) in Lenapehoking, the homeland of the Lenape people. The MLA pays respect to the original stewards of this land and to the diverse and vibrant Native communities that continue to thrive in New York City.

Approaches to Teaching World Literature 181
ISSN 1059-1133

Library of Congress Cataloging-in-Publication Data

Names: Restrepo, Luis Fernando, editor. | Jáuregui, Carlos A., editor.
Title: Approaches to teaching Cabeza de Vaca's "Account" and other texts / edited by Luis Fernando Restrepo and Carlos A. Jáuregui.
Description: New York : The Modern Language Association of America, 2025. | Series: Approaches to teaching world literature, 1059-1133; 181 | Collection of essays by Rolena Adorno and 13 others. | Includes bibliographical references.
Identifiers: LCCN 2024050195 (print) | LCCN 2024050196 (ebook) | ISBN 9781603296861 (hardcover) | ISBN 9781603296878 (paperback) | ISBN 9781603296885 (EPUB)
Subjects: LCSH: Núñez Cabeza de Vaca, Alvar, active 16th century. Relación y comentarios. | Núñez Cabeza de Vaca, Alvar, active 16th century—Translations—History and criticism. | Explorers—America—Study and teaching. | Explorers—America—Biography—History and criticism. | Explorers—Spain—Study and teaching. | Explorers—Spain—Biography—History and criticism. | America—Early accounts to 1600—History and criticism. | America—Discovery and exploration—Spanish—Study and teaching. | America—Discovery and exploration—Spanish—Early works to 1800—History and criticism.
Classification: LCC E125.N9 A77 2025 (print) | LCC E125.N9 A77 2025 (ebook) | DDC 970.01/6071—dc23/eng/20250203
LC record available at https://lccn.loc.gov/2024050195
LC ebook record available at https://lccn.loc.gov/2024050196

CONTENTS

Acknowledgments vii

PART ONE: MATERIALS

Classroom Texts 3
The Instructor's Library 6
Online Resources 9

PART TWO: APPROACHES

Introduction: Teaching and Unteaching Cabeza de Vaca 13
Luis Fernando Restrepo and Carlos A. Jáuregui

Cabeza de Vaca's *Account*

Cabeza de Vaca: His Life, Work, and Legacy 25
Rolena Adorno

Unteaching Cabeza de Vaca; or, How to Question the Culture of Conquest 39
José Rabasa

Mala Cosa, C'est Moi 52
Carlos A. Jáuregui

Intersectional Perspectives

Hidden in Plain Sight: Reading a Complex Esteban in and around *Naufragios* 68
Kathryn Joy McKnight

Gender, Transgender, and Queer Inbetweenness in the *Relación* 82
Paola Uparela

Other Accounts

The Southern Fiasco: Law and Writing in *Comentarios* 101
Loreley El Jaber

Colonial Reckoning: The Problem with Cabeza de Vaca 114
René Carrasco

Cabeza de Vaca across Disciplines

Early Spanish Expeditions in La Florida and the Archaeology of Conquest   124
   George Sabo III and Jeffrey M. Mitchem

North American Space in the *Relación*   135
   Vanina M. Teglia

Food Studies and *Naufragios*   148
   Mariselle Meléndez

Hispanic Literatures, Border Studies, and Digital Humanities

Between Land and Sea: The *Relación* as New World Literature   161
   Ralph Bauer

Naufragios and the Creation of a Latino Literary Canon   174
   Lázaro Lima

From the Desert to the Digital World: Adapting Cabeza de Vaca   188
   Luis Fernando Restrepo

Notes on Contributors   199

Survey Respondents   203

Works Cited   205

ACKNOWLEDGMENTS

In editing this volume, we acknowledge the foundational scholarship of Rolena Adorno, José Rabasa, Margo Glantz, Enrique Pupo-Walker, Beatriz Pastor, Sylvia Molloy, and Maureen Ahern. Their rigorous studies over decades have paved the way for subsequent scholars, including us. We appreciate their contributions to the field and aim to build upon the academic groundwork they have established. This collection is also the result of a collaborative effort and dialogues with our contributors, to whom we are forever indebted.

The research for this work has been made possible thanks to the support of the Kellogg Institute for International Studies; the University of Notre Dame Institute for Scholarship in the Liberal Arts (ISLA); and the Latin American and Latino Studies Program and the Department of World Languages, Literatures, and Cultures of the University of Arkansas, Fayetteville, which generously provided funds to support the editing process. We are indebted to our colleagues at the MLA's LLC Colonial Latin American Forum and the Latin American Studies Association Colonial Section for their feedback and support.

We would also like to thank the following individuals for their intelligent and generous critiques and commentary: James Hatch, Michael Simon, and Zahra Brown, who patiently guided us through the editorial process at the MLA; Juliet Lynd, who read and helped us with the editing and translation of many of the essays; Susana Rudas, who designed the maps of the Narváez and Cabeza de Vaca expeditions and diligently read *Naufragios* to better understand the geography of the conquest; David M. Solodkow and Lisa Voigt for their intelligent suggestions and enthusiasm for this endeavor; and of course the anonymous peer reviewers for their careful reading of the manuscript and thoughtful suggestions. We are also deeply grateful to those who responded to the initial survey by the MLA, helping to gauge interest in this volume. Their feedback was instrumental in shaping the direction and content of our work. Moreover, we extend our gratitude to our students. Their curiosity and fresh perspectives informed our questions. Much of the inspiration and insight for this volume emerged directly from our classroom interactions with these young intelligences and readers.

In the quiet spaces between words and thoughts, we find the echoes of time not spent with our loved ones. To our families, who gracefully filled these absences with understanding and patience, we owe a depth of gratitude that words can scarcely convey.

Part One

MATERIALS

Classroom Texts

Álvar Núñez Cabeza de Vaca's account of the expedition led by Pánfilo de Narváez into present-day Florida and of the survivors' journey through the southern and southwestern United States and northern Mexico (fig. 1) was originally published in 1542 (*Relación que dio Álvar Núñez Cabeza de Vaca*). The *Relación* (*Account*) has been widely known and published as *Naufragios* since Andrés González de Barcia's 1749 edition. Although that is not the original title, the word *Naufragios* ("Shipwrecks") appeared in the running heads and the table of contents of the 1555 second edition (*Relación y comentarios*). The second edition also included the *Comentarios* (*Commentaries*), which provides an account of Cabeza de Vaca's South American expedition written down by the secretary Pero Hernández under Cabeza de Vaca's direction (fig. 2). Organized into chapters, the second edition of the *Relación* seems more readable than the 1542 text. Thus, while most editions of *Naufragios* serve well in the classroom, instructors and students will be better equipped to read the work if they understand the differences between the first two editions and the importance of including the *Comentarios*. Here, we provide a short list of recommended editions.

Most modern Spanish editions that include both *Naufragios* and *Comentarios* seem to be out of print. That is the case with the editions of *Naufragios y comentarios* published by Espasa-Calpe and the two-volume paperback published by Historia 16 in the Biblioteca Americana series. One edition currently available is the paperback *Naufragios y comentarios* published by Editorial Porrúa, which is a budget edition with a brief introduction.

Regarding the *Relación*, there are several critical editions suitable for the classroom. Published in 2016 and available as an e-book, Vanina Teglia's *Naufragios* offers an informative introduction, text annotations, and an appendix with documents related to Narváez's expedition (Cabeza de Vaca, *Naufragios* [Teglia]). In 1992 Enrique Pupo-Walker published a well-annotated edition with Castalia, also available as an e-book (Cabeza de Vaca, *Naufragios* [Pupo-Walker]). Another well-prepared—though not widely available—paperback edition is the one edited by Trinidad Barrera for Alianza Editorial (Cabeza de Vaca, *Naufragios* [Barrera]). There is a 2018 edition by Eloísa Gómez-Lucena and Rubén Caba published by Cátedra (also available as an e-book), but we hesitate to recommend it because it glorifies Cabeza de Vaca and because its references omit most scholarship from the Americas.

For more advanced classes, a digital copy of the 1542 edition of the *Relación* is available online from the New York Public Library (digitalcollections.nypl.org/items/140251e0-ae8f-0130-223a-58d385a7b928), and the 1555 edition of *Relación y comentarios* is accessible through the *Biblioteca Digital Hispánica* (bdh.bne.es/bnesearch/detalle/bdh0000092765). A useful edition was published in 1906 by Manuel Serrano y Sanz under the title *Relación de los naufragios y comentarios de Alvar Núñez Cabeza de Vaca, adelantado y gobernador del Río de la Plata*, available in the *Biblioteca Digital Hispánica*. It includes several

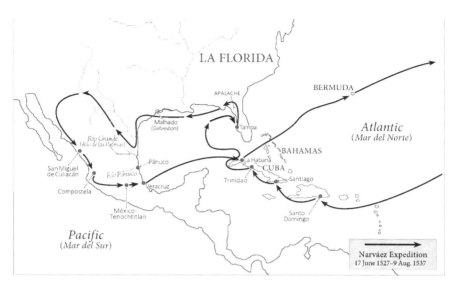

Figure 1. Narváez expedition. Map by Susana Rudas.

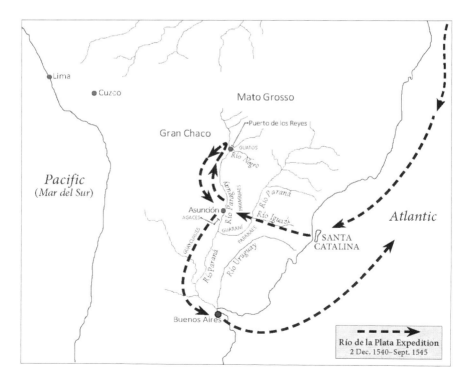

Figure 2. Río de la Plata expedition. Map by Susana Rudas.

important archival documents related to Cabeza de Vaca in the second volume as well as valuable onomastic and topographic indexes. Other documents related to Cabeza de Vaca's legal battles after the Southern Cone fiasco were published by José Rodríguez Carrión, Juan Francisco Maura, and Irala and Quevedo.

There are several editions available in English, though no paperback offers both the *Account* and *Commentaries*. Among the editions of the *Relación*, we highlight Rolena Adorno and Patrick Pautz's paperback *The Narrative of Cabeza de Vaca*, a carefully edited scholarly translation based on the 1542 princeps edition, with an excellent introduction and a well-documented set of annotations that also reference the 1555 edition (Cabeza de Vaca, *Narrative*). Next in rigor and accessibility is Pupo-Walker's *Castaways* (Cabeza de Vaca, *Castaways*; also available as an e-book). In 1993, Arte Publico Press published Martín Favata and Jose Fernández's annotated translation *The Account: Álvar Nùñez Cabeza de Vaca's* Relación. In their introduction, the editors express that they sought to capture the storytelling qualities of the original narrative (Cabeza de Vaca, *Account*). There is a Penguin Classics edition, *Chronicle of the Narváez Expedition*, based on Fanny Bandelier's 1905 translation, edited by Harold Augenbraum and introduced by Ilan Stavans (Cabeza de Vaca, *Chronicle* [Augenbraum]). The Cabeza de Vaca portal of Texas State University (exhibits.library.txstate.edu/cabeza/) provides an English version of the *Relación* in which the 1555 Spanish edition is paired page to page with the aforementioned Arte Público Press translation.

We would also like to highlight a couple of translations of the Southern Cone narrative, *Comentarios*, which is about Cabeza de Vaca's governorship of the Spanish province Río de la Plata. In the nineteenth century, Luis Domínguez published the *Commentaries* together with the narrative of Ulrich Schmidl, a German soldier who provides a first-hand account of Cabeza de Vaca's governorship; this work is accessible digitally through *ProQuest* and other online sources (Domínguez et al.). There is a more recent free translation of the *Comentarios* by Baker Morrow, published by the University of New Mexico Press under the title *The South American Expeditions, 1540–1545*, which we recommend for classroom use (Cabeza de Vaca, *South American Expeditions*). There are other materials published in English regarding Cabeza de Vaca's legal imbroglio, such as the 1551 short sentence against him translated by Morris Bishop (285).

There are two key, complementary primary sources related to Cabeza de Vaca's North and South American experiences: the royal instructions, or *capitulaciones*, for the Narváez expedition to Florida and the document marking Cabeza de Vaca's appointment as governor of Río de la Plata. Both texts were published by Milagros del Vas Mingo (234–37; 362–66). There is also a lost joint report of the Narváez expedition rendered by three of its survivors—Cabeza de Vaca, Andrés Dorantes, and Alonso del Castillo—upon their arrival in New Spain in 1536. The historian Gonzalo Fernández de Oviedo had access to the joint report from the audiencia of Santo Domingo, from which he produced his summary of the Narváez expedition in book 35 of his *Historia general y natural de las Indias* (*The General and Natural History of the Indies*; 2: 579–618). English translations of Oviedo's summary of the Narváez expedition can be found in the University of South Florida Digital Commons collection, edited and translated by Catherine Johnston (Oviedo "Joint Report"), and as appendix 2 in Alex Krieger's *We Came Naked* (243–301).

After Cabeza de Vaca and his companions arrived in Mexico City, one of them, Esteban, an enslaved African Christian known as Estevanico, was enrolled as a guide and mediator for the expedition led by the Franciscan friar Marcos de Niza, which went north in search of Cíbola. Esteban, who traveled ahead of Marcos, was reportedly killed by the Zuni Indians. Various accounts of the events leading to his death can be found in the second volume of George Hammond and Agapito Rey's *Narratives of the Coronado Expedition, 1540–1542*. Finally, for an alternative first-hand account of the events surrounding Cabeza de Vaca's governorship of Río de la Plata, instructors can assign the narrative by Schmidl, mentioned above.

The Instructor's Library

This section provides a brief selection of key critical readings in Spanish and English about Cabeza de Vaca and a list of general background readings. A fundamental resource is the three-volume edition *Alvar Núñez Cabeza de Vaca: His Account, His Life, and the Expedition of Pánfilo de Narváez*, by Rolena Adorno and Patrick Pautz. Volume 1 includes an informative set of maps; an annotated transcription of the 1542 *Relación* in Spanish, accompanied by a translation into English; and a well-documented summary of Cabeza de Vaca's life. Volume 2 provides a detailed description of Narváez's expedition; a step-by-step account of the disastrous journey, from its preparatory stages to Cabeza de Vaca's return to Spain; and a recounting of the expedition survivors' fate. Volume 3 covers the textual history of the *Relación* and the *Comentarios*, including informative discussions of the lost joint report and the ample paper trail of the expedition; early modern readers of the *Relación* and the *Comentarios* from the sixteenth to the eighteenth century; the modern Spanish editions; translations into Italian, French, English, German, and Russian; unpublished archival sources; and historical background on the colonization of the region, from the Caribbean, Florida, and the northern coast of Mexico to the Pacific. Adorno and Pautz's three-volume work is an essential reference tool for teaching Cabeza de Vaca.

As the essays in this volume demonstrate, there is an ample and growing corpus of scholarship on Cabeza de Vaca. However, for the purpose of guiding instructors, we mention here a handful of critical approaches related to both the North American and South American experiences of Cabeza de Vaca. We include in this "starter toolkit" the classic reading of *Naufragios* by Beatriz Pastor (*Discursos narrativos* and *Armature*), who contrasts Hernán Cortés's heroic narrative and the conquest of Mexico with Cabeza de Vaca's narrative about the disastrous Narváez expedition and who proposes that such failure triggered an empathetic view of the indigenous peoples. This line of inquiry is further developed by Yolanda Martínez–San Miguel, for whom Cabeza de Vaca "embodies an imperial and a colonial perspective" and a transculturated subjectivity marked by "ideological ambivalence" (78; 71–100).

An important place in the instructor's library should be reserved for Maureen Ahern's groundbreaking essay "The Cross and the Gourd: The Appropriation of Ritual Signs in the *Relaciones* of Alvar Núñez Cabeza de Vaca and Fray Marcos de Niza," available also in Spanish ("Cruz y calabaza"). Ahern treats skeptically the celebrated exceptionality of Cabeza de Vaca, and her essay paved the way for postcolonial readings of the *Relación*. In her essay, she also draws attention to Esteban's role as a Black conquistador and mediator between the survivors and the indigenous groups. Adorno also has produced an important corpus of scholarship, including the erudite and influential essay "The Negotiation of Fear in Cabeza de Vaca's *Naufragios*." Instructors will find quite useful Adorno's introduction to the paperback edition in English coedited with Patrick Pautz (Cabeza de Vaca, *Narrative*). Glantz's collection on Cabeza de Vaca offers several articles suitable for class, including the contributions by Glantz on the symbolic dimensions of nakedness ("Cuerpo"), Silvia Molloy's reflections on alterity and recognition (219–41), and Juan Bruce-Novoa's essay on Cabeza de Vaca's text within the tradition of Chicano literature ("Naufragios" and "Shipwrecked").

There is an abundant bibliography on the miraculous and supernatural events narrated by Cabeza de Vaca, a topic appealing to many students and studied by Jacques Lafaye ("Los Milagros") and by Robert Goodwin ("Texts"), among others.

Against the grain of most criticism, José Rabasa's *Writing Violence on the Northern Frontier* questions the peaceful conquistador image of Cabeza de Vaca and underscores the imperial policies at play in the narrative accounts of the Spanish expeditions to the American South and Southwest. Along those lines, see Claret Vargas's analysis of the warfare references in the *Relación*; the critiques by Alan Silva, Ralph Bauer, David Rojinsky, and Carlos Jáuregui ("Going Native"; "Cabeza de Vaca") of the celebrated hybrid subjectivity and empathetic ethnography of Cabeza de Vaca; and Kun Jong Lee's study of the Pauline emplotment of the *Relación*—that is, Cabeza de Vaca's use of Paul's episodic narratives to model the encounter with the other.

Instructors teaching the *Relación* from the perspective of race or gender can find several specialized studies on those topics. For example, on the Black conquistador Esteban, see Goodwin (*Crossing the Continent*), Dennis Herrick (*Esteban*), and Richard Gordon ("Following Estevanico"). On the relatively understudied issue of gender in the *Relación*, see the articles by Mariah Wade and Carmen Gómez-Galisteo and also Paola Uparela's work in this collection.

For Cabeza de Vaca's Southern Cone experience, the scholarship is surprisingly less abundant, though the instructor can find good introductory essays such as "The Rivers Plate and Paraguay," by Hugh Thomas; *The Guaraní under Spanish Rule in the Río de la Plata*, by Barbara Ganson; "Las expediciones de Conquista

("Conquest Expeditions"), by Silvio Zavala; and two lengthy and thorough chapters by Enrique de Gandía: "El gobierno de Álvar Núñez" ("Álvar Núñez's Governorship"; *Historia* 95–178) and "La prisión de Álvar Núñez" ("Álvar Núñez's Imprisonment"; *Historia* 179–221). The historical context of the *Comentarios* is complex, and at the same time it is essential to understanding the narrative. More concise readings include articles by María Juliana Gandini ("Experiencias" and "Fuerzas locales"), Milagros Arano-Lean, and Loreley El Jaber (*País*; "Álvar Núñez Cabeza de Vaca"). A suggestive view of the interaction of Cabeza de Vaca and Spanish conquistadores with the Guarani people (a central issue in the *Comentarios*) is provided by the historian Shawn Austin. Austin documents how through *cuñadasgo* ("in-law relationships") the Guarani used marriages of Native women with the conquistadores to form key political alliances (precisely the relationships, both domestic and political, that Cabeza de Vaca sought to eliminate).

Finally, we suggest the following general works on colonial Latin America. For those unfamiliar with the period, a good starting point are two books from the Oxford Very Short Introductions series: Matthew Restall and Felipe Fernández-Armesto's *The Conquistadors* and Adorno's *Colonial Latin American Literature*. In addition, Restall's *Seven Myths of the Spanish Conquest* is a valuable resource that questions some of the commonplaces about the Spanish conquest. The fact is that much of the received knowledge about the Spanish conquest in the Anglophone world comes filtered by the Catholic-Protestant rivalries that fueled the anti-Hispanic Protestant propaganda known as the Black Legend, depicting conquistadores' greed and cruelty (Greer et al.). Also, the general understanding in the United States of the Spanish American past comes from nineteenth-century historiography, which presented the colonial past through powerful narratives of individualized heroes and villains. A nuanced general overview of the period is provided by Restall and Kris Lane. More in-depth and up-to-date discussions on the period can be found in *The Routledge Hispanic Studies Companion to Colonial Latin America and the Caribbean, 1492–1898*, edited by Santa Arias and Martínez-San Miguel.

To continue and broaden the hemispheric and comparative approach required to understand Cabeza de Vaca's colonial experiences in North and South America, we recommend Bauer's *The Cultural Geography of Colonial American Literatures* and Jorge Cañizares-Esguerra's *Puritan Conquistadors: Iberianizing the Atlantic, 1550–1700*. Cañizares-Esguerra challenges the received notion of a peaceful North American conquest compared to the stories of ruthless and gold-thirsty Spanish conquistadores. The violence of the colonization of the Americas shed light on the darker sides of Western modernity, as has been argued by Walter Mignolo in several works that examine the geopolitics of knowledge, including *The Darker Side of the Renaissance*. For a comparative discussion of European imperialism that includes the colonial ventures by the Spanish, British, French, Dutch, and others in the Americas, we recommend Anthony Pagden's *The Burdens of Empire: 1539 to the Present*. The ideology of universalism and the project of universal human rights are heirs to the legacies of Western empires. Studies such as Mignolo's and Pagden's allow us to see that although Cabeza de Vaca's vivid narrative may draw us into that rough trek across the North American continent or up the Paraná River in South America, it is important for us to take a step back to see how Cabeza de Vaca's story is part of a larger imperial global framework.

Online Resources

In addition to the digitized 1542 princeps edition of the *Relación* at the New York Public Library and the digitized 1555 edition of the *Relación y comentarios* in the *Biblioteca Digital Hispánica*, many other online versions of the *Relación* are available in Spanish and English, including scans of print editions accessible through universities and libraries. Both the *Relación* and the 1555 edition of the *Comentarios* can be read online at the Biblioteca Virtual Miguel de Cervantes (www.cervantesvirtual.com/nd/ark:/59851/bmch1534), and an open-access English translation of the *Relación* is available online from the Wittliff Collections at Texas State University (exhibits.library.txstate.edu/cabeza/). Additional resources and information about Cabeza de Vaca presented with that English edition include sections on environmental history, traditional medicine, and Native American lifeways; a suggestive list of critical questions and research topics; and several informative short videos on Cabeza de Vaca and the expedition by Frank de la Teja. The website *Texas beyond History*, oriented toward a general audience, is an educational portal developed by the Texas Archeological Research Laboratory at the University of Texas, Austin, in partnership with the Department of Anthropology at Texas State University and other institutions across the state to offer "a virtual museum of Texas' cultural heritage" (www.texasbeyondhistory.net). The section dedicated to the Spanish conquistadores is titled "Learning from Cabeza de Vaca" (www.texasbeyondhistory.net/cabeza-cooking/index.html). The multimedia *Conquistadors* website, hosted by the Public Broadcasting Service and based on the book and the four-part documentary by Michael Wood, devotes one section to Cabeza de Vaca, with resources and activities for instructors and students. These materials are problematic because they frame the expedition to conquer Florida as a "marvelous adventure" (www.pbs.org/conquistadors/devaca/devaca_flat.html). However, the PBS site presents instructors with the opportunity to address many ethnographic stereotypes and myths of the conquest.

Part Two

APPROACHES

Introduction:
Teaching and Unteaching Cabeza de Vaca

Luis Fernando Restrepo and Carlos A. Jáuregui

Álvar Núñez Cabeza de Vaca is best known for his epic, eight-year journey across North America. He had been part of Pánfilo de Narváez's disastrous expedition to La Florida and had been presumed dead together with the three hundred men that disembarked in Tampa in 1528. Only four of those men returned: Cabeza de Vaca, Alonso del Castillo Maldonado, Andrés Dorantes de Carranza, and Esteban, an enslaved African Christian from Azemmour, Morocco, who is often dismissively called "Estevanico" in historical accounts, a point examined by Kathryn McKnight in this volume. Cabeza de Vaca, who was the treasurer of the expedition, published his account *Relación que dio Álvar Núñez Cabeça de Vaca de lo acaescido en las Indias en la armada donde iva por gobernador Pánphilo de Narbáez, desde el año de veinte y siete hasta el año de treinta y seis que bolvió a Sevilla con tres de su compañía* (*The Account That Álvar Núñez Cabeza de Vaca Gave of What Occurred in the Indies on the Expedition of Which Pánfilo de Narváez Served as Governor, from the Year 1527 to 1536, When He Returned to Seville with Three Members of His Company*) in 1542. A second and better-known edition of his colonial ventures was published in Valladolid in 1555 with some significant changes, divided into chapters, and accompanied by the *Comentarios* (*Commentaries*), a vindicating text written down by his amanuensis, Pero Hernández, on the failed governorship of Cabeza de Vaca in the province of Río de la Plata in South America, from which he was returned to Spain in chains (*La relación y comentarios del governador Álvar Núñez Cabeça de Vaca, de lo acaescido en las dos jornadas que hizo a las Indias* [*Account and Commentaries of the Governor Álvar Núñez Cabeça de Vaca, regarding the Events of His Two Journeys to the Indies*]).

Narváez embarked on his expedition to Florida with the expectation of finding another Mexico (that is, a rich and populated land) but instead was met with hardships, starvation, and ultimately his own demise. Yet, despite the catastrophic failure of the expedition, Cabeza de Vaca, in the best tradition of Hispanic vindication of failure, successfully exploited his somehow aggrandized misfortunes to get yet another colonial gig. In the proem, addressing the Spanish monarch, he stressed that his *Relación* offered valuable information about vast unknown territories and numerous indigenous groups that could be conquered, in a narrative that absolved him of the bad decisions leading to the collapse of the expedition—and instead blamed Narváez. Furthermore, he presented himself as a savvy merchant, messianic figure, and miraculous healer who had been followed across the desert by large indigenous crowds. His account worked, to some extent. Cabeza de Vaca did not get the second chance in Florida that he wanted, but he got a consolation prize: he was appointed to the governorship of Río de la Plata, which consisted of present-day northern Argentina, Uruguay, and Paraguay. In 1541, Cabeza de Vaca arrived in the Southern Cone, where he led several incursions inland. He met strong resistance from the Spanish settlers in the region, who accused him of treason and sent him back to Spain. He would spend eight years litigating to clear his name. He also dictated to Pero Hernández, his secretary, the *Commentaries*, an account presenting Cabeza de Vaca's side of the scuffle with the Spaniards in Asunción, in today's Paraguay. The *Commentaries* were published in 1555 with the second edition of the *Relación*. Their publication brought together two marginal regions of the Spanish Empire quite different from Mexico and Peru. La Florida and Río de la Plata were, if not yet completely conquered, incorporated by colonial writing into the empire.

Edited numerous times in Spain, Latin America, and the United States and translated into many languages, Cabeza de Vaca's narrative has also inspired historical novels, films, music, and artworks, which are discussed by Luis Fernando Restrepo in his essay in this volume. The *Relación* has become a staple reading in Latin American, Latino, and early American studies and has captured the imagination of readers from the colonial period to the present. They have read the *Relación* through diverse lenses as an exemplary survival story, a gone-native narrative, an empathetic ethnographic account of the indigenous peoples encountered by Cabeza de Vaca, a monumental epic of man against nature, a humanitarian text, a story about crossing borders, and more. However valid these interpretations may be, they must be constantly revised and challenged in class. At the same time we must critically assess what is needed to better understand and teach or, more important, unteach this early colonial narrative today. Unteaching entails making explicit and questioning the ideological preconceptions informing the reading and teaching of canonical texts; thus, this assessment is both an academic endeavor and a pedagogical one with political implications.

The *Relación* has received considerable attention in scholarship and in classrooms, and it has been considered a unique colonial text. However, for all its apparent uniqueness, it is part of a complex history of Spanish imperialism and devastation of indigenous peoples in the Americas, and it is related discursively, legally, and historically to many other narratives of "discovery" and conquest. In fact, the *Relación* is a rather ordinary text. It is poorly written and infamously confusing for students. Other accounts of the same events are easier to read and teach but are rarely included in the curriculum. For instance, in *Historia general y natural de las Indias*, Gonzalo Fernández de Oviedo wrote a contemporary transcription of the lost joint report of the three Spaniards that survived Narváez's expedition: Cabeza de Vaca, Castillo, and Dorantes. Esteban's account was deemed unreliable and legally invalid since, as an enslaved person, Esteban was considered alieni juris, or subject to another's control, akin to a child or a woman: incapable of offering legal testimony. In any case, the joint report (or its summary) provided by Oviedo is better organized, better written, and syntactically and discursively more intelligible than Cabeza de Vaca's *Relación*. Yet we teachers insist on teaching only the *Relación*.

We should then start this volume by asking ourselves why we have given so much importance to Cabeza de Vaca's *Relación*. Considering the vast number of similar accounts housed at the Archivo General de Indias (General Archive of the Indies) in Seville, Spain, why should we rely on this one? We suspect that any answer to these questions will have much more to do with our contemporary political and academic sensibilities than with the text itself. As we teach sixteenth-century texts, we should be aware of how much we are discussing, debating, and sometimes justifying our present.

The *Relación* is taught mainly through the second edition and often separated from the *Commentaries* and other important documents related to the Spanish colonization of the Americas, in approaches that have tended to focus on the individual experiences of the four survivors and on texts related to the present US territory. That is the state of the teaching of Cabeza de Vaca. This volume reflects such a state of affairs and at the same time challenges it, inviting readers to consider a richer textual archive. Embracing a wider corpus that includes the Southern Cone narrative *Commentaries* is not an easy task but has the advantage of giving the figure of Cabeza de Vaca a continental breadth more attuned with the realities of sixteenth-century Spanish imperialism.

The fact is that to teach Cabeza de Vaca's writings, instructors must take into consideration the legal, economic, religious, and social structures of Spanish colonialism. The *Relación* is part of a large collection of official conquest reports and bureaucratic documents that were both addressed to and produced by the Crown and that followed certain protocols. Thus its authorship, content, goals, and hierarchical overdeterminations are better understood when we take into consideration the weight and formalism given to written documentation produced by Spanish colonial agents. Conquest expeditions had to be approved by the Crown through legal contracts known as *capitulaciones* that stipulated the expedition's leadership, goals, and territories to be conquered as well as mutual obligations and the privileges and rewards that were to be granted to the conquistadores for their services to the Crown. Those rewards included official posts like a governorship, economic benefits, and the allotment of tribute-paying Indian communities known as repartimientos or encomiendas (Gibson 48–67).[1] In other words, the *capitulaciones* awarded the right to conquest and plunder and assigned certain duties such as the implementation of the evangelical mission and the obligation to produce a detailed account of the expeditions. Although the *capitulaciones* granted by the Crown to Narváez for the conquest of Florida (*CDI* 22: 224–44; Vas Mingo 234–37) and the *capitulaciones* granted to Cabeza de Vaca for the governorship of Río de la Plata (Vas Mingo 362–66) are seldom taught and not available in English, these texts provide us with invaluable material that could be translated, analyzed, and debated in class. The Crown sanctioned but did not finance these conquering ventures and imposed the royal fifth—that is, twenty percent of the loot. The Spanish Crown's authority to grant these rights to conquest was a point of contention between the European powers of the time. Very early on, Spain sought papal support to legalize its rights over the Indies.

As a result, on 3 and 4 May 1493, Alexander VI issued three bulls: *Inter caetera* (*Among other works [pleasing to the Divine Majesty]*), *Eximiae devotionis* (*The highest faith*), and the second *Inter caetera*, followed by *Dudum siquidem* (*Not long ago [we donated]*) on 25 September 1493. Known as the Alexandrine Bulls of Donation, they entrusted "each and every land and island" ("todas y cada una de las tierras e islas") recently discovered to the Spanish Crown for evangelization purposes (Las Casas, *Tratados* 2: 1279).[2] These bulls became the basis for a legal instrument developed by the Spanish jurist Juan Lopez de Palacios Rubios in 1513 known as the Requerimiento (War Ultimatum). As a protocol of conquest, before the conquistadores entered the target territories, local indigenous groups were supposed to be given the option to surrender to the Spanish Crown and embrace Catholicism. If they resisted, a so-called just war could be waged against them. They could also be enslaved and their possessions could be taken away (Castañeda-Delgado 396–98). Moreover, legislation such as the Indian labor regulations, known as the Laws of Burgos, which were established in 1512–13, and the 1526 Ordenanzas sobre el buen tratamiento de los Indios (Ordinances Regarding the Good Treatment of the Indians) sought to rationalize colonial violence and sugarcoat it with the language of imperial love, as José Rabasa has argued (see also the essays by René Carrasco and by Ralph Bauer in this volume). The 1526 ordinances—included in Narváez's *capitulaciones*—required, among other things, the good treatment of the Indians and a detailed account of lands, peoples, and customs encountered.

Taking into consideration the intertextual and legal connections between Cabeza de Vaca's texts and the papal bulls, the Requerimiento, the Laws of Burgos, the *ordenanzas*, and the *capitulaciones*, we can ask, What is Cabeza de Vaca's *Relación* but the glorified and printed fulfillment of a series of precise legal duties? In other words, the *Relación* is the semiscripted answer to a royal mandate rather than a text from an autonomous individual. Despite all the misfortunes and failures of Cabeza de Vaca's North American venture, this narrative renders an account of a loyal subject who shows strict and almost a heroic adherence to the *capitulaciones* and the law (he follows the *ordenanzas* to the letter). Likewise, *Comentarios* tries to justify Cabeza de Vaca's numerous deviations from his legal contract with the Crown and from the law. It always refers implicitly or explicitly to the imperial legal frame that regulated conquest, the plundering of riches, the gathering of geographic and ethnographic information, and the treatment of the Indians. It is worth noting that *Comentarios* not only tells a series of events but also revisits Cabeza de Vaca's legal troubles following his tenure as governor of Río de la Plata (see the essays by Loreley El Jaber and by Carrasco in this volume).

Cabeza de Vaca's texts and other well-known colonial classics such as Hernán Cortés's *Letters from Mexico* and Bartolomé de las Casas's *Short Account of the Destruction of the Indies* need to be read against this legal, contractual, and meritocratic background. In this context, it is not uncommon to see the Requerimiento cited in many conquest accounts (e.g., loosely paraphrased in chapter 35 of the *Relación*). Moreover, seeking royal rewards on behalf of their authors, these documents often allege efforts that individual conquistadores made for the benefit of the Crown and for the evangelization of the Indians. Not surprisingly, conquistadores would stress in their reports their heroic deeds of conquest, the difficulties they endured in their ventures into unknown lands, and the value of the information they provided for the advancement of the empire and the faith. Most important, these texts not only narrate deeds but also document conquistadores' actions vis-à-vis the law (by way of constant references to ceremonial acts, written documents, *probanzas* or testimonies, certifications, notaries accompanying the expedition, etc.).

Beyond the legal framework, what happened on the ground was *harina de otro costal*, as it is said in Spanish ("flour from a different sack," i.e., a different matter). Yet writing was an integral and consequential part of an Iberian culture of conquest that goes back to the *Reconquista*, the Christian wars against Muslim Iberia or Al-Andalus. This longer view of Iberian history is evident in the writings to the Crown where Cabeza de Vaca highlights that his ancestors had fought in the *Reconquista* and also in the conquest of the Canary Islands (*Relación*, "Proemio" and ch. 38).

Teaching Cabeza de Vaca Today

In this volume we propose taking two apparently contradictory roads: a contextualizing reading of the colonial archive and a critical intervention in the reproduction of the canon. That is, one road involves considering the *Relación* and *Commentaries* and other related documents in their larger historical context as part of Iberian imperialism and the European Atlantic expansion from the fifteenth century onward, and the other road involves extracting this corpus from the cultural and pedagogical traditions that place it within a series of organized events and texts that reproduce certain colonial grammar and justify our present as the necessary result of colonial modernity. An example of how our scholarly traditions and ideologies drive research and teaching is the preeminence they give to the *Relación* over the *Commentaries*. The unequal attention given to the former over the latter cannot be attributed to the importance in the sixteenth century of one region (North America) over another (the Southern Cone), since both texts are narratives of Spanish activity in peripheral zones of the empire that did not result in the conquest of great cities or the appropriation of great treasures.

We suspect that a great part of the appeal of the *Relación* (in approaches obliterating the *Comentarios* and other accounts) is that it can be deceptively framed as the opposite of certain narratives of conquest in which bloodshed, pillage, and plunder make it difficult for today's readers to identify with the main characters. Cabeza de Vaca could represent the purportedly good conqueror that we can cope with, the suffering and surviving hero that anticipates Daniel Defoe's Robinson Crusoe and even the successful contestants of survivalist reality shows. Cabeza de Vaca's North American narrative allows readers to identify with a benevolent conquering subject compatible with certain contemporary liberal sensibilities, such as those promoted today by the naive embrace of multiculturalism so acutely criticized by Alain Badiou (*Ethics* 20). These sensibilities, however, have not completely extinguished a resilient historical tradition celebrating conquerors of the kind of Julius Caesar, Gengis Khan, and Cortés. The problem with *Commentaries* is that its main character is neither a peaceful suffering hero nor a glorious conquistador.

In this age of toppling down monuments of conquerors and oppressors, and for the last four decades, Cortés-like heroes have been tough to sell—at least in academia, where we reread the chronicles of the conquest with an awareness of the erasing of other peoples, cultures, and memories. *Commentaries*—better organized and better written than the *Relación*—does not seem to fit the expectations of a humanist curriculum that can handle Jesus or Julius Caesar but struggles with an unrecognizable hybrid that is neither chicha nor lemonade. On the other hand, Cabeza de Vaca's canonical and popular but rather hard-to-read *Relación* has a safe, recognizable, and already instrumentalized emplotment. This narrative of Cabeza de Vaca's North American misadventures is often referred to as the story of a subject that ceases to be a conquistador and engages in ethnographic empathy, language acquisition, multicultural exchanges, and so on. This anticonquistador, then, lends himself to political correctness and shows up in our classes enjoying both a celebrity and an impunity that obscures the colonial structures of the present. Let us be clear. We are the heirs of colonial modernity, and our institutions are part of the history of colonial deterritorialization and dispossession of indigenous lands and of the instrumentalization of life through exploitation of labor; in other words, we read these texts from within a world that is founded on the destructive colonial and capitalist appropriation of cheap labor and cheap nature (see Moore). On the surface, the narrative subject of the *Relación* appears not to subdue nature but merely to survive it, the text is not about the appropriation of riches but about so-called dispossessed Europeans in the New World, and, finally, Cabeza de Vaca is portrayed as a figure that does not exploit indigenous peoples but instead makes a humanitarian argument for their good treatment. These three ideological axes have allowed generations of teachers and students to find in the *Relación* (and not in *Commentaries*) an alternative and convenient genealogy of colonial modernity. Paradoxically, the less readable text has become the most read. And the more teachable *Commentaries* is seldomly taught. One of the challenges for us teachers is to reflect on this asymmetry and also to disrupt it—that is, to find what *Commentaries* can tell us about important issues such as the formation of imperial reason, the ethnographic matrix of the representation of the other, or the complex politics of sex in forging strategic alliances with indigenous groups (see Austin). *Commentaries* also sheds light on the largely ignored but ubiquitous agency of women setting the course of imperial domination and resistance, the tension between humanitarian Christian discourse and the reality of colonial desire and primitive accumulation (the never-ending search for riches), the force and violence of the law, and, conversely, the instrumental role of illegality and illicit acts in the establishment of the transatlantic Iberian Empire. *Commentaries* makes visible the foundational crimes that led to the Latin America we know today. For instance, in the *Commentaries*, we learn that Cabeza de Vaca breaches the royal mandate to rescue a group of Spaniards in Buenos Aires in order to instead pursue the promise of inland riches.[3] In this sense, *Commentaries* could be a very disruptive text. As mentioned below, two essays in this volume address this text. We would like to invite further scholarship and teaching of the *Commentaries*.

In class, we should try a radical interruption of canonical readings of Cabeza de Vaca's works (especially those complacent readings referred to before) and at the same time propose a contextual understanding of these texts. There is no intrinsic value for any text, no matter how classic it may seem. As educators, we can keep certain texts in our syllabi as an act of deference to tradition, or we can try to find approaches that question or make relevant the colonial archive for today's students. Thus, to interrupt canonical readings, this volume offers a collection of historically and culturally competent perspectives on Cabeza de Vaca's *Relación*, *Commentaries*, and other related documents, informed by postcolonial studies, gender studies, critical race theory, and environmental and transatlantic studies. For example, Kathryn McKnight's essay in this volume on the Black conqueror Esteban challenges both the centrality of Cabeza de Vaca's role in the expedition and the stereotypical imagination of subalternity; Esteban is both a subaltern subject and an agent of empire, a Black African and a Christian subject to the Spanish king, an enslaved individual and a conqueror. There are no political guarantees or ready-made positions predetermined by identity, since all identities are enmeshed in history. Paola Uparela's essay suggests a queering of the *Relación* that may help instructors and students to recognize the fluidity of sexual roles and reject the seduction of this text's hypermasculine encoding. After all, women and transgender individuals have an important presence in the text, and there are many instances of inversion of sexual roles. Moreover, we should consider with our students what sort of erasures may be at play in the conspicuous absence in the text of any mention of sex between Europeans and Indians in the eight years that the four survivors of Narváez's expedition lived among them.

For students, walking from Tampa to Mexico sometimes seems easier than thoroughly reading Cabeza de Vaca's rambling and disorganized narrative in the *Relación*. The conquistador's writing would hardly earn a passing grade in our classes. Studying the *Relación* is an arduous task even in comparison with other lengthy, four-hundred-year-old texts that are full of legal jargon, archaic expressions, and odd syntax and that were written for bureaucratic purposes, such as Cortés's *Letters*. Given these challenges, why and how should we teach the *Relación* and other related texts? This volume proposes several answers to these questions.

Essays in the Volume

Approaches to Teaching Cabeza de Vaca's Account *and Other Texts* brings together thirteen well-grounded essays by renowned and emerging scholars teaching in the United States and Latin America, offering perspectives and background information on Cabeza de Vaca's texts. This volume facilitates an informed and productive incorporation of these colonial narratives into the curriculum in various disciplines, including Hispanic studies, Latin American studies, comparative literature, ethnic studies, Native American studies, early American studies (history and literature), anthropology, and geography. The essays are divided into five sections.

The first section, "Cabeza de Vaca's *Account*," opens with an essay by Rolena Adorno, a leading scholar in colonial Latin American studies and coauthor of the three-volume critical bilingual edition of the *Relación* (Adorno and Pautz); the essay provides an overview of the life, writings, and legacy of Cabeza de Vaca. Adorno traces the historical readings of the *Relación* that led to its inclusion in the Latin American and early American canon. Next, José Rabasa critically examines the scholarship presenting Cabeza de Vaca as engaged in "peaceful conquest" and highlights how the writer of the *Relación* disguises violence with "love speech." He proposes a critical understanding of empire building, colonial modernity, colonial writing, and the violence inherent to the colonial world. In the third essay, Carlos Jáuregui revisits the tale of Mala Cosa (Evil Thing)—a small, hairy, mysterious, foreign, and terrifying sorcerer—that helps establish the figure of Cabeza de Vaca as a good Christian healer. Jáuregui refutes the supposed ethnographic contrast between Cabeza de Vaca and Mala Cosa and maintains that the latter could be read as a mirror image of the Spanish conquistador and of colonial violence.

In the section "Intersectional Perspectives," two essays decenter the whiteness and the masculinity of Cabeza de Vaca's text. McKnight traces the figure of Esteban as an African conquistador and negotiator in Cabeza de Vaca's narrative within the larger context of early modern slavery, conquest, and racialization and the history of Black Africans in Spain and the New World. This move is not motivated by political correctness; there is no correction for the violence of past conquests and colonization. But instructors can help students participate in a wider, ongoing critical conversation on systemic racism. For example, Esteban's complex experience as an enslaved Black African and a Spanish conquistador could illuminate the challenges of the politics of race in academia, the classroom, and society at large.

Uparela examines the understudied presence of indigenous and Spanish women in the *Relación* and the multiple gender and cultural roles that Cabeza de Vaca assumes in the narrative, as androgynous shaman and merchant, queer food collector, dancer, and cross-dresser. As a result, the subjectivity that emerges in the *Relación* exceeds the normative social and gendered roles of Iberian society at the time. Queering the *Relación* disrupts what has been the hegemonic teaching of hypermasculine colonial texts, toppling the monumental figures of the conquistadores and prompting a less androcentric understanding of cultural history.

The section "Other Accounts" includes two essays that propose a series of pedagogical detours, textual as well as historical, from the *Relación* and the image of Cabeza de Vaca that it cultivates. Loreley El Jaber examines the *Commentaries*, which narrates Cabeza de Vaca's Southern Cone expedition and is overlooked by most critics. El Jaber takes us into the legal battles that Cabeza de Vaca endured trying to clear his name after his tumultuous experience as governor of Río de la Plata. After those battles, the *Commentaries* constitutes a literary and historical redundancy: the text seeks to clear the record for good and to restore Cabeza de Vaca's honor. Although examining the vast paper trail that informs *Commentaries* could be overwhelming, the bottom line is that this is a predictable colonial text in which Cabeza de Vaca whitewashes his ruthless and failed governorship to present himself as a model imperial subject. His humanitarian persona—so successfully crafted in the North American narrative—does not hold water here. Given the conflictive nature of his tenure in the Southern Cone, he clearly is not the savior of his compatriots or the protector of the Indians that he claims to be.

René Carrasco weighs the political and ideological debts that instructors have incurred by teaching Cabeza de Vaca's text as a narrative of peaceful conquest and as a literary text somehow related to the popular tradition of magical realism. Following the steps of Rabasa's critique of the prevalent scholarship on Cabeza de Vaca, Carrasco underscores a series of problems that reproduce colonial culture in the classroom. The implication of presenting the *Relación* as a peaceful and magical-realist work would be that we are facing an exceptional text: one that allows us to identify with a benevolent colonial tradition somehow disconnected from the foundational violence of Hispanic imperialism. The supposed proto–magical realism of the text corresponds to the literary aestheticization of colonial ethnography and violence.

The section "Cabeza de Vaca across Disciplines" grapples with two things: first, that Cabeza de Vaca's texts hardly fit the contemporary notion of literature, even after the revolution of cultural studies, and, second, that even though we mostly teach these texts within the context of Latin American early literature, or literatures of the early Americas, in the sixteenth century there was no Latin America or idea of the Americas. Latin America is a late-nineteenth-century construct reinvented by area studies in the United States in the past fifty years; "the Americas" is a problematic idea historically linked to both nineteenth-century pan-Americanism and contemporary neoliberalism, which is widely despised south of the Rio Grande. Still, these texts can be legitimately appropriated within contemporary debates that work with notions such as Latin American literature, provided that we do not forget that these texts are historically and disciplinarily characterized by their readers across continents, languages, and disciplines, who include historians, anthropologists, theologians, legal scholars, and, of course, literary critics. We must also consider that a growing number of our students come from disciplines beyond literature and the humanities.

In the first essay of this section, George Sabo III and Jeffrey Mitchem provide an overview of the current archaeological research on Cabeza de Vaca's journey as well as on other sixteenth-century expeditions, such as those led by Tristán de Luna, Hernando de Soto, and Francisco Vázquez de Coronado. This essay is a valuable resource for instructors to better understand the spatial dimension of the colonial encounters between Europeans and the indigenous peoples of the North American continent. Sabo and Mitchem bring to our attention that a text such as Cabeza de Vaca's is just one of the million lost traces that a historical experience or individual leave behind and that often other texts and readings—such as archaeological findings and speculative archaeology—can fill in many blanks in our understanding of the past. Material culture left by colonial interactions that survived the erasure of time offers us a panoply of reading materials inaccessible through written accounts. The traces of *rescates* (beads and other commodities) provide an illustrative record of plunder and unequal colonial exchanges that are often described as peaceful interactions in the written colonial records. There are many tasks ahead for our students, such as mapping indigenous groups and interactions in the *Relación* and *Comentarios* in order to reinstate a reflection about the peoples and cultures that have been erased from maps, history, and life.

Understanding sixteenth-century codifications of space is the topic of Vanina Teglia's essay. Teglia examines the geographic descriptions in the *Relación*, paying attention to the representations of landscapes, climate, and territories. Reading space and colonial processes of reterritorialization in Cabeza de Vaca's texts helps our students understand larger and broader issues in areas such as geography, tourism, political science, and environmental sciences. The colonial production of geographic space in the *Relación* is a complex symbolic operation that incorporates and tries to negotiate early modern and Renaissance preconceptions of the world and imaginary and mythical narratives with the uncertainties of unknown territories and the empirical knowledge emerging from the expeditions. Teglia proposes using online mapping tools and period maps to make some sense of the vague textual geographic references in the *Relación*.

Food and hunger are not small potatoes. Food is not a choice; it is a basic material condition of existence and, for millions, a persistent, life-threatening issue. As liberation theology's founder, Gustavo Gutierrez, reminds us, hunger in the world is not a natural phenomenon like an earthquake but a human-made injustice, a product of pillage and capitalism. In the *Relación*, the failed search for gold leads the conquistadores to plunder Native villages to sustain their invading army, which soon collapses and leaves a few survivors searching for—and stealing—food.

Mariselle Meléndez approaches the *Relación* from the perspective of food studies and draws attention to its multiple references to hunger, food scarcity, and harsh terrain. Facing hunger, the Spaniards could not be picky eaters; Native food made its way by necessity into the narrative, presenting us and our students with a problematic and fascinating menu that challenges Western notions of civilization. Native food is presented by Cabeza de Vaca as scarce, strange, and sometimes repugnant but always needed to survive. It is not surprising that the conquistadores are the only cannibals in the *Relación*, inverting the common colonial trope of the man-eating American savage.

The last section, "Hispanic Literatures, Border Studies, and Digital Humanities," places Cabeza de Vaca's texts in relation to an ample corpus of literary traditions and cultural artifacts. This extended literary and cultural archive is not only a product of the so-called discovery of the New World and its otherness but also the reiteration of European sameness. The *Relación* and *Commentaries* appropriate and recycle medieval and Renaissance tales and tropes about survival and also other accounts and legal records. The two editions of the *Relación*, for example, retell versions of several testimonies rendered to the audiencias in Mexico and in Hispaniola, and *Commentaries* is the third-person account of Cabeza de Vaca's troubles in Río de la Plata within the context of the legal and political imbroglio mentioned above. This section presents readers with a richer and wider group of texts to consider for teaching Cabeza de Vaca in Hispanic, Latin American, and Latino studies classes. First, Ralph Bauer examines the interplay of two genres from the Hispanic narrative traditions present in the *Relación*: the medieval romance of chivalry and the classic shipwreck narrative. Bauer traces the enduring rhetorical power of these two genres that express land-based and seafaring experiences that work as metafictional devices. Land-based narratives solidify identities whereas seafaring accounts, associated with the sixteenth-century imperial expansion, unsettle cultural identities. Cabeza de Vaca somehow follows but also complicates such a pattern: American land becomes a sea of otherness and hybridity.

Lázaro Lima revisits Cabeza de Vaca's controversial inclusion in the Latino studies canon. This approach was proposed first by Luis Leal in the 1970s, in the context of a contrastive affirmation of Puerto Rican and Chicano identity vis-à-vis so-called American literature, and thereafter by many other critics, such as Juan Bruce-Novoa, who canonized Cabeza de Vaca's *Relación* as a foundational text of Chicano literature ("Naufragios" and "Shipwrecked"). Cabeza de Vaca became, in Bruce-Novoa's view, a struggling immigrant *avant la lettre*. Thereafter, critics such as Héctor Calderón and José David Saldívar debated the genealogical inclusion of Cabeza de Vaca as a Hispanic immigrant as the product of an anachronistic reading and an appropriation and inscription of the canonical Latin American text into Latino and Chicano studies. Leal and Bruce-Novoa—on two different sides of the debate—have an important common ground: the attempt to decolonize the academy and the canon of literary studies in the United States. Drawing on the work of Francisco Lomelí and others, and taking critical distance from the inclusion/exclusion debate, Lima proposes to go beyond such dead-end streets. He invites us instead to reckon with the legacies of settler colonialism, exploitation, and the modern formation of racial, cultural, and ethnic identities.

In the last essay, Luis Fernando Restrepo examines adaptations of Cabeza de Vaca's *Relación*, including Haniel Long's *The Marvelous Adventure of Cabeza de Vaca*, Abel Posse's *El largo atardecer del caminante* (*Walking into the Setting Sun*), Leila Lalami's *The Moor's Account*, Nicolás Echevarría's film *Cabeza de*

24   INTRODUCTION

Vaca, the Arizona artist Ettore DeGrazia's book of paintings *DeGrazia Paints Cabeza de Vaca*, Colin Matthews's musical piece *The Great Journey*, and works of public art such as Raúl Ayala Arellano's statue of Cabeza de Vaca in Ciudad Juárez. These artifacts complement and sometimes compete with the scholarly interpretations of the *Relación* and give students an opportunity to reflect on how Cabeza de Vaca and his works have been interpreted. These adaptations play with the familiar and the new, and underscore how, historically, new reading communities creatively appropriate and transform received texts in an ongoing process that renders new meanings to the past. Nonetheless, many of these adaptations reproduce the problematic figure of the humanitarian conquistador and the suffering hero. For example, George Antheil's important but understudied cantata *Cabeza de Vaca* magnifies the affective power of the vast American landscape and portrays the transformative spiritual journey of a suffering subject, thus reproducing the myths of the gone-native conquistador and the peaceful conquest. Adaptations expand the repertoire of class materials and pedagogical activities. Students, for example, can debate the affective power of art and music and the relations between the aesthetic appeal of certain narratives, pictures, and musical compositions and the political implications of those artifacts.

Altogether, the pedagogical resources and the thirteen essays included in this volume provide valuable interdisciplinary approaches to teaching the *Relación* and related texts in the classroom. More than just taking a historicist perspective, this collection brings forth key ethical and political questions on teaching and unteaching a classic. Rather than paying homage to a series of colonial texts that we have become too complacent with and that reproduce institutionalized violence, racism, sexism, and other inequities, this volume proposes that we unteach these texts. Thus, this pedagogical effort does not celebrate or dismiss the offensive legacies of the past and does not shun the uncomfortable task of teaching them. Rather, we strive to critically question these texts in order to decolonize the present and imagine a future in which we can recognize alternatives to a long, ongoing, and unsettled colonial history.

NOTES

1. Throughout this volume, we often employ the historical term *Indian* (over *Amerindian*, *Native American*, and so on), which corresponds to a legal, theological, and ethnographic category found in colonial records, historiographic works, legislation, religious documents, and other texts to refer to the multiple and heterogeneous peoples of the New World.

2. "The Indies" refers to Las Indias, meaning all the territories under the Spanish dominion from the voyages of Columbus onward.

3. Other major crimes include Vasco Núñez de Balboa's unauthorized foundation of Santa María la Antigua del Darién, Cortés's insurrection against Diego Velázquez and regicide of Cuauhtemoc, Francisco Pizarro's execution of Atahualpa and his own alleged rebellion against the Spanish king, and Lope de Aguirre's defiance of the Crown.

CABEZA DE VACA'S *ACCOUNT*

Cabeza de Vaca: His Life, Work, and Legacy

Rolena Adorno

Teaching *Naufragios* (*Shipwrecks*), also known as the *Relación* (or *Account*), of Álvar Núñez Cabeza de Vaca can be deceptively simple. On the face of it, *Naufragios* seems to be a continuous narrative that begins when Cabeza de Vaca departs on the Pánfilo de Narváez expedition and ends when he returns to Spain. Because of its brevity, it can be read in a single sitting. Because of its elliptical, allusive character, it suggests any number of engaging topics, such as those considered in the essays of this volume. Here I review five matters: Cabeza de Vaca's life and the initial publications of his work, in 1542 and 1555; allusiveness and omissions in *Naufragios*; time and space in *Naufragios*; curing episodes and Mala Cosa; and Esteban in history and fiction.[1]

Two preliminary observations will be helpful. First, in the sixteenth century the Spanish designation *Florida* or *La Florida* referred to the vast lands north of New Spain that extended across North America, east to west, from the Florida Peninsula to the Pacific coast and that were inhabited by various Native peoples. Florida today is a small part of that vast territory (fig. 1). To differentiate between the two geographic entities, I use "Spanish Florida" when referring to the historical region. Second, the Native groups with which Cabeza de Vaca's party had contact did not constitute a single monolithic, undifferentiated mass of Indians but rather consisted of several ethnic groups with distinctive customs that Cabeza de Vaca endeavored to describe. Chapters 23 through 26 of *Naufragios* include such descriptions for the ethnic groups of the shoreline and coastal interior of Texas, where Cabeza de Vaca and his companions spent six and a half years, and chapters 27 through 30 set out the practices performed by Native groups in their encounters with the Spanish party as it journeyed to the Pacific coast over a period of ten months. If prompted, attentive students can appreciate these differences. Although those ethnic groups cannot be identified with groups that exist

26   LIFE, WORK, AND LEGACY

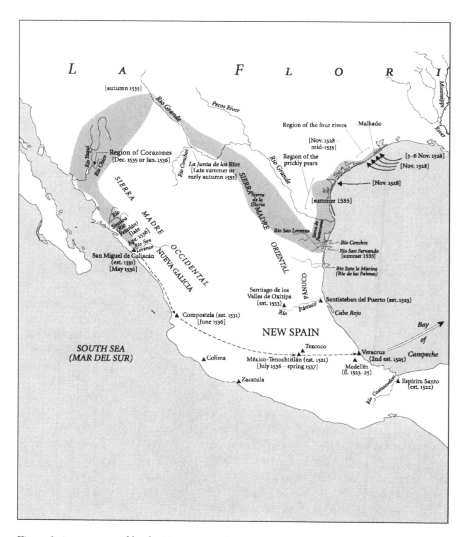

Figure 1. Areas traversed by the Narváez expedition (1527–28) and its four overland survivors (1528–36). From Adorno and Pautz, vol. 1, pp. xxvi–xxvii. Reproduced by permission of the University of Nebraska Press.

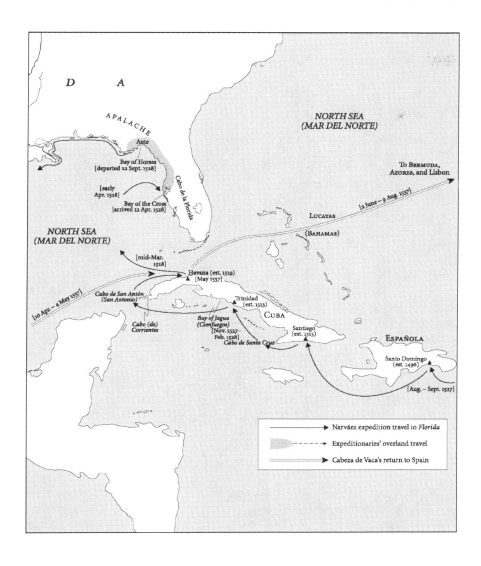

today—because they were wiped out by disease or other factors or were, at best, displaced and renamed before modern anthropology could keep track of them—one of the lessons learned from *Naufragios* is its author's pragmatic attempt to understand cultural diversity among Native populations.

The Life of Cabeza de Vaca

Cabeza de Vaca was a venerable surname in Spain's long history of caballeros and hidalgos (untitled nobility). The rank of the Cabeza de Vaca line was well established in the chronicles of Christian Spain's reconquest of lost territories from the armies of Islam, and by the seventeenth century the family was the object of encomiastic genealogical studies (Adorno and Pautz 1: 298–323). One apocryphal legend proclaims that *Cabeza de Vaca* was an honorific title granted by the king to a poor shepherd. The Cabeza de Vaca line comes into view around 1200, when Doña Inés Pérez Cabeza de Vaca and her husband, Rodrigo Rodríguez Girón, had a son, Fernán Ruiz Cabeza de Vaca, who, when grown, was one of two notable Cabeza de Vaca caballeros who participated in the 1236 reconquest of Córdoba from the Muslims. Álvar Núñez Cabeza de Vaca was born in the late 1480s or early 1490s.[2] Even though his paternal grandfather, Pedro de Vera, completed the Spanish conquest of Gran Canaria in the Canary Islands and served as its military governor, Cabeza de Vaca chose to use the surname of his mother, Doña Teresa Cabeza de Vaca (a common practice in those days), because her surname was the more distinguished of the two. Naming both forebears at the end of his account (Cabeza de Vaca, *Narrative* 176; ch. 38), Cabeza de Vaca must have assumed that their prestigious longevity and recent military prowess augured well for his prospects in the South—that is, in the continuing struggle against the Muslims of North Africa.

But Cabeza de Vaca instead went west, where fresh opportunities seemed to lie. Because of his background as a hidalgo, he was able to secure a commission as the *tesorero* ("chief ranking officer") of the royal treasury team that was part of every outward-bound Castilian conquering expedition to the Americas. He was responsible for reporting on the treasure found (they found none) as well as on the newly traversed territories and their Native inhabitants. In that capacity, he participated in the preparation of at least four known official reports, which are now lost. The most significant is the so-called joint report, which was collectively authored in 1536 by the three surviving hidalgos—Cabeza de Vaca, Andrés Dorantes, and Alonso del Castillo Maldonado—and submitted to the Audiencia of Santo Domingo in 1537, where Gonzalo Fernández de Oviedo read it. Oviedo later used the joint report as the basis for his account of the Narváez expedition in his *Historia general y natural de las Indias* (*General and Natural History of the Indies*; Cabeza de Vaca, *Narrative* 22–24; Adorno and Pautz 3: 8–12).

After a sojourn of ten years in North America on a journey that crossed the Atlantic, lingered in the Caribbean, spanned the breadth of the lower part of the North American continent, and recrossed the Atlantic, Cabeza de Vaca arrived home in 1537. He raced to the royal court in Valladolid, hoping to be awarded the royal commission for the next major expedition to North America. He was too late. At court he met Hernando de Soto, a captain of the recently successful Spanish invasion of Peru that had felled the reigning prince of the Inca Empire. De Soto had just been awarded the coveted Spanish Florida commission. Knowing that Cabeza de Vaca's experience would be a plus, De Soto offered him a post on his forthcoming expedition. Cabeza de Vaca refused.

Cabeza de Vaca instead sat down to write the now-famous account *Naufragios*. Published in 1542 and 1555 under the title *Relación*, it was titled *Naufragios* in its eighteenth-century editions. At the time, *naufragio* referred not only to shipwrecks but, more broadly, to calamities of any sort. Two of the Narváez ships were wrecked, not while at sea but when anchored off the coast of Cuba, trying to weather a hurricane (*Narrative* 49–52; ch. 1). Nevertheless, given later events, the translation "calamities" is a better fit. More than the memoir of a failed expedition, the account Cabeza de Vaca produced in the years 1538–40 was the means by which he hoped to land a commission to lead the next major outbound conquest expedition, and in 1540 he was awarded the royal contract for the governorship of the province of Río de la Plata in the South American interior. Before he departed on his South American expedition in December 1540, Cabeza de Vaca deposited his narrative account with his Cabeza de Vaca kinsmen in Zamora, where it was published in 1542.

His South American sojourn turned out to be his second doomed expedition experience. After taking up his royal appointment in Río de la Plata, he created enemies, both Christian and Native, such that in 1545 he was sent back to Spain in chains (see Adorno and Pautz 1: 382–402). But that is another story, not to be taken up here. Only its sequel is of interest: Cabeza de Vaca's ultimate restoration of his good fortune and good name and the second publication of his *Relación*. After his exoneration by the Royal Council of the Indies for criminal charges lodged against him regarding his actions in Río de la Plata, Cabeza de Vaca reestablished his residence in Jerez de la Frontera and in 1559 cosponsored the ransom payment of his distant cousin Hernán Ruiz Cabeza de Vaca, who was one of twelve thousand Spanish soldiers captured by Algerian troops in a failed expedition against the Ottoman Turks in 1558. The date of Cabeza de Vaca's death is uncertain, but circumstantial evidence suggests that he was buried, like his paternal grandfather, in the family vault in the Real Convento de Santo Domingo in Jerez (1: 407–13).

For the fresh publication of the *Relación* in 1555, a running head was introduced along the top of the folios and on the contents page identifying the twin accounts, Cabeza de Vaca's North American *Relación* plus Pero Hernández's apologetic history of his governance of Río de la Plata, together titled *Relación y comentarios* (1: 286–87, 3: 111–14). The fact that Cabeza de Vaca was able to bring his *Relación* into print for a second time is proof of his personal and professional vindication and an indication of the prestige of the Cabeza de Vaca line. His editorial success was unique for his time. In the first half or so of the sixteenth century, only two other works by Spanish authors who wrote about American affairs were repeatedly published, and they were of much broader scope: Oviedo's *Historia general y natural de las Indias*, in 1535 and 1547, and Francisco López de Gómara's *Historia general de las Indias y la conquista de México* (*General History of the Indies and the Conquest of Mexico*), in 1552, 1553, and 1554, the third edition of which included the conquest of Peru. Cabeza de Vaca's distinction was in having personal experience that spanned both North and South America.

There are differences between the first and second editions of Cabeza de Vaca's account. For the 1555 edition, Cabeza de Vaca divided his account into chapters. This converted his continuous, uninterrupted report to the royal court into a segmented narration that was easy for any curious reader to read at leisure. Another difference is that Cabeza de Vaca recast (and exaggerated) his personal role in events. This includes his claims that he had been a more prudent and responsible leader than Narváez and that as a healer he was bolder and more daring than his companions (*Narrative* 57–59, 118–19; chs. 4, 22; see Adorno and Pautz 3: 84–97).

The legacy of Cabeza de Vaca's *Relación*-cum-*Naufragios* is enormous. It is one of the only works from the Spanish-conquest era that is still in print to this day on three continents: in Europe and both Americas. Whether Cabeza de Vaca is identified as a sojourner of Spanish territories now in the United States or in South American republics, interest in his *Naufragios* continues to be high. It started in the sixteenth and seventeenth centuries, when it was valued by Spanish conquistadores for potentially useful information that it contained about Native peoples and territories beyond the northern reaches of New Spain. In the eighteenth century it was viewed by Spanish-language missionary writers as an inspiring, providential tale about the potential for the evangelization of Native peoples. Importantly, the work's first modern edition—and the first to use *Naufragios* as its title—appeared at this time: Andrés González de Barcia published it in a now-lost edition in 1731 and again in his *Historiadores primitivos de las Indias* (*Early Historians of the Indies*), in 1749 (Adorno and Pautz 3: 180–89, 38; Cabeza de Vaca, *Narrative* 33–36). In the nineteenth century *Naufragios* attracted English-language writers interested in the Spanish past in North America. Since then, interest in the work has proliferated. Cabeza de Vaca's *Naufragios* has inspired novels, epic poems, lyric poetry, a feature-length film, a choral cantata, and much more (see Adorno, "Cabeza de Vaca Phenomenon").

Allusiveness and Omissions in Naufragios

Upon his return to Spain in 1537, Cabeza de Vaca faced the challenge of recalling, interpreting, and putting into words his experiences of a world entirely unknown to his readers. Before studying *Naufragios*, students can profitably read works (or portions of them) that dramatize the problem. For example, Abel Posse's novel *El largo atardecer del caminante* (*The Long Twilight of the Wan-*

derer) features as its protagonist an aged Cabeza de Vaca, who, long back from his transatlantic trials and tribulations, continues to be hounded for information about his North American experience: "They say you have a secret version, a third version of your journey" ("Dicen que ud. tiene una versión secreta, una tercera versión de su viaje"; my trans.; 30). Annoyed, the old man responds silently to himself later, "I have no patience for the prestigious lies of exactitude" ("No tengo paciencia con la prestigiosa mentira de la exactitud"; my trans.; 35).

Similarly, Jorge Luis Borges's 1969 short story "The Ethnographer" features as its protagonist a young doctoral student, Fred Murdock, who studies Amerindian languages. After spending two years living with a Native community in prairie country and having plumbed the depths of his indigenous hosts' linguistic knowledge and affective experience, Fred returns to campus to inform his mentor that he will not write the expected doctoral dissertation. He explains that what he has learned is inexpressible and that it must be personally experienced to be understood. Fred then abandons his studies, marries, divorces, and ends up as one of the librarians at Yale, where no expectations for arcane personal disclosure are placed upon him. The terrible "prestigious lies of exactitude" and a subject's inner thoughts are not to be found in *Naufragios*, but by reading Borges's short story and key selections from Posse's novel, students can appreciate the power of what is not said.

Time and Space in **Naufragios**

The relationship between time and space in the narrative is a fundamental topic. Too often the account is misunderstood as a continuous journey of wandering, when in fact there were years-long stationary periods. Ultimately, Cabeza de Vaca, Dorantes, Castillo Maldonado, and Esteban, who was enslaved to Dorantes, traversed the North American continent east to west, Texas to Sonora, in a mere ten months. Despite acknowledging Posse's fictional Cabeza de Vaca's disdain for "the prestigious lies of exactitude" (35), the reader of *Naufragios* can benefit from knowing the approximate loci of actions-in-time.

Consisting of nearly six hundred people and heralded as a major expedition for the purpose of conquering and settling the northern rim of the Gulf of Mexico, the Narváez expedition was a short-term historical failure with long-term literary consequences. It began when the expedition members departed Sanlúcar de Barrameda in Spain in June 1527, and it ended in September or October 1528. Some one hundred and forty men abandoned the expedition as soon as it reached the island of Santo Domingo (Hispaniola) in August 1527 (Cabeza de Vaca, *Narrative* 48; ch. 1). After taking some three hundred men ashore into present-day Florida in the hope of finding wealth to match that of Moctezuma's Mexico (59–74; chs. 5–8), and later, in 1528, being unable to locate the expedition's three ships that were waiting at the coast, Narváez ordered the construction of five rafts to carry the men across the Gulf of Mexico to the northernmost reaches of New Spain and beyond—all before abandoning his command while rafting in Gulf waters (71–82; chs. 8–10). Narváez was never heard from again. The expedition's aftermath lasted from 1528 to 1536—that is, from the arrival of the rafts on the shores of eastern Texas in November 1528 to Cabeza de Vaca and his party's reunion with Spanish slavers in northwestern Mexico in spring 1536 (159–60; chs. 33–34).

To visualize Cabeza de Vaca's experience for students and to help them follow the geography and chronology of narrative events, I show them a map (fig. 1) and a table (table 1). The map shows approximate locations and dates of travel in the Caribbean, along the Gulf of Mexico coast, and inland and overland from the Gulf Coast of Texas to Mexico's Pacific coast and then inland to the capital of New Spain.[3] The table also charts the time and place of events but links them to the chapters of *Naufragios* in which they appear so that readers can follow along using any edition (see also Cabeza de Vaca, *Narrative* 17). Start to finish, the total time elapsed in *Naufragios* is ten years and two months. A simple, vivid way to put in mind the experiences of Cabeza de Vaca and his three companions is to think in terms of winters. They spent the first winter in Cuba, then seven winters in eastern coastal Texas, followed by one winter during their crossing of Mexico, and one winter—their last together—in the capital of New Spain. As table 1 indicates, these events occupy chapters 1–36 and take place from 1527 to 1536. After Cabeza de Vaca describes his arduous journey home to Spain in chapter 37, chapter 38 narrates what Cabeza de Vaca learned upon arriving in México-Tenochtitlan in 1536—namely, that the one hundred persons who had stayed with the ships in 1528 first attempted to find the overland contingent but then gave up and sailed on to New Spain, arriving in 1529.[4]

All told, Cabeza de Vaca and his three companions experienced, in effect, three separate journeys. The first was the sea-and-land journey from Spain through the years of their habitation in eastern Texas, covering the years 1527–35. The second was the party's overland journey from southeastern Texas and northeastern Mexico to the west coast of Mexico and southward, then southeastward, to the capital of New Spain (México-Tenochtitlan, today Mexico City), in the years 1535–36. The third was Cabeza de Vaca's voyage home. The ship was beset by storms and delays in the Caribbean, encountered French privateers in the Azores, and was rescued near the island of Corvo by a Portuguese armada homeward bound from India; Cabeza de Vaca finally arrived in Spain in 1537 (Cabeza de Vaca, *Narrative* 169–73; ch. 37).

There were one hundred other survivors of the Narváez expedition who had better luck. In 1528 they stayed with the expedition's three surviving ships in the coastal waters off present-day Florida's northern shore, and after unsuccessfully searching for the expedition members who had gone inland into Spanish Florida, they ultimately crossed the Gulf to New Spain's capital in 1529. Cabeza de Vaca's party of four encountered them there after their arrival in 1536. Narrated in chapter 38, this finale also includes the prophecy of the Moorish woman from Hornachos, which offers an unnerving commentary about the Narváez expedition as having been fated to fail (Cabeza de Vaca, *Narrative* 173–75).[5]

Table 1. Sequence of events in *Naufragios*

Naufragios chapters	Time period	Events and locations
1–2	June 1527 to February or March 1528	The Narváez expedition makes the Atlantic crossing from Sanlúcar de Barrameda, Spain, and sojourns at Havana, Cuba.
3–4	March to May 1528	The expedition gets lost when it sails from Havana but then reaches the Florida coast at Tampa Bay.
5–8	May to September 1528	Captain Narváez and three hundred men, including Cabeza de Vaca, go ashore at Tampa Bay and travel on foot to Apalachee Bay.
9–10	September to November 1528	Some two hundred and fifty men in the overland contingent travel by raft from Apalachee Bay to coastal Texas. (Narváez relinquishes his command and is lost at sea.)
11–28	November 1528 to mid or late summer 1535	Cabeza de Vaca, Castillo Maldonado, Dorantes, and Esteban spend six and a half years traversing the area along the Gulf Coast between Galveston Bay, Texas, and Río San Fernando in Tamaulipas.
28–31	Mid or late summer to early autumn 1535	Cabeza de Vaca and his three companions travel overland from Río San Fernando to La Junta de los Ríos on the Texas-Chihuahua border.
31–33	Early autumn 1535 to late spring 1536	The Cabeza de Vaca party continues overland from La Junta de los Ríos to the Río Petatlán in Sinaloa.
33–36	Spring to 23 July 1536	The Cabeza de Vaca party completes its overland travel from the Río Petatlán to México-Tenochtitlan, the capital of New Spain.
37	23 July 1536 to 9 August 1537; autumn 1537	Cabeza de Vaca travels home from México-Tenochtitlan, sailing to Lisbon and going overland to Castile.
38	May 1528 to July 1529	The seaborne contingent of one hundred persons that never left the ships at Tampa Bay searches for survivors of the inland expedition and then travels directly to New Spain.

Curing Episodes and Mala Cosa

Cabeza de Vaca's tale of his party's experience as healers and his account of the mysterious figure Mala Cosa (Bad Thing) always fascinate readers. In sixteenth-century Spain the tradition of the *saludador*, or folk healer, was not controversial to the Catholic Church. And the party's reported acts of curing were not Inquisitorial offenses. The careful reader will note that Cabeza de Vaca never makes direct personal claims about the success of the four men's efforts as healers or about Mala Cosa. Instead, he always attributes such testimony to the Native peoples (*Narrative* 164–65; ch. 35).

The healing episodes, which range over chapters 15–35 of *Naufragios*, are attractive for classroom use because they can help students engage the central issue of how to parse and weigh the power of Cabeza de Vaca's narrative, regardless of whether the account is historically accurate (which is unknowable). Such scenes morph from initially tense encounters with Native people who insist that the four men perform curative rituals and heal their maladies (93; ch. 15) into joyful gatherings in which the four men carry out their healing rituals among Native groups who pass the four men from one group to the next; by this means, the Cabeza de Vaca party was led across southwestern Texas and into northern Mexico from late summer 1535 through spring 1536 at a swift and steady pace (113–14; ch. 20). As Cabeza de Vaca tells it, these encounters further evolved into ritual pillaging by one Native group of another (135–39; ch. 28) as those communities sought to express their apparently fearful, astonished regard for Cabeza de Vaca and his party (138–65; chs. 28–35). Taking advantage of the Native people's respect for talismanic items, the four men began carrying gourds (139; ch. 29), which Cabeza de Vaca later characterized as "our principal insignia and emblem of our great estate" ("nuestra principal insignia y muestra de gran estado"; 165, ch. 35; Adorno and Pautz 1: 256).

In narrating these events, Cabeza de Vaca tells how Native communities reported the existence of a shadowy figure called Mala Cosa, who some fifteen years earlier had terrorized the peoples of the region (*Narrative* 119–21; ch. 22). Although Cabeza de Vaca says that he and his fellows never encountered Mala Cosa personally, they found the apparent evidence of his earlier presence to be disturbing.[6] Instructors can highlight this episode for students by furnishing them a glimpse of similar ancient accounts documented in North American and Mesoamerican anthropology, cited below, that speak to one of humanity's oldest inventions: the trickster figure.

The account that Cabeza de Vaca gives of Mala Cosa's deeds is strikingly vivid. Appearing at the door of a house with a burning firebrand, Mala Cosa would enter the dwelling, select a victim, and perform two surgical operations, using a sharp flint to inflict three large incisions in his victim's upper torso. He would then place his hand in the wounds, pull out the entrails, cut off a piece, and throw it into the fire. Afterward he would make three cuts in the victim's arm, the second at the crook, thus dislocating it. Mala Cosa would then reset the dislocated limb and place his hands over the open torso wounds; later, the Native peoples report, they saw that the wounds were healed. When Cabeza de Vaca and his companions dismiss the tale with a laugh, the Native peoples bring forward Mala Cosa's purported victims; a perplexed Cabeza de Vaca acknowledges having seen the scars of the healed cuts, located in the places and in the manner they claimed (*Narrative* 120–21; ch. 22).

The tale of Mala Cosa represents the ancient tradition of the trickster figure. With a nearly universal distribution that included the cultures of the ancient Greeks, the Chinese, the Japanese, and the Semitic world, the trickster figure's earliest, most archaic forms—and also its modern ones—have been found among the indigenous peoples of North America. In its North American manifestations, according to the classic study by Paul Radin (xxiii–xxv, 132–46, 155–69), selections of which I recommend assigning as an adjunct to the Mala Cosa episode, the trickster was a creator and a destroyer, one who duped others and was himself duped; knowing neither good nor evil, he was responsible for both. Possessing no social or moral values, he existed at the mercy of his passions and appetites. He remained isolated from society and had the ability to appear to transform himself sexually. In short, the significance of the trickster figure consisted of its embodiment of "the vague memories of an archaic and primordial past, where there as yet existed no clear-cut differentiation between the divine and the non-divine. . . . His hunger, his sex and his wandering belonged neither to the gods nor to man" (Radin 168; see Adorno and Pautz 2: 272–85).

In order to introduce students to the complex cultural traditions of the indigenous Americas, I recommend that students read Cabeza de Vaca's Mala Cosa account alongside other indigenous myths collected in Mesoamerica in the sixteenth and subsequent centuries that offer accounts of magical bodily dismemberment and restoration. For the Nahua cultures of New Spain, the Franciscan friar Bernardino de Sahagún offers pertinent examples in his *Historia general de las cosas de Nueva España* (*General History of the Things of New Spain*), in which he collected materials about Native magicians and mountebanks (904–09). One such figure, *el destrozador* ("the destroyer"), cut off hands, feet, and other body parts of his lordly victims, then covered the dismembered appendages with a red mantle, after which he would reveal the restored body, which appeared as if it had never been dismembered (906). The *Popol Vuh*, which is the sacred book of the highland Quiché Maya, records the myth of corporeal dismemberment and restoration in the hero cycle of the sacred twins Xbalanque and Hunahpu (136–37). Xbalanque sacrificed Hunahpu by extending his arms and legs, decapitating him, and tearing out his heart. Xbalanque then danced alone before commanding his dismembered brother to arise. Hunahpu got up restored, and much rejoicing followed (137). These accounts can encourage students to explore the all-too-neat dichotomy between myth and history, and instructors can also point out to them, by way of Radin and his cited sources, the endurance of Amerindian traditions.

Esteban in History and Fiction

No member of the Narváez expedition has aroused more interest than Esteban, identified by Cabeza de Vaca in the last line of *Naufragios*: "The fourth is named Estevanico; he is an Arabic-speaking black man, a native of Azamor" ("El quarto se llama Estevanico; es negro alárabe, natural de Azamor"; *Narrative* 176; ch. 38; Adorno and Pautz 1: 279; 278). He was named for Stephen, the first saint of the Roman Catholic Church, who was martyred by being stoned to death (such may have been Esteban's fate, too). The diminutive form of his name, "Estevanico," was the usage commonly applied to enslaved people and interpreters—whether African, indigenous, or mestizo—by the Spaniards they served.

Less is known about the historical figure of Esteban than is attributed to him in fiction. Both versions are essential, in my view, to the task of engaging students' interest. The presence of Esteban and an additional unknown number of enslaved Africans on the Narváez expedition followed a practice that began with Columbus. Enslaved Africans had been introduced into the Spanish Caribbean since at least 1501, when Queen Isabel limited the already-swelling passage of enslaved Black Africans to those who had been born and raised under Christian tutelage. A little later, enslaved Black Africans arrived in the territory of the current United States, but this arrival predated the Narváez expedition, and claims that Esteban was this country's first enslaved Black presence are erroneous. On the contrary, Juan Ponce de León's expedition arrived at the Florida Peninsula in 1513, and in 1520 and 1521, Ponce de León and Lucas Vázquez de Ayllón separately attempted to establish settlements there (Adorno and Pautz 3: 215–18, 270–78). There is no question that such efforts included enslaved Black Africans, who were alleged to possess great strength and would have been considered essential for the hard labor required.

Esteban was born in the city of Azemmour in the province of Doukkala, Morocco. Azemmour was noted for its fishing bounty, its production of wheat, and especially its Portuguese-run slave market.[7] Portugal had taken Azemmour in 1486, lost it in 1502, and retaken it in 1508; it remained a Portuguese protectorate from that date until 1540. Esteban was probably born just prior to, or sometime early in, this second period of Portuguese domination. Andrés Dorantes may have purchased Esteban in Seville as part of the preparation for his planned settlement in Spanish Florida, or he may have brought him, already enslaved, from his home in the north, Béjar in Old Castile, also known as Extremadura at the time (Adorno and Pautz 2: 408, 416).

As a member of the Cabeza de Vaca party, Esteban played a crucial role as scout and mediator. On the overland trek, he was regularly sent ahead of the others to gather information and communicate with the Native peoples (Cabeza de Vaca, *Narrative* 153; ch. 31). Esteban's expertise as a guide also played a large role in his fate after the Narváez expedition. The viceroy of New Spain, Antonio de Mendoza, purchased him from Dorantes after the four men's arrival in the city of México-Tenochtitlan, then the viceregal capital. Mendoza sent Esteban north with the friar Marcos de Niza's expedition, which departed from San Miguel de Culiacán (in today's Sinaloa) in March 1539. Esteban never returned, evidently having been killed by the Native peoples of the northerly areas traversed by the exploring party or while scouting ahead of the party.

Niza reported, at second hand, that Esteban had been the victim of a massacre that claimed the lives of three hundred Native allies who had accompanied the expedition. Francisco Vázquez de Coronado claimed, at third hand, that Esteban's death could be blamed on his cruelties, particularly his assaults on Native women. The Hernando de Alarcón expedition destined for the South Sea (the Pacific Ocean) offered yet another account. The "bearded negro" had given threatening information to his Native interlocutors about his "infinite number of arms-bearing brothers" (Hammond and Rey 2: 141, 145). In this scenario, Esteban was killed by the Native people to prevent him from revealing their location to his powerful kin. As to the time and place of Esteban's death, it probably took place in northern Sonora sometime in April 1539 (Adorno and Pautz 2: 414–22).

The major interpretative point I like to make with students about Esteban is this: In that long (I call it "liminal") period from 1528 to 1536, when Cabeza de Vaca and his companions were out of contact with their countrymen and had little or no hope of ever rejoining Spanish-style civilization, Esteban took the lead. Although Cabeza de Vaca followed the rigid racial and social hierarchies of his day and had no intention of portraying Esteban as their leader (invariably calling him "el negro" [Cabeza de Vaca, *Narrative* 96; ch. 16] and much less frequently "Estevanico" [101; ch. 17] and recounting orders they gave him), he acknowledged that Esteban was the one who was most uniquely capable of communicating and negotiating with Native groups. Given Esteban's talismanic—perhaps charismatic—qualities as seen by the indigenous communities that interacted with him, it is likely that he (not Cabeza de Vaca, who lays claim to the deed) led the small party to its fervently desired destination: the lands of Spanish settlement (159–60; ch. 33). Cabeza de Vaca's limited and allusive characterization of Esteban's role has facilitated—even made plausible and attractive—today's cultural reckoning with this North African figure. Esteban lives on in novels narrated in the first person: he is "Estebanico" in Helen Rand Parish's *Estebanico*, "Estevan" in Daniel Panger's novel *Black Ulysses*, and, much more recently, "Mustafa al-Zamori" in Laila Lalami's Pulitzer Prize–nominated *The Moor's Account*.

All this goes to show that the uncertain, unstable literary domain inhabited by the early Spanish writings about the New World offered—and continues to offer—old and new ways of approaching the mysteries of human experience. The literary tenure of the figure of Esteban is the best indication of this point, which underscores the main themes of this essay: the medieval heritage and modern legacy of Cabeza de Vaca, the stark contrast between his party's crossing of the North American continent in ten months after spending six and a half years in easternmost Texas and Mexico, the Native peoples' attribution of magical powers to Mala Cosa and healing prowess to Cabeza de Vaca and his three companions, and the paradoxical role of the enslaved Esteban as the account's most effective leader. Ellipses, allusions, and omissions are the major catalysts in these writings that blur the distinction between history and fiction, allowing these works to cohabitate in unexpected places, thus making possible ever-new readings.

NOTES

1. Citations of *Naufragios* refer to the translation by Rolena Adorno and Patrick Charles Pautz (Cabeza de Vaca, *Narrative*) and include the chapter numbers used in the 1555 Spanish edition (*Relación y comentarios*). The translation aims to provide a strong impression of Cabeza de Vaca's prose without embellishing it, and it offers philological annotations that take into account the respective variants in the 1542 and 1555 editions, as well as explanatory notes that identify geographic, historical, and cultural references. All such observations are based on Adorno and Pautz, vol. 2.

2. Determining Cabeza de Vaca's exact birth date has proved impossible; see Adorno and Pautz 1: 343–50.

3. Patrick Pautz and I created this map using our detailed analysis of Cabeza de Vaca's narrative account, which can be found in Adorno and Pautz, volume 2. The map is reprinted in Cabeza de Vaca, *Narrative* 38–39.

4. For a closer look at the narrative complexity of Cabeza de Vaca's account, see *Narrative* 12–17.

5. On the Muslim and Morisco enclave in Hornachos, Extremadura, and the erudite and popular traditions of Muslim and Morisco prophecy, see Adorno and Pautz 2: 403–04.

6. The tale of Mala Cosa was one that Oviedo refused to include in his own *Historia general* after having read Cabeza de Vaca's published *Relación* of 1542. The episode had undoubtedly been left out of the now-lost report submitted jointly by Cabeza de Vaca, Dorantes, and Castillo Maldonado in 1536 to the Audiencia de Santo Domingo. See Adorno and Pautz 3: 12–22.

7. Portugal had begun its West African slave trade in the mid–fifteenth century; Boxer 21–31.

Unteaching Cabeza de Vaca; or, How to Question the Culture of Conquest

José Rabasa

Para Ismael

Influential studies of the literary character of the so-called *crónicas* ("chronicles") of Spanish conquest in the Americas, and in particular of Álvar Núñez Cabeza de Vaca's *Naufragios* (*Shipwrecks*), have broadened our understanding and appreciation of their rhetorical and aesthetic sophistication.[1] It is my belief, however, that we ought to step back and consider wherein lies the literary quality and charm of conquest narratives before we define a literary canon that would tend to perpetuate—in the classroom as it has in most of the related scholarship—a whole array of ethnocentric terms (e.g., the uncritical use of evolutionary stages from savagery to civilization), the reduction of the corpus of Spanish-American literature to texts written in Spanish, and a definition of literary value that exclusively follows Western conventions.[2] Furthermore, we should note that even though Cabeza de Vaca portrays himself as a benevolent colonial official, he nonetheless reproduces on a symbolic level the colonial myths and structure and articulates the same violence that he condemns. His denunciations, for instance, reiterate the belief in the natural subordination of Native Americans to Spanish rule, the definition of cannibalism as a culinary aberration, and the reduction of Native knowledge to sham and superstition inspired by the devil. Even when we can read ambivalence and playful reversals in Cabeza de Vaca's stock images of Indians, we need to understand, for example, how in the *Comentarios* (*Commentaries*) the denunciation of Spanish terror uses these same images to accentuate the illegality and rampant abuse of Indians in Río de la Plata. Current preferences for a Cabeza de Vaca who undergoes a conversion from what can only be a stereotype of a greedy conquistador to a reformed character who embodies a panoply of apparently good traits—critic of empire (Pastor, *Discursos*), advocate of peaceful conquest (Adorno, "Negotiation," "Discursive Encounter," "Peaceful Conquest"), and first Spanish transculturador (someone who enacts transculturation) of Indian culture (Spitta, *Between Two Waters* 29–54), who is also the first Chicano (Bruce-Novoa, "Naufragios" and "Shipwrecked"; Valdez and Steiner)—suggest a need for a homey *Madre Patria* ("Motherland"), for a counterdiscourse to the *leyenda negra* ("Black Legend"), for a founding moment of Latin America and modernity where imperialism was not always bad. Thus, these readings manage to critique imperialism while retaining a redeemable view of Spanish colonialism in exceptional individuals. Have we been seduced by Cabeza de Vaca into an uncritical reproduction of the culture of conquest?

With all this in mind, we must not *teach* Cabeza de Vaca's work but *unteach* it, by looking critically into the terms, concepts, and topoi that the work supposedly inaugurates and by ceasing, once and for all, our reproduction of the culture of conquest. We must thoroughly examine these concepts, among them notions like peaceful conquest and the benign, loving, or good empire, and we must reframe them under the logic of love speech that is representative of what I have elsewhere termed "writing violence."

Peaceful Conquest, an Oxymoron

Well-known critics in literary studies have critiqued the concept of the literary as an elitist category that serves to undermine the cultural contributions of non-Western cultures and thus perpetuate a closed canon (see Beverley; Bourdieu; Derrida). On the other hand, the preference put forward by critics for anthropological or historical readings that accentuate the uniqueness of *Naufragios* as a founding text of Latin American heterogeneity or of Cabeza de Vaca as an exemption to the colonial ethos of the conquistadores would seem to confirm the seductive power of the literary in *Naufragios* (see Adorno, "Peaceful Conquest"; Pupo-Walker, "Sobre el legado retórico"; Spitta, *Between Two Waters*). We have come to understand the literary as a construct, but we have failed to take this insight further by analyzing the force of the aesthetic—its violence.

It seems to me that the seductive powers of *Naufragios*—that is, what makes it a brilliant literary piece—have led historians, critics, and the creators of literary and cinematic adaptations of the work to argue that Cabeza de Vaca underwent a personal transformation that enabled him to formulate and exemplify a peaceful conquest. Take, for instance, Rolena Adorno's assessment of the differences between Nuño de Guzmán and Cabeza de Vaca: "In contrast [to Guzmán], Cabeza de Vaca provided what was, to date, the most successful and the most peaceful of conquests. It was the prototype of expeditions that were to be called, according to Phillip II's 1573 laws, not conquests but 'acts of pacification'" ("Negotiation" 191). By reading *Naufragios* in the legal context of the 1526 Ordenanzas sobre el buen tratamiento de los indios (Ordinances for the Good Treatment of the Indians), regulating exploration and conquest, we come to question the purported originality of Cabeza de Vaca's advocacy of peaceful colonization. We need, moreover, to attend to the ways in which the oxymoron *peaceful conquest* manages to negotiate dominance with hegemonic consent: the right kind of treatment will ensure that potentially hostile Indians will turn out servile. The oxymoron also remains blind to, hence complicitous with, the rhetorical slippages in Cabeza de Vaca's texts, where ideology (hegemonic will) gives way to violence (dominance). Although toward the end of *Naufragios* Cabeza de Vaca outlines an ideal form of imperialism and casts himself as an equally ideal servant of the Crown, it is in the *Comentarios*, an account of his political fiasco in Río de la Plata recorded by his amanuensis, Pero Hernández, that the conquistador dwells at length on his efforts to enforce colonial law in an outpost ruled by terror. The power of *Naufragios* resides in the story of shipwreck, of complete loss of material civilization, of becoming a shaman, and of immersion in an Indian world. Colonial laws, nonetheless, constitute a subtext of *Naufragios*.

Why privilege *Naufragios* over the *Comentarios*, which, despite Cabeza de Vaca's pathetic return to Spain in chains, presents his account of Río de la Plata as an exemplary history with moral and political lessons? What reading patterns inform literary appraisals of colonial texts, in particular *Naufragios*, to the point of ignoring their colonialist impulse and their reduction of Native Americans to either servile or hostile characters in the Spanish imperial plot in the Americas? What deeply embedded historiographical prejudices keep these readings alive and prevent readers from recognizing the right of indigenous peoples to violently oppose Spanish invasions?

Cabeza de Vaca is without a doubt one of the most romantic of the conquistadores. His writings inaugurate some of the most vivid and familiar topoi in representations of colonial encounters. By *topoi* I mean those discursive spaces and places of memory—barbarism, cannibalism, superstition, and the evolutionary stages from savagery to civilization, as well as the shipwreck, saintliness, and going native—that written accounts reelaborate in the construction of a Western self and its others. *Naufragios*, however, also stands out for its reversals of the stock images used in representing the Spanish and the Indians: the Spaniards eat each other, undergo a complete loss of material civilization, suffer a political and ethical breakdown, and depend on Indian knowledge for survival. In this story, shipwreck becomes a metaphor for the movement from order to chaos (Pranzetti). This metaphor underlies the fascination this text has produced for modern critics, teachers, and students, leading them to raise it to the status of literature, and the anxiety it provoked among some of Cabeza de Vaca's contemporaries, leading them to censor passages in official chronicles (i.e., by Gonzalo Fernández de Oviedo and by Antonio de Herrera y Tordesillas). If there is in Cabeza de Vaca's narrative a self-conscious hesitation to spell out figurative meanings, other autobiographical gestures and novelesque episodes interrupt the straightforward chronicle of events and thus call our attention to an expected tropological reading (Tyler 132; White, *Tropics* 1–25). For a sixteenth-century European audience avid for adventure stories in exotic places, the wanderings across oceans, rivers, deserts, and jungles were not just traces on the face of the earth, to be reproduced in maps and written accounts, but events with a transcendent significance. Indeed, explorers and conquerors wrote and designed their narratives anticipating that allegorical meanings would be drawn from the events. The conquistadores knew that their feats would be read as if they were inscriptions in gold letters on the pages of history. Therein lies the power of seduction of their self-consciously elaborate narratives and their contribution to the culture of conquest in colonial myths and anthropological categories that still haunt Western ethnography, literary criticism, and fiction.

Empire and Its Subjects

Love speech often informs the language of conquest. According to the twentieth-century rubber boom baron Julio César Arana, the "word 'Conquistar,' from what I have been told in English, sounds very strong. We use it in Spanish to attract a person, to conquer their sympathies" (qtd. in Taussig 28). The language of the 1526 *ordenanzas* mentioned above, included in the *capitulaciones* ("contract") between Pánfilo de Narváez and the Crown for Narváez's expedition, mirrors Arana's definition of *conquista* ("conquest"). But the subtle passage from the language of love into a regime of (legal or criminal) terror seems to have escaped the good conscience of the critics of the rubber boom and the current celebrators of Cabeza de Vaca alike (Morales Padrón, *Teoría y leyes de la Conquista*). The terms *calidad* ("quality") and *habilidad* ("ability") establish the criteria for an anthropological assessment of the most appropriate modes for subjecting Indians to the Crown, or, if necessary, for exterminating them. *Razón* ("reason") and *derecho* ("right" or "law") are used to justify war as well as its consequences—that is, slavery, massacres, and extermination.

As the title of the *ordenanzas* underscores, it is the Crown that defines the proper behavior of Spanish conquistadores toward Indians. And in Cabeza de Vaca's account the laws serve as background in the sense that they are constitutive rules of truth and rightfulness. The laws also structure the questionnaires in the *probanzas* ("depositions") taken upon his return from Río de la Plata. If in writing *Naufragios* Cabeza de Vaca assumes familiarity with the *ordenanzas* (though they are never explicitly mentioned), what are we to say about the privilege critics have granted to the Crown's love speech in current readings of *Naufragios* as a model for peaceful colonization, a transcultural text, or a critique of empire? What in our postcolonial sensibilities keeps us from seeing the flip side of law and rightfulness, a menacing regime of terror, in Cabeza de Vaca's language?

The inclusion of the legal instrument known as the Requerimiento (War Ultimatum) in the *capitulaciones* signals the priority of political subjection over religious conversion. The most primitive version of the Requerimiento offers a path to peace by explaining the Indians' obligation to recognize Spain's sovereignty over their lands as the condition for preventing or ending war (Castañeda-Delgado 396–98). The formal version included in the *ordenanzas* was first read aloud to local peoples by Pedrarias Dávila in Darién in 1514, and later by other conquistadores such as Hernán Cortés in Mexico, but it was not a legal stipulation in the *capitulaciones* granted by the Spanish Crown to conquistadores until 1526.[3] Cortés, given his need to justify mutiny, mentions its reading extensively to highlight the legality of his enterprise as well as to assuage the conscience of the Crown. In the *capitulaciones* with Narváez, the Crown's response to his request to enslave warlike Indians makes enslavement conditional on the reading of the Requerimiento previous to any attack (*CDI* 22: 224–44; Vas Mingo 234–37). Lest we want to idealize Cabeza de Vaca's emphasis on love as a unique formulation of peaceful colonization, we should trace this legal subtext in his writings. The force of *Naufragios* and the *Comentarios* resides as much in Cabeza de Vaca's circumscription of the events and his acts according to the law as in the colonial topoi of shipwreck, going native, and becoming a shaman. From Cabeza de Vaca to Arana in the twentieth century, and beyond, the colonial world has conveyed fascination and repulsion regarding the intertwining of law, aesthetics, and violence.

Cabeza de Vaca participated as treasurer in Narváez's expedition to Florida. This is the same Narváez who tried to topple Cortés at the beginning of the conquest of what is now Mexico. The expedition sailed from Sanlúcar de Barrameda on 17 June 1527, stopped in Santo Domingo and Santiago de Cuba, and tried to sail from Trinidad to Havana when a wind blew the ship toward Florida, where it landed on 12 April 1528. Thus began a disastrous expedition in which hundreds of men were lost and only four survived, stumbling into Culiacán, Sinaloa, in March 1537 after crossing Texas and what are now the Mexican states of Chihuahua and Sonora. The Spanish slave-raiding party that encountered them there—"so strangely dressed and in the company of Indians"—were left speechless and amazed, as Cabeza de Vaca explains: "[t]hey remained looking at me for a long time, so astonished that they neither spoke to me nor managed to ask me anything" ("tan estrañamente vestido y en compañía de indios. Estuviéronme mirando mucho espacio de tiempo, tan atónitos que ni me hablavan ni açertavan a preguntarme nada"; Adorno and Pautz 1: 245; 244; ch. 33)

Images of this kind convey the mythic stuff of Cabeza de Vaca's story and its attractiveness to both a sixteenth- and a twenty-first-century audience. In Tzvetan Todorov's typology of attitudes toward otherness, *Naufragios* exemplifies an evolved ethnographic viewpoint: "Cabeza de Vaca also reached a neutral point, not because he was indifferent to the two cultures, but because he had experienced them both from within—thereby, he no longer had anything but 'the others' around him; without becoming an Indian, Cabeza de Vaca was no longer quite a Spaniard. His experience symbolizes and heralds that of the modern exile" (*Conquest* 249). Todorov's narrative of an evolving ethnographic consciousness manifests a need for Western subjects to believe in their privileged capacity to understand other cultures. It is far from obvious whether Cabeza de Vaca would have recognized the value of not being the other and yet not quite the same, in Todorov's characterization, but he does represent himself as a benevolent, enlightened colonial official dutifully pursuing the interest of the Crown. Cabeza de Vaca sought the governorship of Florida, but by the time he returned to Spain in 1538, it had already been assigned to Hernando de Soto. Nevertheless, Cabeza de Vaca did gain the title of *adelantado* (appointed "civil and military governor") of Río de la Plata, which he sailed to in November 1540. Five years later, Cabeza de Vaca returned to Spain, accused of crimes ranging from such minor offenses as robbing the inhabitants of the Canary Islands of three cows on his outward journey to more serious ones like murdering friendly Indians, confiscating the property of Spaniards, and, the ultimate crime of sedition, calling himself king of the land; he was first jailed and then held under house arrest in a Madrid inn for a total of eight years (Bishop 276–78). The *Comentarios* tell us about these political failures.

Although *Naufragios* and the *Comentarios* are often published together, only *Naufragios* has been singled out as one of the most accomplished narratives about the Spanish conquest from a literary point of view. With the exception of Juan

Francisco Maura, who reads *Naufragios* as a series of trumped-up events intended to gain the writer political favors, literary critics generally agree in finding a tension between the work's historical accounts of events and the novelesque episodes, between an exceptional capacity to relate simply what was seen and a notable autobiographical projection (Pupo-Walker, "Pesquisas"; Pastor, *Discursos*; Dowling; Lewis; Lagmanovich). Scholars generally find these separations clear-cut and insist that *Naufragios* can be studied as literature or as a chronicle. Accordingly, critics identify a series of short stories that they see as intercalated in the account of real events. Drawing mainly from the work of Mircea Eliade, however, Spitta has argued that those passages read by critics as novelesque actually contain anthropological information on shamanism and testify to the deep immersion of Cabeza de Vaca in Native culture (*Between Two Waters* 29–54).

According to Lee Dowling the supposed distinction between story (the chronicle of events) and discourse (the commentary on the events) is debatable and not inherent in the text but a product of our reading (97). Furthermore, that distinction does not make sense if we want to read *Naufragios* as fiction. The tension between fiction and history would, in the end, be the tension between seeing *Naufragios* as similar either to adventure stories or to autobiography and historical account.

Despite the problems with reading *Naufragios* as fiction, it seems to me that displacing the tension to a historical reading creates, in turn, a false opposition (White, *Content*; Lewis 686). *Naufragios* is not simply an account of what happened, because the significance of its facts depends on factors such as the instructions from the Crown, the required numerous readings of the Requerimiento, and an ideology of conquest that defines not only a legal framework but also parameters of prudence and chivalry.

We must insist that Cabeza de Vaca's task is not simply to convey New World phenomena to a European audience but to convey a sense of the uncanny that underlies his experience of the magical. Indeed, we can read *Naufragios* as a text that brings to light what should have remained secret through a process of repression, and it is marked by ambivalence (Freud 225–26, 241). Shipwreck in Cabeza de Vaca's narrative marks the transition to a primordial time signified by physical nakedness and the revelation that European civilization is a thin veneer, easily discarded. This transition entails not only a complete loss of material civilization but also complete dependence on Amerindian knowledge—including the plurality of possible worlds in which magic makes sense and works. I would add that the irony in *Naufragios* is not accidental.

In identifying a tension between fiction and history in the work, critics have assumed that there is an antithetical relation between these terms. The concept of allegoresis, as defined by Hayden White, enables us to surpass this binary opposition:

> Precisely insofar as the historical narrative endows sets of real events with the kinds of meaning found otherwise only in myth and literature, we

were justified in regarding it as a product of *allegoresis*. Therefore rather than regard every historical narrative as mythic or ideological in nature, we should regard it as allegorical, that is, as saying one thing and meaning another. (*Content* 45)

White follows Quintilian's definition of ironic allegory, in which the meaning is contrary to that suggested by the words (bk. 8, ch. 6, line 54; 3: 333–35). What is crucial to allegory is the simultaneity of at least two equally valid readings. We can further complement the meaning of allegory in ethnographic work with James Clifford's observation that allegory (from the Greek *allos*, "other," and *agorevein*, "speak") is "a representation that 'interprets' itself" (99). The allegorical as defined by White and Clifford opens *Naufragios* to at least two double registers: passages that "[say] one thing and [mean] another" and "representations [that] interpret themselves."

In praising or condemning the novelesque elements of *Naufragios*, commentators (at least since Oviedo) have negated Cabeza de Vaca's testimony of experiences that are alien to Western rationality. Beyond being simply an aesthetic, the *real maravilloso* ("magic realism") in *Naufragios* betrays just how ridden with contradictions is the representation (the magic of realism) of another culture (the reality of magic) when one takes into consideration the fact that in the contact zone there is an encounter of at least two sociolects (practices that define reality for a given social group), whose conceptions of the world are often radically incommensurable. Radical incommensurability, however, does not preclude the existence of two (incommensurable) worlds in one consciousness without incurring a contradiction. Rather, contradiction results from the attempt to translate one world into the other. Depending on the register, Cabeza de Vaca at once conveys the notion that magic exists and that magic does not exist. Critics have consistently repressed the uncanny existence of two worlds in *Naufragios*.

The force of the ethnographic texts, according to Clifford Geertz, "has less to do with either a factual look or an air of conceptual elegance than it has with their capacity to convince us" (*Works* 4–5). If an ethnographic text is a testimony of an experience of "being there," its writing necessarily happens in a "being here," in a world of libraries, seminars, lecterns, blackboards, and, above all, disciplinary expectations. In the case of Cabeza de Vaca's work, the audience consists of the secular and ecclesiastical authorities of Charles V's Spain. The language of the real consists of accepted images, concepts, and categories that had become sedimented in chronicles of the New World. The preferred storyline tells of the triumphs of the empire. Thus, the "capacity to convince" depends on the balance between the two understandings of allegory outlined above: narratives endowing meaning to events and self-interpretations in representations. *Naufragios* is at once a story that transforms failure into success and a series of narrative loops whereby Cabeza de Vaca corrodes stock images of the New World and its inhabitants. The ambivalence of the uncanny as defined by Sigmund Freud would seem to be at work in these transformations, where *heimlich* ("homely, familiar") "finally coincides with its opposite, *unheimlich* ['uncanny']" (Freud 225–26). Nothing has been more repressed in readings and teaching of Cabeza de Vaca than his immersion in Amerindian worldviews embedded in magic. In this process, interpreters of *Naufragios* (such as José Miguel Oviedo, Adorno, and Roberto González-Echeverría, just to mention a few) identify magic with Cabeza de Vaca—that is, with the European individual who alternately performs miracles, negotiates fear, and possesses healing powers. The shuttling back and forth between the canny and the uncanny must be seen as integral to what makes *Naufragios* an allegorical text.

Reading Cabeza de Vaca

Several drafts anticipated the version of *Naufragios* we know today. These reflect the transformation of what would have been one more account of events by one more functionary of the Indies into a self-consciously labored text with literary pretensions. Two early versions, written in collaboration with the other survivors, were submitted to the viceregal authorities of New Spain upon the author's arrival at México-Tenochtitlan. There is a fragment with the title "Relación de Cabeza de Vaca, tesorero que fue en la conquista" ("The Account of Cabeza de Vaca, Treasurer Who Went on the Conquest"), which also includes the instructions to Cabeza de Vaca (*CDI* 14: 265–79), and we have Fernández de Oviedo's summary of and commentaries on the lost joint report by Cabeza de Vaca, Alonso del Castillo Maldonado, and Andrés Dorantes (G. Oviedo, *Historia* 2: 579–618). *Naufragios* was first published in 1542 as *La relación* (*The Account*), with neither *privilegio* ("license") nor chapter headings, and was published again in 1555, with further revisions and with the *Comentarios*, as *La relación y comentarios*. Although the term *Naufragios* appears in the table of contents of the 1555 edition, it was not used as a title until 1749.

If the *Relación*'s revisions seem particularly obsessive, the work's impulse to draw a universal message does have illustrious antecedents among the narratives of successful expeditions—for example, Christopher Columbus's *Diario* (*Diary*) of the first voyage and Cortés's letters to Charles V (*Letters from Mexico*), which relate their particular feats as unique events that would affect world history. Columbus and Cortés knew that their enterprises would be read as key parts of an emerging historical plot. Passages in their accounts underscore the uniqueness of their enterprises, but for the most part, narrative is subordinated to an inconclusive chronological account. Cabeza de Vaca faced another task in *Naufragios*: while retaining a truthful, open-ended account characteristic of the *relación* genre, he projects into the sequence of events the plot structure of romance. Emplotment, the constitution and organization of facts by means of a narrative structure, endows otherwise univocal statements with figurative meanings: nakedness, hunger, shipwreck, and healing are given political, religious, and moral interpretations (Pastor, *Discursos* 294–337). To prevent the account from being filed away as one more report of a failed expedition,

Cabeza de Vaca must underscore the uniqueness of his story by means of a narrative. By creating the *relación*-like, inconclusive representation of events in time, as well as the narration's apparent autonomy, Cabeza de Vaca allows for several readings. His ethnographic register names and geographically situates the peoples within a narrative of evangelization and conquest whose meanings, in turn, exceed the adventures of Cabeza de Vaca and the other survivors.

The adoption of the title *Naufragios* illustrates the tropological field in the text. We may wonder why the editor of the 1749 edition chose *Naufragios* and not *Milagros (Miracles), Peregrinajes (Pilgrimages)*, or even *Las aventuras de Cabeza de Vaca (The Adventures of Cabeza de Vaca)*, which would perhaps have been the closest to the title of Defoe's famous 1719 novel *The Life and Strange Adventures of Robinson Crusoe*. Although the nature of the so-called *milagros* and Cabeza de Vaca's capacity to perform them have been the subject of debate, the metaphor of the shipwreck is the strongest motif; it dates to antiquity and recurs in the works of such prominent figures as Homer, Dante, and Defoe. Indeed, shipwrecks have a long tradition as vehicles for conveying the spiritual travails of saints. Because Cabeza de Vaca undergoes a shipwreck, his account immediately lends itself to a religious reading, among others. Shipwreck entails a loss of material civilization, a transition to chaos and social anomie, but also a transition to a world where Western reason faces its limits and founders. Cabeza de Vaca's experience of magic is the element of his account that most resists interpretation. Readers of *Naufragios* have repressed magic, turning magic into miracles effected by God and reading Cabeza de Vaca as a saint of the conquest, and they have celebrated Cabeza de Vaca as a manipulator of fear or gullibility, turning him into an astute as well as benevolent, savvy colonial frontier type, when he is not a *pícaro* ("rogue").[4] Spitta's careful comparison of those passages purported to be fictions with shamanic practices described by Eliade and others spares us the need to analyze these practices in detail (50). Let us simply say that it is equally valid to speak of divine miracles, an opportunistic conquistador, and a Spaniard transculturating shamanism.

Almost a Whole Nation

Haniel Long's novella *The Marvelous Adventures of Cabeza de Vaca* inspired Guillermo Sheridan's screenplay of Nicolás Echevarría's film *Cabeza de Vaca* (Sheridan 23). If Long sort of follows *Naufragios*, anchoring his version of Cabeza de Vaca's meditations on key passages in the source text, Sheridan shrugs off bibliographic materials, seeing in their lack a challenge and a blessing that gives him the license to invent. Sheridan's screenplay and Echevarría's film are not fictions but fantasies. If we can hold fiction accountable—especially historical fiction that aims for verisimilitude—for the accuracy of its representations, a historical fantasy would seem to operate according to rules that allow it to produce images and situations at will.

In Echevarría's film, images with a symbolic aura, with murky or luminous surfaces, are carefully crafted to affect our sensibility. They say much while blinding us to their significance. Does Echevarría know what these images mean? As an example of epistemic murk, take the scene that first depicts the Indian world, where slime and muck invest nondescript cultural objects with the powers of witchcraft. Echevarría's purpose in this scene might have been to reproduce the cultural shock of the Spaniards, but why do it at the expense of Amerindian cultures? After all, that is what the slime and muck stand for. As for examples of the luminous, those takes of Cabeza de Vaca wandering in the desert against a huge blue sky with dramatic cloud formations are obvious instances. They tell of his vulnerability and spiritual grandeur, but what are we to make of them? Perhaps that Cabeza de Vaca holds a unique place in the field of the Lord, one verified by a tree that suddenly bursts into flames at the end of the film. But Mala Cosa (Evil Thing) is also luminous, weeping after having grasped the uniqueness of Cabeza de Vaca, sensitized to his own evil after being mysteriously touched by Western values. It is never made clear what, if anything, this legless and armless dwarf[5] is supposed to stand for: a symbol for Indian culture before Christian redemption? the intuition of the Christian God? One also wonders what is gained by this seemingly arbitrary transformation of the Mala Cosa of *Naufragios*, whose practice of slashing bodies and lifting houses into the air is reminiscent of characters in other Native American texts such as the *Popol Vuh*, where the twins Xbalanque and Hunapuh, after acquiring fame for performing parallel collective illusions, defeat the lords of Xibalba by cutting up their bodies for real (*Popol Vuh* 150).

In his prologue to Sheridan's screenplay, the Colombian novelist Álvaro Mutis gives us a clue as to how to read these images: "What makes this story a beautiful parable of all human destiny is that we learn, at the end, that converted again to what they were before, the Spanish depart and the natives remain in the midst of their precarious condition of a survival bordering inanition and the darkness of primitive chaos, without escape" ("Lo que hacede esta historia una hermosa parabola de todo destino humano, es el saber que, al final, los españoles parten convertidos de nuevo n olo ue eran antes y los nativos se quedan en medio de sus precarias condiciones de sobrevivencia al borde de la inanición y las tinieblas de un caos prmitivo y sin salida"; my trans.; Sheridan 8). We have here a violent response to murk that reduces Indian life to inanition, darkness, and primitive chaos, "without escape." The reader may be baffled when Mutis states that while reading the screenplay or watching the film, "we are struck by that unsettling realization that, for the first time, we have been told the story as it really happened" ("tenemos esa inquietante certeza de que, por primera vez, nos han contado las cosas como fueron"; my trans.; Sheridan 8). Nothing less than the real thing! What do the images say about Indians who have survived the past five hundred years of oppression? The task, then, is to identify how images act—and on what social reality or form of life.

Does the Indian world as presented by Sheridan and Echevarría provide a visual text that would pretend to illustrate *Naufragios*? The film and the screenplay build on passages from Cabeza de Vaca's work (and borrow freely from Long), so they are not completely arbitrary, but for the most part the film fabricates images with no connection to *Naufragios*. Again, if we read it as a fantasy, it doesn't really matter whether it is faithful to the original. Sheridan and Echevarría draw from a wide variety of sources that include depictions of healing practices common among shamans as well as acts of witchcraft.

We must now ask what Echevarría and Sheridan are doing to and with Cabeza de Vaca. I would say that when this film was produced, on the eve of the Columbian quincentennial in 1992, its ideological effect (at least on Mutis) was to counter, if not undermine and silence, the urgency that Indians felt throughout the Americas to condemn the invasion and colonization of the New World. The portrayal of Native Americans as Stone Age peoples who engage in sorcery, are aggressively loud, and utter incomprehensible grunts, among other stereotypes, hardly provides a just representation of Indian culture. If Echevarría's film, as Gustavo Verdesio has pointed out, is a parody of sixteenth-century chronicles, it reproduces—if not exacerbates—the cultures of conquest that existed then and still plague our discourse today (195). Let us now examine some of the preferred metaphors among literary critics.

Hostile Paleolithic Indians

As noted above, according to Pranzetti, the shipwreck functions as a metaphor that marks a transition from order to chaos. The tendency among critics, however, has been to read chaos as an original or primitive state attributed to Indian cultures (in the manner of Mutis) and not simply as a complete loss of material culture on the part of the Spaniards. Enrique Pupo-Walker and David Lagmanovich have separately defined what they perceive as a historicotemporal voyage in *Naufragios*: primitive chaos is but one step further from the characterization of Cabeza de Vaca's journey into North America as "a hallucinatory itinerary that took him from the culture of the Renaissance to the hostile barbarism of the American Paleolithic Age" ("un alucinante itinerario que lo llevó de la cultura renacentista a la barbarie indócil del paleolítico americano"; my trans; Pupo-Walker, "Pesquisas" 539) or "a journey in time, from European civilization of the sixteenth century to the Stone Age" ("un viaje en el tiempo, de la civilización European del siglo XVI a la edad de piedra"; my trans.; Lagmanovich 32).

If any group in Cabeza de Vaca's narrative lacks refinement, it is the Spaniards; for instance, when they are faced with the task of building ships, not one of them has the knowledge or the skills: "we didn't know how to make them" ("nosotros no los sabíamos hazer"; Adorno and Pautz 1: 69; 68; ch. 8). Moreover, if the Indians are hostile, one need not wonder why; the Spaniards raid villages for food, "although not without fights and skirmishes with the Indians" ("no sin contiendas y pendençias con los indios"; 1: 71, 70; ch. 8). Additionally, to the astonishment of the Indians, the Spaniards resort to cannibalism out of hunger: "they ate one another until only one remained. . . . The Indians became very upset because of this and it produced such a great scandal among them that without a doubt, if at the start they had seen it, they would have killed them, and all of us would have been in grave danger" ("se comieron los unos a los otros hasta que quedó uno. . . . Deste caso se alteraron tanto los indios y huvo entre ellos tan gran escándalo que sin duda que si al principio ellos los vieran los mataran, y todos nos viéramos en grande trabajo"; 1: 107; 106; ch. 14). There is a certain irony in Cabeza de Vaca's insistence on the fact that there was no one left to eat the last Spaniard. In their abhorrence of Spanish cannibalism, the Indians embody European values, for Cabeza de Vaca imagines them inflicting death as a punishment.

Thus, the Indians' character is one more component of the plot that depends on the attitude of the Spanish. Yes, the peoples of Florida were hostile to Narváez's invading army. It is also true that Cabeza de Vaca eventually comes into contact with nomadic peoples, but there is no justification, even if the term *Stone Age* were applicable, for the qualifier "indocile barbarism" (Pupo-Walker, "Pesquisas" 539). One can make a reference to indocility only from an imperialist perspective. Indocility would read as resistance in a nonethnocentric reading of Indian responses to the Spanish invasion of their land. As literary critics we should not contribute to the culture of conquest by framing the right to make war against the invaders as hostile barbarism.

In today's studies of colonial texts we can do without the trope of time travel from European civilization to the Stone Age. On the other hand, immediately after introducing his time travel metaphor, Lagmanovich asserts that *Naufragios* is the account of "a progressive identification with the indigenous world that he [Cabeza de Vaca] had come to conquer" ("una progresiva identificación del autor con el mundo que había partió para sojuzgar"; my trans.; 32). In this sense, *Naufragios* suggests a transition and conversion to an overarching critique of the Spanish conquest of the New World. Following these indications by Lagmanovich, Pastor has elaborated a detailed close reading of *Naufragios* as an inversion of the Spanish imperial project (*Discursos* 211–38, 240–44, 250–55).

In treating the discursive violence that the culture of conquest perpetrates through its reading and interpreting of colonial texts, I reiterate the lack of attention literary readings pay to indigenous resistance. The vulnerability of the four survivors in *Naufragios* does not lend itself to the acknowledgment of several instances of resistance, nor does Cabeza de Vaca's almost exclusive concern with the political conflict with the sordid world of Domingo de Irala, who had assumed the leadership of Río de la Plata in the *Comentarios*. But forms of resistance can be reconstructed from descriptions of military encounters in the so-called *entradas* ("raids") without resorting to the imperialistic topos of the hostile Indian. As scholars and teachers, we should also resist the impulse to define Cabeza de Vaca's function as a shaman in *Naufragios* with the topos of the Western hero whose perspicacity enables him to play the role of a quack doctor and manipulate the supposed indigenous perception of the Spaniards as "children of the sun" ("hijos del sol"; Adorno and Pautz 1: 165; 164; ch. 22).

It is precisely because the topoi of ignorant natives and warlike Indians have played an integral function in colonialist literature that they lend artistic and literary value to *Naufragios*. But in following Cabeza de Vaca's conception of the Indians, literary critics also lose track of the rhetorical devices that enabled him to convey knowledge of Native American cultures and personal experiences that questioned European taboos. Cabeza de Vaca's self-representation as a law-abiding colonial official and conquistador may coexist with his role as a colonizer whose writing occurs in a "being here" and has an exceptional story to tell about "being there." Only when we make room for the paradoxical coexistence of an imperial and an empathetic perspective will we be able to trace voices of resistance in Cabeza de Vaca's work.

NOTES

I would like to acknowledge René Carrasco's contributions and help with crafting this essay.

1. See, for example, Maura; Pupo-Walker, "Pesquisas"; Pastor, *Discursos*; Molloy; Barrera; Dowling; Barrera López and Mora Valcárcel; Lewis; and Lagmanovich, among others.

2. Mignolo draws an extensive critique of the reduction by literary critics of the multicultural reality of the Americas to Spanish and other Western cultural norms; "Lengua."

3. Students would benefit from reading the Requerimiento and paying attention to the colonial language of peaceful submission in *Naufragios*.

4. For a summary of the bibliography on the debates over Cabeza de Vaca's cures versus miracles, see Rabasa 54n16, 295–97; Lafaye; Pupo-Walker, "Pesquisas"; Goodwin, "Texts."

5. The movie's casting for the Mala Cosa character implies notions of teratology relevant to both the colonial text and the film, which reenact colonial ideology and stereotypes. In the *Relación*, Mala Cosa is described merely as a small being (of short stature).

Mala Cosa, C'est Moi

Carlos A. Jáuregui

Teaching is, in a certain sense, a repetition of decisions that precede us regarding what we teach and why and the selection of relevant passages, translations, definitions for context, and previous interpretations. We know that the meaning of a text crosses through what Heidegger called *Vorgriff* ("preconception"), or "what we grasp in advance" (41). What is fundamental to the pedagogical exercises of teaching a classic like the *Relación* (*Account*) by Álvar Núñez Cabeza de Vaca is not avoiding preconceptions but rather maintaining critical consciousness of that which determines our understanding.

Cabeza de Vaca is often treated as the conqueror conquered by otherness, a transculturated European who represents the indigenous world with empathy and humanitarianism: an advocate for a so-called peaceful conquest. Following the work of José Rabasa, Maureen Ahern, and Ralph Bauer, numerous critics—myself included—have pointed out the imperialism and Eurocentrism threaded throughout the *Relación* (Jáuregui, "Going Native" 175–77 and *Espectros* 91–94), and certainly today critical readings of Cabeza de Vaca as a "mighty whitey" who is generous, transculturated, and empathetic toward the indigenous world are much less common.[1] Yet in class, hermeneutic-pedagogical traditions persist that perpetuate ideas of colonial humanitarianism and the ideology of *mestizaje* ("miscegenation"). For this reason, the introduction to this volume proposes the notion of unteaching, according to which we must put forth multiple readings of the *Relación* that challenge these preconceptions.

I suggest that we begin by appreciating the disconnect between the perception of the canonical value of the *Relación* held by teachers and the experience of our students. What many instructors consider a fascinating story of an extraordinary adventure on an incredible continent and among unknown indigenous peoples is for many of our students a heavy slog of a reading assignment. The language of the text, with its devilish syntax, is consistently difficult; the narration of events is confusing and constantly interrupted by ethnographic disquisitions. Let's face it, Cabeza de Vaca was not a gifted storyteller.

I have found that students' negative reactions to the text can be productive, and what excites many of them is not so much slogging through a dense classic but rather unreading it, armed with an irreverent and corrosive hermeneutics of distrust (Ricœur, *Freud and Philosophy* 27; Gadamer). My students have posed a whole set of irreverent questions: How tall was Cabeza de Vaca, and why does he say that the Indians seemed like giants? Did he eat human flesh? Why does the narrator maintain such a neutral tone when talking about Spanish cannibalism? In the eight years of his experience abroad, did Cabeza de Vaca never have sex, not even once? Ever? When he finds out that his prayers resurrected a Susola Indian, why does he not freak out? Why doesn't he go to verify the report? Were the Spanish healers frauds? Discussing these questions with intelligent young people who are irritated by the text has informed my own understanding and research.

This essay examines the episode of Mala Cosa (Evil or Wicked Thing), in which Cabeza de Vaca tells a story that he supposedly heard from the Mariame and Avavare Indians about a man with supernatural powers, described as a kind of small, hairy, mysterious, foreign, and terrifying sorcerer. The tale is typically taught as a representation of indigenous shamanism and myths, as a rare fantastical or literary episode, or as the deployment of a contrastive character who helps establish Cabeza de Vaca as a good Christian healer. Against these pedagogical preconceptions, I propose we refute the strangeness of this episode and the supposed ethnographic contrast between Cabeza de Vaca and Mala Cosa.

Something Very Strange

The *Relación* mentions several strange events, including the indigenous story of Mala Cosa.[2] In the summer of 1534, Cabeza de Vaca, Andrés Dorantes, Alonso del Castillo Maldonado, and Esteban (a.k.a. Estevanico), fleeing from the Mariames and the Yguazes, arrived at the lands inhabited by the Avavares, and shortly thereafter the Spaniards carried out a series of healings and pseudomiracles that include the supposed resurrection of a Susola Indian. Cabeza de Vaca says then that the Avavares and the Mariames "told us something very strange" ("nos contaron *una cosa muy estraña*"; Adorno and Pautz 1: 165; 164; ch. 22; emphasis added): the story of Mala Cosa, a bearded foreigner of short stature, an enigmatic agent of magical powers who had shown up some fifteen or sixteen years prior. He sometimes dressed as a woman and other times as a man, he terrorized the Indians and submitted them to magical-surgical procedures, he dislocated their arms and later put them back in place, and he lifted their houses into the air. The Spaniards are skeptical, but the conquistadores' doubts end when the informants show them evidence of the cuts on their bodies.

One traditional way to approach a reading of the "strangeness" of Mala Cosa is to interpret it as literary and, therefore, a manifestation or foreshadowing of a premodern Latin America, which is conceived as an inherently fantastic, magical-realist, and transculturated continent. This colonial genealogy of Latin American literature tends to produce an identification with the culture of the Conquest, as Rabasa has pointed out (31–83), and it builds on the idea that the *Relación* is an antecedent to magical realism when actually the opposite is true: magical realism retrospectively offers certain parameters for preconceiving the colonial text.

On the other hand, several critics have concluded that the story represents aspects of the culture of the Mariames and Avavares, such as shamanism (Pupo-Walker, "*Naufragios*" 765, 772; Spitta, "Chamanismo") or the universal myth of the trickster, as Adorno supposes: "I am sure that the myth of Mala Cosa pertains to the mythical cycle most widespread in North America, which is to say that of the 'trickster' in its most ancient and archaic forms, found among the Indians of North America" (*De Guancane a Macondo* 56–57).

These are reasonable hypotheses, but they run the risk of unintentionally reiterating a colonial point of view. Independent of whether we characterize the story as fictional or ethnographic—or both, as Clifford Geertz might (*Works* 1–24)—to affirm that the episode of Mala Cosa is protoliterary and fable-like or the narration of a myth in its most archaic forms is the equivalent of saying that the Indians are mythical-magical and archaic storytellers. This claim posits that the others are in effect others and that the ethnographic ego is juxtaposed to that so-called primitive indigenous subjectivity. We must keep in mind that ethnography insists on the "I" in a way that is both stubborn and tautological. Mala Cosa and Cabeza de Vaca would be ethnographically opposed to one another. This is—let us reiterate this point—what the colonial text explicitly proposes. But that division between the "I" and the other is not solid. Even supposing the indigenous origin of the tale of Mala Cosa, it comes to us profoundly mediated, both linguistically and culturally. First of all, whatever the indigenous name of this character may have been, the name *Mala Cosa*—in Spanish—suggests that this is not simply an indigenous story but at best the Spaniards' retelling and translation of an indigenous narration. Second, the name is used as a descriptor, suggesting that this "cosa," or "thing," is inherently bad, wicked, evil: an alter-ego to Cabeza de Vaca, the good being. This self-proclaimed tautological difference must be taken with a grain of salt. Let us suspend both the idea of strangeness and the contrast between Cabeza de Vaca and Mala Cosa, and start to notice their similarities: let's inquire into the *cabezadevacaness* of Mala Cosa and the *malacosaness* of Cabeza de Vaca.

Small, Bearded, Cross-Dressing, and Other

In the *Relación* the Mariames and Avavares say that Mala Cosa "was small in body and . . . had a beard" ("era pequeño de cuerpo, . . . y tenía barvas"; Adorno and Pautz 1: 167; 166; ch. 22). While some critics refer to Mala Cosa as a dwarf (Maura 59–60; Paniagua-Pérez 152), and the unfortunate filmic version by Nicolás Echevarría presents him as such, the text simply notes that, in comparison with the Indians, Mala Cosa was short in stature and bearded—physical characteristics that could also be attributed to Cabeza de Vaca.

Now what does it mean that Mala Cosa was "small"? A brief and politically incorrect survey of stereotypes regarding the height of diverse human groups would reveal the racialization of size as a sign and that in processes of othering, size matters. Cabeza de Vaca generally describes the Indians as "of large build" ("crescidos de cuerpo"; Adorno and Pautz, 1: 63; 62; ch. 7), "of great stature" ("grandes"; 1: 95; 94; ch. 11), and "large and well proportioned" ("grandes y bien dispuestos"; 1: 107; 106; ch. 14), such that, "from a distance, they appear to be giants" ("desde lexos paresçen gigantes"; 1: 63; 62; ch. 7). The fact that Cabeza de Vaca calls attention to this particularity is indicative of the astonishment that the size of the Indians produced in the Europeans. There are numerous testimonials about the elevated stature of the indigenous people of the Southeast, but the osteometric archaeological evidence indicates an average height of just five feet, seven inches (Iscan and Kessel 73–78). Today this does not seem extraordinary, considering the average height of Spanish men is about five feet, eight inches (Martínez-Carrión and Puche-Gil 445, 449). However, in the sixteenth century their average height was only five feet, three inches (Cook and Borah 142)—that is, four inches shorter than the Indians. This fact presents an opportunity to remind our students that many physiological and even aesthetic features of the body are relative and their cultural meaning arbitrary, that nutrition has an impact on stature, and that such a difference—so often mentioned today when talking about race—is not necessarily genetically determined. The difference in height certainly baffled Cabeza de Vaca, who at one point insinuates that he could have had a false perception motivated by fear and the precarity of his own situation on Malhado Island (Adorno and Pautz 1: 94–95; ch. 11). Fear is a powerful amplifying lens. All this to say that the size of Mala Cosa does not distinguish him from Cabeza de Vaca.

Neither can Mala Cosa's facial hair be seen as a trait that differentiated him from Cabeza de Vaca, who we certainly suppose to be bearded like the majority of the conquistadores. The question seems minor, but it is not. A class discussion or a research assignment will not only allow students to discover books like *Of Beards and Men*, by Christopher Oldstone-Moore, and *The Bearded Lady Project*, edited by Lexi Marsh and Ellen Currano, but will also teach them some of the cultural, historical, and ethnographic dimensions of the beard. They will learn, for example, how before the Conquest, beards in Iberian culture were associated with masculinity, adulthood, virtue, and wisdom, and the lack of a beard implied a feminine, infantile, and ignorant nature. This semiotic distribution between adulthood and boyhood allowed facial hair to become a sign of distinction between the Europeans and indigenous peoples in the Americas. Pietro Martire d'Anghiera synthesizes the stereotype: "All of the barbarians from those nations are beardless and are horrified by and fear the bearded men"; 2: 568; my trans.). Like frightened children, the beardless Indians are represented as afraid of the civilized, bearded Spaniards. The relation between signifier and signified is obviously arbitrary: Mala Cosa is indigenous and bearded, and this ethnographic anomaly indicates that differences (bearded/beardless) are not as important as what those differences signify. The beard has meant many things in different eras and places: civilization, masculinity, and sainthood, but also a lack of hygiene, aggression, poverty, monstrosity, and even barbarism. The beard is a floating signifier that is assigned meaning by history, much like skin pigmentation, the shape of the nose, or stature. What is important in the ethnographic distinction is not a physical difference itself but rather what it signifies—that is, to live or to die, to be seen as a child, to be the object of conquest, and so forth. None of these meanings is naturally related to the beard but is a product of the historical (and colonial) processes of signifying difference.

Mala Cosa's facial hair does not signify virility, masculinity, and Christian virtue, as facial hair does for the Europeans. The *Relación* suggests that Mala Cosa was indigenous, occasionally dressed as a woman (i.e., was not fully masculine), and was evil. Mala Cosa's beard and his clothing are in tension with one another in representing an anomalous gendered condition: "he appeared among them, sometimes in the costume of a woman, and other times dressed as a man" ("muchas vezes cuando bailavan aparesçía entre ellos, en hábito de muger . . . y otras como hombre"; Adorno and Pautz 1: 167; 166; ch. 22). Let us first clarify that Mala Cosa is not "a hybrid composite (*hermaphrodite*)" ("un compuesto híbrido [hermafrodita]"), as Glantz argues ("Cuerpo" 425–26), "a hermaphrodite being that lived underground" ("un ser hermafrodita que vivía bajo la tierra"), in the words of Maura (59), or a trickster who can "sexually transform" ("transformarse sexualmente"; Adorno, *Polemics* 257–58 and *De Guancane a Macondo* 56–57). The text itself does not speak of hermaphroditism, genitals, or sex but rather of performance, appearance, and gender roles ("hábito"). Mala Cosa is simply presented as an occasional *travesti*;[3] Cabeza de Vaca also changes his gendered appearance and is even said to change skins "like serpents . . . twice a year" ("a manera de serpientes mudávamos los cueros dos vezes en el año"; Adorno and Pautz 1: 171, 173; 170, 172; ch. 22). Whatever benefits and enjoyment Cabeza de Vaca may have derived from the gender ambiguity he inhabited, he reports that he regularly assumed tasks typically—according to him—assigned to women while he lived among indigenous groups: gathering food, firewood, and water; making combs and weaving rugs; treating hides; and, especially, trading with and mediating between enemy groups (1: 108–09, 140–41, 168–69, 172–73). It is notable that after a year of working, Cabeza de Vaca abandons Malhado Island and joins the Charrucos, among whom he became a "merchant" ("mercader"), a job that garnered him respect, good treatment, and freedom of movement along the coast up to forty or fifty leagues (1: 121; 120; ch. 16). This mobility coincides with that of indigenous women, who, he says, "are at liberty to communicate and converse with their in-laws and relatives" ("tienen la libertad para comunicar y conversar con los suegros y parientes"; 1: 111; 110; ch. 14)—that is, without the restrictions of taboo. Even more important, "women can mediate [and trade] even when there is war" ("pueden contratar aunque aya guerra"; 1: 217; 216; ch. 30). Cabeza de Vaca recounts various instances of feminine mediation, such as when after an armed conflict "the women of the ones who were called Quevenes came and negotiated between them and made friends with them" ("vinieron las mugeres de los que se llamavan Quevenes, y entendieron entre ellos y los hizieron amigos"; 1: 183; 182; ch. 24). In the final part of the *Relación*, Cabeza de Vaca says that the Christians constantly reconcile antagonistic groups and that their presence incites peace: "those who were at war with one another later made friends in order to come to receive us. . . . And in this manner we left the entire land [in peace]" ("los que tenían guerras con los otros se hazían luego amigos para venirnos a reçebir. . . . Y desta manera dexamos toda la tierra en paz"; 1: 233; 232; ch. 31). According to the text, men are not peace brokers: "men do not intervene" ("hombres no entran a despartirlos"; 1: 179; 178; ch. 24). We must not miss the opportunity to reflect on the representation of indigenous and European female subjectivity as associated with complex maneuvers, spells, and diplomacy, among the skills required for the roles of cross-cultural and political intermediaries.

In addition to being small and bearded and assuming different gender roles, Cabeza de Vaca and Mala Cosa are both others with respect to the Indians. With the exception of the years between 1529 and 1533, when he lived first on Malhado Island and then as a merchant among the Charrucos on the mainland, Cabeza de Vaca, is, as is Mala Cosa, a subject in transit who—contrary to what is often alleged—remains foreign and textually separated from the indigenous peoples. Both are itinerant foreigners with strange powers; the Indians receive both of them with an ambivalent mix of hospitality and fear, with festivities, dances, and gifts. It is said of Mala Cosa that "many times when they danced, he appeared among them" ("muchas vezes cuando bailavan aparesçía entre ellos"; 1: 167; 166; ch. 22). Likewise, when the Christians begin to practice healing among the Avavares, the Indians "began to dance and make their areitos and celebrations" ("comenzaron a bailar y hazer sus areitos y fiestas"; 1: 155; 154; ch. 27). The Christians are regularly welcomed with dances and invitations to perform as healers (1: 194–97, 200–01, 204–05, 222–23). All these dances, feasts, and healing performances function in the *Relación* as welcoming ceremonies for strangers who have no bond with the community to which they arrive. Cabeza de Vaca stands midway between being received as a hostile other and as a guest, and therefore his strangeness is coded and dealt with by ambivalent rituals and representations. One is obliged to welcome the arriving other by the norms of hospitality. At the same time, one is to fear such arrival. Is the stranger a benefic or malefic presence? Welcoming rites assume both possibilities could be true. Dancing, healing, and offerings function as performative signs of love and hate, peace and war, health and illness; they both invite and repel the arriving stranger.

Like Mala Cosa, Cabeza de Vaca comes from another world. Cabeza de Vaca, following a long tradition among "mighty whitey" conquistadores, puts words in the mouths of the Indians about his own origin: "they said that truly we were the children of the sun" ("dezían que verdaderamente nosotros éramos hijos del sol"; 1: 165; 164; ch. 22); later, after a session of healings, he declares: "among all these peoples, it was taken for certain that we came from the sky [heaven]" ("entre todas estas gentes se tenía por muy çierto, que veníamos del çielo"; 1: 233; 232; ch. 31). The first edition of the *Relación* explains that "all the things that [the Indians] do not know the origin of, they say come from the sky" ("todas las cosas que ellos no alcançan, ni tienen notiçia de donde vienen, dizen que vienen del çielo"; 1: 233; 232; ch. 31). In other words, the phrase simply indicated that, for the Indians, the Spaniards were unknown and foreign (like Mala Cosa). Nevertheless, this clarifying passage was suppressed in the 1555 edition (Adorno and Pautz 1: 233n2), and the origin of the Christians stopped being unknown and instead became celestial: *cielo* as sky becomes *cielo* as heaven.

In contrast to Cabeza de Vaca's origins, the indigenous informants say that Mala Cosa comes from the underworld: "[the Indians] asked him [Mala Cosa] where he came from and where he had his house, and he showed them a cleft in the earth and said that his house was there below" ("le preguntavan dónde venía y a qué parte tenía su casa, y que les mostró una hendedura de la tierra y dixo que su casa era allá debaxo"; 1: 167; 166; ch. 22). According to Roger Bartra, in the sixteenth century the "definition of alterity, [and] of externality . . . [were] conceptually dependent on a vertical axis that had the infernal underworld and heavens above as opposite poles" ("la definición de la alteridad, la externidad y la anormalidad, . . . dependía conceptualmente de un eje vertical que tenia como polos opuestos el inframundo infernal y el supramundo celestial"; 67; my trans.). Initially, the Spaniards do not believe the story of Mala Cosa and mock it; when they see the scars on the Indians, Cabeza de Vaca recounts, "We told them that he was an evil being" ("Nosotros les diximos que aquél era un malo") and that if they believed in "Our Lord" ("nuestro Señor"), Mala Cosa would not hurt them, nor would he show up again so long as the Christians were there (Adorno and Pautz 1: 169; 168; ch. 22).

The ethnographic opposition between sameness and otherness is thus founded on a Manichean symbolic economy that opposes the heavenly above and the underworld, Christianness and devilishness, healing and witchcraft. The text explicitly posits that Mala Cosa (malefic, from underground, harmful, and deceitful) is opposed to Cabeza de Vaca (benefic, of celestial origins, healer, and truthful). However, these oppositions are unstable and even interchangeable. Ultimately, they point to the same cultural exteriority. Cabeza de Vaca and Mala Cosa come from places plotted on the same cosmogonic axis. Furthermore—despite the contrast that the text proposes—the Indians also saw Cabeza de Vaca as a harmful figure with mysterious powers, who caused sickness and death and pillaged Indian communities.

Miraculous Healer and Evil Sorcerer

Cabeza de Vaca describes indigenous healing practices by way of an episode on Malhado Island (1528–29), when the Indians supposedly forced the Christians to become *físicos* (literally, physicians; in context, healers). At this point he distinguishes between the way *they* cure illness and the way *we* do. The passage must be read in class, and students should pay attention to the rhetorical insistence on ethnographic contrast. They will notice that despite the text's explicit tautological contrasts, the similarities are evident between the description of indigenous and European forms of healing: the Indians cure illnesses by blowing on the sick and using their hands, and the Spaniards do it by "making the sign of the cross over them and blowing on them" ("santiguándolos y soplarlos, y rezar un Pater Noster y un Ave María, y rogar lo mejor que podíamos a Dios"; Adorno and Pautz 1: 115; 114; ch. 15); indigenous medicine is remunerated, and the Christian physicians also hope for and receive payment; and the indigenous perform surgeries and extractions, and so do the Spaniards. Cabeza de Vaca tells us later on in the story how he extracted the point of an arrow from near the heart of a man (1: 208–09; ch. 29); Spaniards and Indians both perform cauterizations with fire. Overcodifying such commonalities as differences, however, the text distinguishes rhetorically between *them* and *us*: they have their ways, and we have ours. Mala Cosa's deeds at times seem to be those of a sorcerer, witch, or shaman, an agent of harm and health. The term *sorcerer* does not correspond to any word in the text ascribed to Mala Cosa; his supernatural powers are described anecdotally in the *Relación*, and to choose a word in English or Spanish to conjures up, as it were, a figure with the ability to heal or cause harm; to inspire fear and to levitate homes into the air and let them fall is to evoke cultural attitudes toward such possibilities. Exercises in translation can also serve to unteach the text and expose our own presuppositions about what is being described in it: how would our students name the role of Mala Cosa or of Cabeza de Vaca? What are the limits of and cultural assumptions attached to any of the possible choices?[24] Coming back to the supposed differences between Spanish and indigenous healing, it must be noted that Mala Cosa's mechanisms for healing correspond as much to the indigenous *them* as to the Spanish *us*. Mala Cosa uses fire, cuts bodies, performs extractions, and "placed his hand into those wounds" ("metía la mano por aquellas cuchilladas") to heal (1: 167; 166; ch. 22). The *Relación* insists on differentiating, even though it presents practices that are similar and complementary.

Although the *Relación* says that after the winter of 1528–29 on Malhado Island the Spaniards were obliged to become *físicos*, the story does not include any reports of healings until after Cabeza de Vaca is reunited with his companions, when they flee from the Mariames and the Yguazes in 1534 and eventually arrive in the land of the Avavares—that is, five years and about six thousand words later: "That same night that we arrived, some Indians came to Castillo and said to him that they suffered a malady of the head, begging him to cure them" ("Aquella misma noche que llegamos vinieron unos indios a Castillo y dixéronle que estavan muy malos de la cabeça, ruegándole que los curasse"; 1: 155; 154; ch. 21). It is important to clarify that initially Cabeza de Vaca stays on the margins of the healings—until his messianic initiation, when he gets lost on an excursion to gather prickly pears and is rescued from the cold thanks to the miraculous apparition of a "tree aflame" ("árbol ardiendo"; 1: 157; 156; ch. 21). He reports how, when he was lost, at night he would bury himself in holes in the earth and warm himself with fire he made from two charred logs he carried with him. Finally, to the surprise of his companions and the Indians, who had given him up for dead, Cabeza de Vaca returns as a practicing healer, with his charred logs and embers, having survived the cold by seeking shelter in holes in the ground. It is then that the Indians bring him five sick people to cure, and Cabeza de Vaca and his companions reinitiate their healings (1: 158–61; ch. 22). Note that Mala Cosa appears in a similar way: he shows up with a "flaming firebrand" ("un tizón ardiendo"), saying that he came from a "cleft underground" ("hendedura de la tierra") and that "his house was there below" ("su casa era allá debaxo" 1: 167; 166; ch. 22).

The passage on Cabeza de Vaca's initiation in the desert draws on central motifs from Exodus and is associated with the saving figure of Moses: signs of divine favor such as the burning bush, escape from bondage, and supernatural use of health and sickness as instruments of liberation. One could say of Cabeza de Vaca, Mala Cosa, and Moses that they are powerful and frightening thaumaturgists who unleash the powers of sickness and health.

Just after the messianic initiation, the *Relación* refers to the resurrection of a Susola Indian. Cabeza de Vaca says that he approached what he thought was a dying man that turned out to be a cadaver. The Spaniards witnessed the mourning of the family members, the body's lack of a pulse, the eyes rolled back in the head, and other "signs of death" ("señales de muerto"). But the fact of death does not discourage Cabeza de Vaca, who makes "the sign of the cross and blows on him many times" ("santiguado e soplado muchas veces"; 1: 163; 162; ch. 22). The Spaniards left the man for dead and returned to their lodging, and later on they learned that this indigenous Lazarus had come back to life. Cabeza de Vaca does not say that he witnessed the resurrection, nor does he affirm that it happened; he merely notes that he heard about it from the Avavare Indians: "they said that that one who had been dead and whom I had cured . . . had arisen revived and walked about and eaten and spoken with them" ("dixeron que aquél que estava muerto y yo avía curado . . . se avía levantado bueno y se avía paseado y comido y hablado con ellos"; 163; 162; ch. 22). Cabeza de Vaca suggests but does not confirm the resurrection of the Susola Indian presumably because such an event straddles the limit between miracle and witchcraft, between divine intervention and diabolical sorcery.

Following the news of the resurrection, Cabeza de Vaca becomes, he says, the most important of the Christian doctors: "we all became physicians, although in boldness and daring to perform any cure *I was the most notable among them*" ("venimos todos a ser médicos, aunque en atrevimiento y osar acometer cualquier cura *era yo más señalado entrellos*"; 165; 164; ch. 22; emphasis added). I must underscore an important point here: although it is precisely after this ambiguous resurrection that Cabeza de Vaca tells the story of Mala Cosa that marks the contrast between the "evil thing" and himself, Cabeza de Vaca and Mala Cosa are still not unalike. Their most evident similarity is precisely their actions as prodigious agents of wonders, endowed with supernatural powers over health and sickness, life and death.

Without getting into a discussion about the typologies that would distinguish the shaman from the witch doctor, the sorcerer, and the healer, one can say that the *Relación* itself proposes the ethnographic framework for such differences: that is, it qualifies the wonders of Mala Cosa as "something very strange" ("cosa muy estraña") or "bad" ("mala"), harmful, and demonic (1: 165; 164; ch. 22), and it qualifies Christian healing as beneficial and miraculous. Still, we are confronted with analogous procedures whose distinction is merely stated. In the end, the difference between the healer and the sorcerer depends on contrary visions and beliefs, hence the ethnographers' frequent inability to differentiate between the figures of the evil witch and the healing shaman (M. Brown 251–54; Harner 197).

The *Relación* states that when Mala Cosa arrived somewhere, people's "hair stood on end and they trembled" ("se les levantavan los cabellos y temblavan"); he took whichever of them he wanted and made "incisions in [their] sides . . . and pulled out their entrails . . . , and afterward he made three cuts in the arm and . . . dislocated it. And . . . afterward, he set it back into place, and he placed his hands over the wounds, and they told us that later they were healed" ("cuchilladas grandes por las hijadas . . . y sacávales las tripas . . . , y luego le dava tres cuchilladas en un braço . . . , y desconçertávaselo. Y dende a poco, se lo tornava a conçertar, y poníales las manos sobre las heridas, y dezíannos que luego quedavan sanos"; Adorno and Pautz 1: 167; 166; ch. 22). Adorno proposes that "[t]hough a terrorist and torturer, he [Mala Cosa] was also a healer. This band of four strangers [the Spaniards], so far as we know, did not harm, but did heal" ("Negotiation" 174). However, this distinction is questionable. The Christian healers also frequently appear as terrorists and agents of evil and, like Mala Cosa, they heal the injuries that they themselves have inflicted. In effect, the text lets us know that the Spaniards cause sickness, or that it arrives with them. For example, during the winter of 1528–29 on Malhado Island, the Spaniards got sick and spread the illness to the Indians. Of the eighty Spaniards that arrived there, only fifteen survived the illness, and among the Indians, half of the people died (Adorno and Pautz 1: 104–07; ch. 14). The Indians initially believed—and they were not wrong—that the Spaniards were the cause of the disaster (1: 106–07; ch. 14). It was there, Cabeza de Vaca declares, that the Spaniards were obliged to become healers (1: 112–13; ch. 15). Both on Malhado Island and later, after the Christians encounter the Avavares, their curative practice cannot be separated from the appearance of the illness.

Mala Cosa is a figure that alludes to Cabeza de Vaca and reveals him to be a *cosa muy estraña* that is harmful and frightening, using magic as an instrument of intimidation, violence, and plunder. According to the *Relación*, Mala Cosa "came in and took whichever one of them [the Indians] he wanted" ("entrava y tomava al que quería") and even took a "buhío, or house, and raised it into the air, and a little while afterward he dropped it and it fell with a great blow" ("tomaba el buhío o casa y subíala en alto, y dende a poco caía con ella y daba muy gran golpe"; 1: 167; 166; ch. 22). This power hyperbolically expresses the behavior of the Christian healers during their travels through southeastern Texas and northern Mexico, where they continued performing as healers, traveling from settlement to settlement, followed by a crowd of Indians, and taking voluntary and sometimes not so voluntary gifts from their patients. Ahern calls these events "ritual pillages" (221). Cabeza de Vaca washes his hands of the matter, saying that the Indians who accompanied them were responsible for the looting and that he opposed it but could not control his companions: "[we] were powerless to remedy it" ("no éramos parte para remediallo"; Adorno and Pautz 1: 197; 196; ch. 28). By his own admission, the Christians were leading a group of bandits.

Cabeza de Vaca repeatedly insists in the *Relación* on the great authority he had over the Indians, but here declares that he has none. What is clear is that Cabeza de Vaca did not interfere with the pillaging, here or later on, when he affirms that the Christians took "a little" ("un poco") of the loot and that "the rest we gave to the lord of the people who went with us, *ordering him* to distribute it among them all" ("lo otro dábamos al principal de la gente que con nosotros venía, *mandándole* que lo repartiese entre todos"; 1: 213; 212; ch. 29; emphasis added). The sharing of loot occurs under the Christians' mandate, which confirms their leadership in the theft. At some point, the pillaging became unnecessary because the terrorized people offered up all their belongings to the bandits (1: 212–15). Healing was less of a beneficent practice than it was a strategy used to put on a show of authority over the Indians. In the final part of the *Relación*, Cabeza de Vaca notes that he and his companions learned and adopted the ritual signs of shamanic power to pacify (i.e., to subject) populations in conflict with the conquistadores in northern Mexico (1: 224–25). The Christians—much like Mala Cosa—inspired "great fear . . . and agitation" ("mucho temor . . . y turbaçión"; 1: 177; 176; see also 195; 194) and the Indians received them "weeping and with great sorrow because they already knew that wherever we went all the people were sacked and robbed by those who accompanied us" ("llorando y con grande tristeza, porque sabían ya que adondequiera que llegávamos eran todos saqueados y robados de los que nos acompañavan"; 1: 203; 202; ch. 28).

Cabeza de Vaca does not attempt to protect or calm the victims. In fact, he takes credit for tactically utilizing fear; he says that in the last part of the journey he and his companions did not eat in front of the Indians: "we walked the entire day without eating until night. And we ate so little that they were astonished [frightened] to see it. . . . We had a great deal of authority and influence over them" ("caminamos todo el día sin comer hasta la noche. Y comíamos tan poco que ellos se espantavan de verlo. . . . Teníamos con ellos mucha autoridad y gravedad"; 1: 233; 232; ch. 31). Note the parallel with Mala Cosa, whom the Indians never saw eating: "They also told us that many times they gave [Mala Cosa] food to eat and that he never ate anything" ("contaron que muchas vezes le dieron de comer y que nunca jamás comió"; 1: 167; 166; ch. 22). Perhaps the best example of the Spaniards' deliberate provocation of terror occurs when they are crossing the Río Bravo for the second time and there is some disagreement with their followers about which route to take: the Christians want to continue westward and then head north, but the Indians refuse, alleging that there is uninhabited terrain to the north. Cabeza de Vaca expresses his annoyance:

> [W]e became angry. And I went one night to sleep . . . apart from them, but later they went to where I was. And they were there the entire night without sleeping and with very great fear . . . , begging us to not be angry . . . [and that] they would take us wherever we wanted to go. And as we still pretended to be angry, and *because their fear did not subside, a strange thing* occurred, and it was that this same day many of them fell ill.

And the following day eight men died. Throughout the entire land . . . there was so much fear of us that it seemed that in seeing us they would die of fear. They begged us not to be angry or to will that any more of them die. And they held it for certain that we were killing them by simply desiring it.
(1: 217, 219; ch. 30; emphasis added)

[N]os enojamos. Y yo me salí una noche a dormir . . . apartado dellos, mas luego fueron donde yo estava. Y toda la noche estuvieron sin dormir y con mucho miedo . . . , rogándonos que no estuviéssemos más enojados, y que . . . nos llevarían por donde nosotros quisiéssemos ir. E como nosotros todavía fingíamos estar enojados, *y porque su miedo no se quitasse, suçedió una cosa estraña*, y fue que este día mesmo adolesçieron muchos dellos. Y otro día siguiente murieron ocho hombres. Por toda la tierra . . . , huvieron tanto miedo de nosotros que paresçía en vernos que de temor avían de morir. Rogáronnos que no estuviéssemos enojados ni quisiéssemos que más dellos moriessen. Y tenían por muy cierto que nosotros los matávamos con solamente quererlo. (1: 216, 218; ch. 30; emphasis added)

This is the second time we encounter the expression "strange thing" ("cosa estraña") in the *Relación*. The first instance precedes the story of Mala Cosa. But here the phrase returns to refer to the Christians' magical causation of sickness and death. The supernatural weapon is anger: in truth, feigned anger. Although the Indians accept the route that Cabeza de Vaca wants, the Christians continue to pretend to be angry so that "their fear did not subside," and this is when the "strange thing" happens: eight Indians die. Fearing that the Indians will abandon them, the Christians beg God for a cure, and those who were ill begin to get better (1: 218–19; ch. 30). As in the case of Mala Cosa, Cabeza de Vaca is a terrifying figure who appears to cause strange things and to manipulate the invisible forces of good and evil. Over the next fifteen days, the Spaniards do not see the Indians cry, speak among themselves, or show any emotion. And when a "baby" ("criatura") cries, "they took the baby very far from there. And with some sharp teeth of a rat they lacerated her from her shoulders to almost the bottom of her legs . . . to punish her because she had cried in my presence" ("la llevaron muy lexos de allí. Y con unos dientes de ratón agudos la sajaron desde los hombros hasta casi todas las piernas . . . para castigarla porque avía llorado delante de mí"; my trans.; 1: 218; ch. 30). This image, properly dialectical,[5] sheds fleeting light on the frightening figure of Cabeza de Vaca and the terror that comes with the evil known as peaceful colonialism.

Interpretive Hypotheses

Mala Cosa functions as a spectral figuration of the conquistador himself, appearing in the *Relación* not just in relation to the Indians, their myths, and their eccentricities but in relation to Cabeza de Vaca and his Christian companions, questioning the supposedly peaceful imperialism and the ethnographic empathy that frame so many readings of the *Relación*. I invite students to start with an almost formalist analysis of Mala Cosa as a character, examining the possibility that, contrary to what the text suggests, Mala Cosa mirrors the conquistador and that it is precisely because Mala Cosa signals an unbearable instance of recognition that he becomes a thing that is estranged and conjured by colonial writing.[6] But the strangeness of Mala Cosa is not so strange ontologically; he is rendered strange by being put through a discursive process that hides his similarity to Cabeza de Vaca. Take, as a point of comparison, the philosophical proposal implicit in Jorge Luis Borges's "Doctor Brodie's Report": the strangest things about the fictional tribe called the Yahoos, upon closer scrutiny, are not essentially different from those of the ethnographer's own culture! The limits between self and other rhetorically affirm difference through the continuous hypostasis of superficial differences and a voluntary blindness with respect to the fundamental similarities. In Borges's story, the others "drink the milk of cats and bats" ("beben leche de gato y de murciélago"; my trans.), they eat repulsive things, they are cannibals, they "go around naked" ("[a]ndan desnudos"; my trans.), and they live in swamps (223). It is only through radical ethnographic relativism that we are able to see ourselves as strange, that we can see such things as drinking the milk of cows and goats, eating certain raw and rotten meats, conducting organ transplants, covering our bodies out of modesty or vanity, attending faculty meetings, and living with air conditioning as bizarre. The strangeness of customs does not come from the otherness of the other but rather from the foreignness of the gaze, as Montaigne and Bartolomé de las Casas noted in the sixteenth century (Montaigne; Las Casas, *Apologética historia sumaria* 2: 637–51).

But if the "difference" isn't so different, why the rhetorical emphasis to mark it? Precisely because of the unbearableness of similarity—particularly in circumstances ideologically marked by radical difference, as during the conquest and colonization of the Americas, where European ethnic, religious, and cultural superiority was assumed a priori. The possibility of recognizing oneself in those who are supposedly inferior and monstrous objects of conquest and subordination is intolerable, unless you are willing to go native. The similarity must thus be marked as difference, but doing so still leaves traces of that which has been negated. Thus the episode about Mala Cosa in the *Relación* functions like a cloudy mirror. Unteaching Cabeza de Vaca can simply consist of unfogging the glass a bit to glimpse some reflections of sameness.

An important question remains: could this story—if not invented by Cabeza de Vaca—be considered a representation of an indigenous myth or tale? The short answer is that in the text there is no indigenous story or tradition. There is only the presence of an absence, and a spectral disruption of colonial writing. I propose that the Avavares and Mariames tell the Spaniards a story about Mala Cosa in which they would recognize themselves; the apparently indigenous story has the power to interpellate the Spaniards to prompt a response. The indigenous tale—of which nothing but a spectral trace remains—would go like this: "see yourself as a terrifying agent of magic; do not harm us, or if you do, repair the evil you have done to us." This hypothesis supposes that the story is narrated by the Indians to the Spaniards not to show them the wealth of their cultural traditions but rather for reasons relevant to the Spaniards' arrival. What is interesting about this story is not what it means but how it functions.

I recall a conversation I had with the media and communications scholar Jesús Martín-Barbero in Pittsburgh. We were talking about the social and cultural circulation of urban legends such as organ trafficking and the political intelligibility of these supposed cultural hysterias. I told him that when I was about seventeen years old, my grandmother Elena Gaviria, with whom I lived at the time, told me horror stories about organ trafficking, which involved attractive women from gangs of delinquents working with criminal doctors to deceive young men in bars by drugging their drinks; the victims would wake up the next morning to find themselves sutured where their kidney had been removed in order to be sold on the black market for transplants. We know that the vast majority of these stories that circulated in the 1980s in the Americas are urban legends, which I have elsewhere related to the social terrors of the dispossession of the body in the neoliberal era (Jáuregui, *Canibalia* 588–603). The important question that touches on the story my grandmother would tell me is not whether these crimes occurred, or if they circulated through a society that felt defenseless against the sinister forces of capitalism, or whether they expressed a gothic mistrust of the medical system. No. Martín-Barbero smiled, as he did when he anticipated one of his marvelous insights, and he said, "I think that your grandmother just wanted to keep you from going out partying all night!" In other words, the horror story had a specific function, and its meaning was not determined by legendary or macropolitical referents: this cautionary tale demanded that I see myself in it so I would stop doing something that was distressing to my grandmother. In the case of Mala Cosa, we must ask ourselves what the storytellers may have wanted to convey. Even if the Indians were narrating an established myth, its function is still relevant.

Claude Levi-Strauss points out something in relation to myths that we can extend to the tale of Mala Cosa: that it is possible that "some of the events they relate are genuine, even if the picture they paint of them is symbolic and distorted" (242). Paul Ricœur affirms that myth is not "a false explanation by means of images and fables" about a remote time but rather a form of understanding the concrete world of the present (*Symbolism* 5). *Mythical* is not synonymous with *unreal* or *ahistorical*. The story of Mala Cosa symbolically enunciates a truth about issues, such as evil, that are not completely intelligible through reason alone. What a myth signifies is largely determined by the present in which it is narrated; it can refer to a remote time but only to articulate it for the present. In sum, a horror story can be and often is the echo of a terror that lurks nearby, an attempt to understand that terror or even to conjure up its danger. The story of Mala Cosa is not an inexplicable cultural fantasy of primitive people afraid of their own shadows; it could be the sediment of concrete experiences and fears that contains, as Levi-Strauss says, a "logical contingency and emotional turbulence" (243). The story expresses tangible affects of confronting evil and concrete cognitions about being submitted to strange foreign powers. These affects and perceptions are historically articulated, symbolically with the colonial experience. Reff rightly observes that the appearance of Mala Cosa "fifteen or sixteen years" before the arrival of Cabeza de Vaca in the land of the Avavares in 1534 roughly corresponds to the 1519 arrival of Hernán Cortés in Mexico, which suggests that the tale of Mala Cosa might be related to colonial activities in New Spain, including New Galicia (126).[7] Reff correctly supposes that Mala Cosa is related to the violence of Spanish colonialism, but for Reff, this is a case of misrecognition: the Indians had initially identified the good Cabeza de Vaca with his bad compatriots ravaging the south. I believe, on the contrary, that there is no mistake, and that the story of Mala Cosa is directly related to Cabeza de Vaca, as can be deduced through the coincident similarities between the two figures.

I think that the figure of Mala Cosa expresses the uneasiness and the fear that Cabeza de Vaca provoked among the indigenous people. So initially the story may have functioned as an attempt by them to conceive of this terror through known categories and tales, such as that of an evil foreigner. The story seems to present the unknown Cabeza de Vaca in the familiar role of a shaman. It may also be an interpellation, as mentioned earlier. The arrival of a stranger in a community implies an undeniable tension between a failed encounter and anagnorisis, through which the benevolent or malignant role of said stranger is negotiated and defined. Cabeza de Vaca would have been seen as an agent of supernatural powers, susceptible to narrative seduction: "Hey, stranger, let me tell you about another stranger . . . ." After all, the Mariames and the Avavares welcome Cabeza de Vaca with a story about a mysterious stranger who terrorizes the community, does damage, and exercises magical powers, but that in the end repairs the altered order: Mala Cosa cut the Indians and "pulled out their entrails," and dislocated their arms but "a little while afterward, he set it [the injured limb] back into place, and he placed his hands over the wounds" and healed them (Adorno and Pautz 1: 167; ch. 22). The story seems to function as a narrative conjuring of evil: a proposition or a request, so that the malevolent sorcerer can become a healer.

The story might also have offered a model that Cabeza de Vaca and his companions took advantage of to instill fear. In other words, the story of Mala Cosa might have offered the Christians ethnographic information that they used in their medical performances, in their use of magical terrorism and tricks, such as not allowing the Indians to see them eat in order to frighten them. The story of Mala Cosa, which tries to conjure the evil and strangeness the Spaniards represented, may have ended up offering the Spaniards magical tools of terror.

These hypotheses are not mutually exclusive: the story of Mala Cosa can be an anti-ethnography or an indigenous tale referring to the conquistador (who would have been taken as a sort of shaman or compelled to become one) and also a tale on which Cabeza de Vaca models his ethnographic competency and causes the Indians terror and submission. In both cases, the figure of the other is the same. Mala Cosa—strange and terrifying—alludes to Cabeza de Vaca.

Mala Cosa is the horror story of the Conquest and a specter we should conjure to unteach the *Relación*.

NOTES

1. In academic terms, the "mighty whitey" trope refers to a narrative device in literature and media where a white protagonist excels in and often surpasses the skills or knowledge associated with a nonwhite, indigenous culture (Bentham 167). This character frequently assumes a role of savior or superior figure, often resolving conflicts or challenges that the native characters cannot. This trope perpetuates colonial and imperialistic ideologies, reinforcing the notion of white superiority and the dependency of nonwhite cultures on white intervention for progress or salvation.

2. Other mysterious events include the encounter in Florida with some crates belonging to Castilian merchants, which were filled with cadavers and which perhaps were the remains from an earlier Spanish incursion fended off by the Indians (see Adorno and Pautz 1: 36–39); the messianic appearance of a burning tree in the desert (1: 154–59); numerous cures carried out by the Spaniards (1: 154–55, 158–59, 160–61, 164–65, 196–97, 208–09, 220–21); an apparent resurrection (1: 160–63); the sudden death of several indigenous people, seemingly caused by Cabeza de Vaca (1: 216–19); and the bad omens of a Moorish woman in Spain who predicted the disaster of the expedition (1: 274–75).

3. The term *travesti* is used loosely as a synonym of *travestido*, which in English would correspond to the term *cross-dresser*, to signal the change of appearance and gender performativity through a change of clothing or change of roles.

4. *Sorcerer* and *wizard* imply someone with healing or harmful supernatural powers; *witch* and *witch doctor* may do the same but are loaded with assumptions about gender, indigeneity, and paganism; and all these terms are steeped in the cultural baggage of Eurocentric narratives. *Shaman* often refers to indigenous healers and practices supposedly antithetical to Western medicine. To refer to Cabeza de Vaca as a shaman reinforces the myth of his acculturation into the indigenous world. To call him a sorcerer or healer, as I do here, is still to evoke the miraculous occurrences reported in the *Relación*. His use of the word *physician* evokes modern medicine, yet the Spaniards were at best Christian healers. None of these words name a person—Mala Cosa or Cabeza de Vaca—who manipulates others' perceptions of seemingly miraculous events (injuring and healing). I am indebted to Juliet Lynd for her insights on this matter.

5. I refer to what Walter Benjamin called *dialectical images* of the past—those that briefly and suddenly illuminate and defamiliarize history, allowing us to remember it in the tradition of the oppressed (198, 199).

6. I refer to the kind of character analysis deployed by Russian formalism, which emphasizes the function and role of characters within the narrative structure, paying close attention to their portrayal through literary devices and language.

7. It is possible that the coastal tribes of Texas would have received news about the violent fall of Tenochtitlan, or about Nuño de Guzmán's campaigns in New Galicia, and that said news would have been incorporated into the storytelling that preceded the arrival of Cabeza de Vaca and his companions (Reff 115–38).

INTERSECTIONAL PERSPECTIVES

Hidden in Plain Sight: Reading a Complex Esteban in and around *Naufragios*

Kathryn Joy McKnight

The Texas African American History Memorial sits on the capitol grounds in Austin, and at its leftmost end stands a bronze representation of Esteban, or Estevanico, identified by the Legislative Reference Library of Texas as "Estevanico de Dorantes (the first African to set foot on Texas soil)" ("New Texas African American Monument"). The bronze figure is dressed as a Spanish soldier, though without armor; he rests his right hand on the hilt of a sword, and his left holds a staff capped by a gourd, from which hang strings of beads. The statue, created by the African American sculptor Ed Dwight, synthesizes the meanings in the legends of Esteban: his presence in the memorial signals his African identity, perhaps more so than the muted visual signs of race; his position speaks to his status as first; his clothing signals his function in bringing Spanish cultural identity and imperial expansion to the Pueblo homelands; and his manipulation of Native symbols to gain authority—the shamanic staff—suggests his skill as a communicator and his importance as an agent in the interactions with Native peoples.

Beginning with this synthetic image invites us to consider the challenges of reading Esteban in Álvar Núñez Cabeza de Vaca's *Naufragios* (*Shipwrecks*), which gives relatively little attention to this key and complex member of the expedition. However, Esteban has inspired many contemporary culture workers to imagine and elaborate his identity and importance, based on these meager details. A sampling from these creators suggests their desire to decolonize a Eurocentric history: the rapper-educator Kalyan Ali Balaven, a.k.a. Professor A. L. I., has identified with Esteban's multilingual abilities and has recorded a rap, "Black Steven Speaks," that evokes rage at the killing of Esteban, prejudices against Muslims in the United States, and the killing of Muslims in the Middle East (A. L. I., "Who" and *Carbon Cycle Diaries*); the Bronx-based muralists Tats Cru created a mural they title *Estevanico* in Azemmour; the Moroccan American novelist Laila Lalami's novel *The Moor's Account* gives Esteban the name Mustafa ibn Muhammad ibn Abdussalam al Zamori and identifies him as Muslim; the American poet Jeffrey Yang's poem "Estevanico" invokes the figure and his origins in Azemmour as well as his importance as the expedition's speaker in a multilingual context; and an article by the *Our Weekly* staff writer Merdies Hayes marks the four hundredth anniversary of "the importation of Africans" into what is now the United States and identifies Esteban as the "first Black person in the New World."[1] A brief Internet search reveals at least a dozen distinct images of Esteban that have also strengthened various elements of his legend.

The names that Esteban has been given matter. In this essay, I use *Esteban* rather than *Estevanico*. Studying the naming practices in the Spanish Antilles through encomienda records, the linguist Silke Jansen notes that Christian names marked verbally the power of the colonizer as well as the named person's new Christian status (175). Persons in subordinate categories were often not assigned a second or family name (172). This situation applies to Esteban, although he is sometimes referred to by his owner's family name, as in "Esteban de Dorantes." Finally, diminutive forms such as *-ico* appear in the records of the time predominantly in relation to people who have been relegated to subordinate status, such as that of an enslaved person or servant (166–69). Curiously, William Phillips, Jr., reports that the diminutive was not in general use in Spain for enslaved people (81). Thus, while I believe it important to use the name *Esteban* to indicate this figure's status as a Christian within the context of conquest, rather than using one of the Muslim names attributed to him, I prefer not to use the diminutive *Estevanico* so as not to reinforce any idea that his humanity is less. One challenge to reading Esteban in *Naufragios* is the fact that while other narratives dedicate slightly more text to him, none develops his identity or contributions in depth. A second challenge for readers who would decolonize this historical narrative is Esteban's relationship to Native Pueblo history: among the Zunis he is remembered as "the first white man" of the conquest (*Surviving* 00:18:36).[2] How, then, can we help students read Esteban's representation beyond the legends, to understand how this enslaved man, taken from Morocco and baptized a Christian in Iberia, contributed to one of the most well-known Spanish expeditions? How did this Black African join a Spanish expedition? Why do the narratives address so little of his identity and activity? How can our awareness of that partial erasure shed light on the greater impact of Black participants on the Spanish conquest and colonization?

This essay offers the following ways of reading Esteban, in order to encourage students to think critically about how Black lives mattered to the conquest and colonization and to imagine how Esteban may have seen himself on the expedition. I begin with *Naufragios* itself, investigating Esteban's contribution to the survival of the four companions as they crossed Texas and northern New Spain. I then move to Esteban's origins and the history of Black Africans in Iberia and Esteban's early experience of forced migration. Next I offer as context examples of the portrayal of Esteban in other texts and of other Black African-born or Afro-Iberian enslaved men and freedmen who participated in the early Iberian expeditions. These representations allow students to better understand the textual politics of the representation of Black Africans in the problematic genres of exploration and conquest narratives. I end with questions about Esteban's significance today in the southwestern United States.

Esteban in **Naufragios**

In the last line of *Naufragios*, Cabeza de Vaca identifies Esteban as a "negro alárabe, natural de Azamor" (Adorno and Pautz 1: 278). Rolena Adorno and Patrick Charles Pautz argue persuasively for translating this description as "Arabic-speaking black man, a native of Azamor" (1: 279). While he has been referred to as Esteban the Moor, the term *Moor* suggests a practicing Muslim, whereas his passage to the Americas would have required that he first be baptized as a Christian. So Adorno and Pautz read "alárabe" to refer primarily to language (2: 416–17).

While racial bias likely provides one explanation for the lack of depth of Esteban's treatment in Cabeza de Vaca's account, the genre itself—the *relación*, which is closely related in purpose and form to the *probanza de méritos* ("account of merits and deeds")—required the author to focus centrally on himself. As Matthew Restall explains, "The very nature and purpose of *probanzas* obliged those who wrote them to promote their own deeds and downplay or ignore those of others" (*Seven Myths* 12). Students can be invited to track the number of times that Esteban appears in *Naufragios* and to compare his characterization with those of the other three members of the group of survivors. Of the nineteen times that he is named, usually as "Estevanico," sometimes as "el negro" or "Estevanico, el negro," about half refer only to his presence or participation in the activity and movements of the group as a whole.

Three of the times that he appears in the text contribute to a deeper understanding of Esteban's talents and importance to the expedition. In the first, sometime around September or October 1534, at the end of the prickly pear season, Cabeza de Vaca, Andrés Dorantes, Alonso del Castillo Maldonado, and Esteban try to leave the prickly pear region, north of the Rio Grande. For the first time, Cabeza de Vaca portrays Esteban in the roles of scout and intercultural communicator: "[W]e saw an Indian who, as he saw that we were coming toward him, fled without wanting to wait for us. We sent the black man after him. And since he saw that [the Indian] was coming alone, he waited for him. The black man told him that we were going to look for those people who were making those spires of smoke" ("[V]imos un indio que, como vio que ivamos a él, huyó sin querernos aguardar. Nosotros embiamos al negro tras dél. Y como vio que [el indio] iva solo, aguardolo. El negro le dixo que ívamos a buscar aquella gente que hazía aquellos humos" Adorno and Pautz 1: 153; 152; ch. 20). Once the four survivors find the dwellings from which the smoke originated, they are welcomed by the inhabitants, whom Cabeza de Vaca identifies as Avavares. Here, Cabeza de Vaca focuses on his and Castillo's work as healers, which is of growing interest to their hosts. Shortly thereafter, he adds the role of healer to Esteban's repertoire as scout and communicator: "Until then Dorantes and the black man had not performed any cures, but on account of the great demands made on us, [the Indians] coming from many places to look for us, we all became physicians" ("Dorantes y el negro hasta allí no avían curado, mas por la mucha importunidad que teníamos, [los indios] veniéndonos de muchas partes a buscar, venimos todos a ser médicos"; 1: 165; 164; ch. 22).

Cabeza de Vaca describes Esteban as a scout, guide, and communicator three more times. Once, Castillo and Esteban encounter a permanent settlement somewhere in northwestern Chihuahua or northeastern Sonora. While Castillo returns to the other Spaniards, Esteban is trusted to remain alone with the local inhabitants, to ensure that they meet up with the three Spaniards (ch. 30). When Cabeza de Vaca recounts a later moment, probably near what is now El Paso, he describes the importance of Esteban's service and expertise and the trust that was placed in him as an agent, with the most detail and emphasis to be found in the entire narrative (1: 229n4). In Cabeza de Vaca's view, Esteban's function as an intermediary allowed the Spaniards to establish greater authority over the Native people on whom they depended.

> We had a great deal of authority and influence over them. And in order to conserve this we spoke to them but few times. The black man always spoke to them and informed himself about the roads we wished to travel and the villages that there were and about other things that we wanted to know. We passed through a great number and diversity of languages. With all of them God our Lord favored us, because they always understood us and we understood them. (1: 233; ch. 31)

> Teníamos con ellos mucha autoridad y gravedad. Y para conservar esto les hablávamos pocas vezes. El negro les hablava siempre y se informava de los caminos que queríamos ir y los pueblos que avía y de las cosas que queríamos saber. Passamos por gran número y diversidades de lenguas. Con todas ellas Dios nuestro Señor nos favoresçió, porque siempre nos entendieron y les entendimos. (1: 232; ch. 31)

In a final note on Esteban's value to the group, Cabeza de Vaca tells how, when he and Esteban encountered Spanish soldiers in New Galicia, while scouting ahead, he gave Esteban the responsibility to guide three horsemen and fifty indigenous captives back to fetch Dorantes and Castillo (ch. 33).

African Diasporic Context

The image of slavery in the Americas that my students bring to class is often limited to plantation slavery, particularly in Brazil and the Caribbean. So, to understand Esteban's forced migration from Morocco to Spain as well as his experience as an enslaved Moroccan in Iberia and his participation within Spanish imperial expansion, students need information on slavery prior to the development of American plantations and the Middle Passage.

Esteban arrived in Spain sometime before 1527, the year the Narváez expedition departed from Sanlúcar de Barrameda with him and his owner, Dorantes, on board. Cabeza de Vaca identifies Esteban's origin as Azemmour, a city on Morocco's southern Atlantic coast. Most Black people in Morocco in the sixteenth century arrived from West Africa via the trans-Saharan slave trade: during the previous nine hundred years, several thousand Black Africans had been brought every year to Morocco via the routes of this slave trade (El Hamel 8, 149). It is probable that Esteban was taken by a Portuguese slave trader from Morocco to Iberia. His arrival in Iberia likely coincided with Portugal's control of the city of Azemmour, beginning in 1513. After Azemmour experienced catastrophic famine and plague in the 1520s, slave trade activity increased from Azemmour to the Iberian peninsula (138, 141). It is possible that Esteban was taken to Iberia during this upswing in the Moroccan slave trade.

Esteban arrived in a society long accustomed to the institution of slavery. Phillips summarizes Iberian slavery thus:

> Slavery was present in the Iberian Peninsula from the beginning of recorded history. It was prominent in Roman times and in the early Middle Ages under the Visigoths. The Muslims maintained a slave system in Iberia as long as they held territory there. The medieval Christian kingdoms of the peninsula all had slaves and laws governing them, and slavery continued in early modern Spain and Portugal before declining and dying out in the eighteenth century. (10)

Enslaved people in Iberia in the late Middle Ages and the early modern period were a racially diverse group. Muslim kingdoms had brought enslaved Slavs, Byzantine Christians, North African Berbers, and sub-Saharan Africans to the peninsula, and they also enslaved Iberian Christians. Societies in Christian-ruled areas enslaved people from the southern and eastern Mediterranean as well as Iberian Muslims. The European pandemic of the mid–fourteenth century, the black death, had decimated the population and created a need for labor, moving European elites to obtain enslaved people from a broader area, including from southeastern Europe all the way east to the Black Sea. In the mid–fifteenth century, Portuguese merchants began to run expeditions down the coast of West Africa and to bring to Iberia larger numbers of enslaved people from sub-Saharan Africa. When Esteban arrived in Spain, enslaved people in Iberia included Moroccans, sub-Saharan Black Africans, inhabitants of the Canary Islands, Moriscos from the Iberian Peninsula, and Muslims from the peninsula and the Mediterranean (Phillips 15–23).

The basis for regulating slavery in Spain was King Alfonso X's Siete partidas (Seven Divisions), a legal code that drew on Roman law (Phillips 21). Enslaved people were considered their owner's property and had no independent legal rights (83). Their treatment at the hands of their owners, however, was regulated, and the owners might be punished by a judge for extreme mistreatment (98–100). A small minority of enslaved people obtained freedom through manumission. Enslaved people could purchase their freedom with money they earned through their work outside of the household or with assistance from their family members. In almost all cases, the enslaved person needed to obtain the master's agreement before purchasing their freedom; exceptions might occur in the case of a master's severe misdeeds. Some enslaved people who succeeded in winning their master's approval might influence the master to manumit them in their will (Phillips 130–34).

Enslaved men and women worked as auxiliaries in households, artisan workshops, and agricultural estates (Phillips 85). Women were employed as laundresses, garbage collectors, and wet nurses (110). Owners might prostitute enslaved women or have sexual relations with them, sometimes resulting in pregnancies (87–89). Men worked as stevedores; in construction, shoemaking, and commerce; and as sailors, ferrymen, and soldiers (110–12). Not all life was work: enslaved people participated in local Christian institutions, especially in religious brotherhoods, or *cofradías*—organizations that provided charity, decent burials, and a community that might retain cultural customs from the members' homelands (94, 96).

Africans and Afro-Iberians as Intermediaries in Exploration and Conquest

While Esteban's functions as cultural intermediary, healer, scout, and guide have captured the imagination of many readers as unique roles, Esteban was one of a number of Black Africans or Afro-Iberians who accompanied Iberian colonizers as auxiliaries, often playing key roles as intermediaries in the imperial project (see Garofalo). Two circumstances bolstered this phenomenon: first, the significant number of people of African descent living in Iberian port cities, and, second, their experience of being moved from one place to another and of adapting to new languages and cultures (Garofalo 30–31). Close to 35,000 West Africans were sold into slavery and arrived in Iberia before the sixteenth century; some ten to twenty percent of the residents in Iberian port cities, including Lisbon and Seville, were Afro-descendants (Garofalo 29; Phillips 10–11). At this time, Afro-Iberians usually traveled to the Americas not in slave ships[3] but as *pasajeros a Indias* ("passengers to the Indies"), either as free persons or accompanying the person who claimed ownership of them. In the Americas, they "helped shape the cultural and physical webs that bound together the African, European, and American continents" (Garofalo 27). They acted "as traders, translators, missionaries, refugees, sailors," and soldiers (30–31).

Esteban was not the first enslaved Black man to accompany an Iberian expedition of exploration or conquest. Among the first was Juan Garrido, a man likely born in West Africa. After some eight years living in Lisbon and Seville, Garrido traveled to the Caribbean in 1502 or 1503 and later accompanied Hernán Cortés to México-Tenochtitlan. Black men served Juan Ponce de León in his 1508 conquest of Puerto Rico, Diego Velázquez de Cuéllar in Cuba in 1511–12, and Francisco de Ibarra in northern New Spain in the 1520s. Cortés took some three hundred Black people with him to Baja California in the 1530s, and Pedro de Alvarado took two hundred Africans with him to Peru in 1534. Afro-Iberians served in varied roles, including as interpreters and soldiers. The latter role was a continuation of patterns established in the wars of Christians against Muslims in the Iberian Middle Ages (Restall, "Black Conquistadors" 181–83, 193–94).

Africans and Afro-Iberians tended to serve in auxiliary roles in Spanish companies, as opposed to the Spaniards' Native allies, who fought in separate units under their own leaders against shared Native enemies (Restall, *Beyond* 19). While official histories, chronicles, and *probanzas de mérito* ignore much of the importance of the Black participants in the expeditions of reconnaissance and conquest, they do provide clues that allow us to consider what might have been omitted from the narratives. These clues include visual representations. Around 1579, Diego Durán completed his *Historia de las Indias de la Nueva España e islas de Tierra Firme* (*History of the Indies of New Spain*), an important ethnographic record of the history of the Mexicas (the Náhuatl-speaking inhabitants of the Valley of Mexico). Eleven chapters tell the story of the Spanish conquest. The accounts of Tlaxcaltecans receiving Cortés (ch. 73) and Moctezuma II welcoming Cortés to México-Tenochtitlan (ch. 74) both include illustrations in which a Black man acts as Cortés's auxiliary. In Durán's picture of the entry into Tlaxcala, the midpoint of the image is a gift proffered by the first of two Tlaxcaltecans, who occupy the right half of the image; the left half is filled by Cortés on horseback and, behind him, the Black man on foot, dressed as a Spaniard and carrying a spear (*Historia de las Indias*, fol. 207r). The Black man is thus given signal importance as one of the four figures in the exchange. Some scholars have identified this man as Juan Garrido, though Restall suggests that the figure likely represents the presence of Black men in general on Cortés's expedition ("Black Conquistadors" 180). In either case, this Black man acts as a personal auxiliary in a military endeavor, in a capacity similar to the one Esteban would fulfill only ten years later.

The next image that Durán offers shows Moctezuma II receiving Cortés: the picture is divided in half, this time by the spear held by a Black man who is dressed as a Spaniard (*Historia de las Indias*, fol. 208v). To the left of the spear, the Black man holds the reins of Cortés's horse, signaling that he serves as an auxiliary. Behind him stands Cortés's horse, and behind the horse, the first of Cortés's Spanish soldiers. To the right of the spear, Cortés advances toward Moctezuma II, behind whom stand two other Mexica lords. Moctezuma II holds out a gift of a garland (fol. 208v). Again, in this image, the Black man's presence is prominent.

While the number of Afro-Iberians who served expeditions of exploration and conquest was less than the number of Spaniards or Amerindian allies, their roles shaped both conquest and colonization. Armed participation by Black men in the Spanish conquest supported the later commissioning of Black militias that were vital to the protection of Spanish interests against English, French, and Dutch privateers (Restall, "Black Conquistadors" 197). Some Black people who assisted in the Spanish conquest sought freedom and autonomy in clandestine *palenques* or *quilombos* ("maroon enclaves"), separate from Amerindians. Others integrated into indigenous communities and at times supported Indian rebellions (200). A few, such as Esteban, whose presence contributed to oral histories and legends, continue to complicate the web of race relations and perceptions in the Americas even today, as the oral history in Zuni Pueblo shows.

Narrative Politics: Clues from Other Representations

As students approach Cabeza de Vaca's representation of Esteban and consider the meanings with which *Naufragios* imbues him as well as the work's silences, it is helpful to examine representations of Esteban and other expeditionaries of African descent and to talk about narrative politics: how the purpose and genre of each text shapes the representation of the African or Afro-Iberian auxiliary. Restall's "Black Conquistadors" and Richard Gordon's "Following Estevanico" are especially helpful to identify primary-text sources. I take the following examples from the many more that these scholars document.

The first epic poem set in territory that is now the United States is Gaspar Pérez de Villagrá's *Historia de la Nueva México* (1610). Here, Villagrá notes Esteban's racial difference while also elevating Esteban's valor to a degree indistinguishable from that of his European companions. In Gordon's analysis, Esteban serves Villagrá's purpose—and that of the epic in general—of emphasizing the heroic deeds that created this outpost of Spanish civilization.

> They show us, with no small astonishment,
> After in Florida they were lost
> For that prolonged time,
> The great and valorous negro Esteban
> And Memorable Cabeza de Vaca,
> Castillo, Maldonado, without peer,
> And Andrés Dorantes, most remarkable,
> All being men most singular.   (Villagrá 18–19)

> Con no pequeño assombro nos mostraron,
> Después que en la Florida se perdieron
> Por aquel largo tiempo prolongado,
> El grande negro Esteban valeroso
> Y Cabeza de Vaca memorable,
> Castillo, Maldonado, sin segundo,
> Y Andrés Dorantes, más aventajado,
> Todos singularísimos varones.   (18–19)

This characterization of a valiant Esteban responds not only to the imperative of the epic but also to a popular image of Black soldiers that emerged from the wars between Christians and Muslims on the Iberian peninsula. Black people were perceived by Spaniards as "natural warriors" (Restall, "Black Conquistadors" 193).[4]

Esteban's importance to the expedition survivors in *Naufragios* and to the legacy of Spanish-indigenous relations becomes clearer in the light of the fuller narratives of Esteban's participation in the subsequent Marcos de Niza expedition. Inspired by Cabeza de Vaca's reports of gold-rich territory, Viceroy Antonio de Mendoza sent an expedition in 1539 to continue exploring to the north. Mendoza could not persuade any of the Spaniards who had recently returned to lead the enterprise, so he purchased Esteban from Dorantes and sent him as a guide to Marcos de Niza. Calling Esteban a "person of reason" ("persona de razón"; qtd in Gordon, "Following" 201n27), Mendoza surely based his decision on the reports of Esteban's value to reconnaissance work given by the three Spanish survivors (Adorno and Pautz, 2: 421; see also Ahern, "Cross").

Marcos de Niza, facing criticism for falsely asserting that he had seen the fabled cities of gold, needed in his narrative to enhance the idea that his expedition was successful despite his lack of material evidence. Niza arguably establishes Esteban as protagonist of his *relación*, particularly since he, Niza, was absent from the key arrival at what he identifies as Cíbola.[5] Having sent Esteban ahead (named Stephen in the translated passage below), Niza enhances Esteban's authority, skill, and success in the narrative and thus communicates the value of the expedition (Gordon, "Following Estevanico" 192–93). Esteban sent messengers to Cíbola carrying with them his calabash to announce his approach and intent to perform cures. But when the lord of Cíbola

> saw the rattles, he flung . . . [the calabash] furiously on the floor and said: "I know these people; these rattles are not of our style of workmanship; tell them to go back immediately or not a man of them will remain alive" . . . [and] remained very angry. The messengers went back sad, and hardly dared to tell Stephen of the reception they had met. Nevertheless . . . he said that they should not fear, that he desired to go on, because, although they answered him badly, they would receive him well. So he went and arrived at the city of Cibola just before sunset, with . . . more than three hundred men, besides many women. The inhabitants would not permit them to enter the city, but put them in a large and commodious house outside. . . . They at once took away from Stephen all that he carried, telling him that the lord so ordered. "All that night," said the Indians, "they gave us nothing to eat nor drink. The next day, when the sun was a lance-length high, Stephen went out of the house and some of the chiefs with him. Straightway many people came out of the city and, as soon as he saw them, he began to flee and we with him. Then they gave us these arrow-strokes and cuts and we fell and some dead men fell on top of us. Thus we lay till nightfall, without daring to stir. . . . We saw no more of Stephen and we concluded that they had

shot him with arrows as they had the rest that were with him, of whom there escaped only us." (Niza, "Relation" 216–17)

y vido los cascabeles, . . . arrojó en el suelo el calabazo y dijo: "yo conozco esta gente, porquestos cascabeles no son de la hechura de los nuestros, decildes que luego se vuelvan, si no que no quedará hombre dellos"; y . . . se quedó muy enojado. Y los mensajeros volvieron tristes, y no osaban decir a Esteban lo que les acaesció, aunque . . . él les dijo: "que no temiesen, que él quería ir allá, porque, aunque le respondían mal, le rescibían bien"; y así se fue y llegó a la ciudad de Cíbola, ya que se quería poner el sol, con . . . más de trescientos hombres, sin otras muchas mujeres; y no los consintieron entrar en la ciudad, sino en una casa grande y de buen aposento, que estaba fuera. . . . Y luego tomaron a Esteban todo lo que llevaba, diciendo que el Señor lo mandó así; y en toda esa noche no nos dieron de comer, ni de beber. Y otro día, el sol de una lanza fuera, salió Esteban de la casa, y algunos de los principales con él, y luego vino mucha gente de la ciudad, y como él los vio, echó a huir y nosotros también; y luego nos dieron estos flechazos y heridas y caímos; y cayeron sobre nosotros otros muertos, y así estuvimos hasta la noche, sin osarnos menear . . . y no vimos más a Esteban, sino que creemos que le flecharon como a los demás que iban con él, que no escaparon más de nosotros. (Niza, *Descubrimiento*)

Maureen Ahern analyzes how Esteban uses symbolic communication both on the Cabeza de Vaca expedition and on the later Marcos de Niza expedition in his key role as scout and cultural mediator. In Cíbola, Esteban employs the gourd as a symbol, believing it will communicate his role and authority as a shaman. Ahern argues that Esteban missed the differences between the peoples he encountered in Texas and those he met in Cíbola. His use of the symbols that had worked to open communication in Texas and Sonora were likely read by the leaders of Cíbola as heralding the threat of cross and conquest arriving from the south (231–33).

Students can understand the concept of narrative politics and apply it especially well to how it shapes representation by contrasting Niza's lengthy account of Esteban's death with the account given by Pedro de Castañeda. In 1540, inspired by the tale Niza told of cities that outshone México-Tenochtitlan, Viceroy Mendoza sent Francisco Vázquez de Coronado as captain of another expedition into northern New Spain. Surprised by the poverty and the meager populations that the Coronado expedition encountered, and now finding Niza's report unbelievable, Pedro de Castañeda maligns Esteban's credibility in order to criticize Niza. Castañeda associates Esteban with the evils of conquest and portrays his death as the result of arrogance and an assumed authority that overstep appropriate behavior for an enslaved Black man:

> After Stephen had left the friars, he thought he could get all the reputation and honor himself, and that if he should discover those settlements with such famous high houses, alone, he would be considered bold and

courageous. So he proceeded with the people who had followed him, and succeeded in crossing the wilderness which lies between the country he had passed through and Cibola. He was so far ahead of the friars that, when these reached Chichilticalli, which is on the edge of the wilderness, he was already at Cibola. . . . As I said, Estevan reached Cibola loaded with a large quantity of turquoise as they had given him and some beautiful women whom the Indians who followed him and carried his things were taking with them and had given him. These had followed him from all the settlements he passed, believing that under his protection they could traverse the whole world without any danger. But as the people in this country were more intelligent than those who follow Estevan, they lodged him in a little hut they had outside their village, and the older men and the governors heard his story and took steps to find out the reason he had come to that country. For three days they made inquiries about him and held a council. The account which the Negro gave them of two white men who were following him, sent by a great Lord, who knew about the things in the sky, and how these were coming to instruct them in divine matters, made them think that he must be a spy or a guide from some nations who wish to come and conquer them, because it seemed to them unreasonable to say that the people were white in the country from whence he came and that he was sent by them, he being black. Besides these other reasons, they thought it was hard of him to ask for turquoises and women, and so they decided to kill him. They did this, but they did not kill any of those who went with him, although they kept some young fellows and let others, about 60 persons, return freely to their own country. (Castañeda, *Translation* 475)

Apartado que se hubo el Esteban de los dichos frailes, presumió ganar en todo reputación y honra y que se le atribuyese la osadía y atrevimiento de haber él solo descubierto aquellos poblados de altos tan nombrados por aquella tierra. Y llevando consigo de aquellas gentes que le seguían procuró de atravesar los despoblados que hay entre Cíbola y lo poblado que había andado. Y habíaseles adelantado tanto a los frailes que, cuando ellos llegaron a Chichieticale, ques principio del despoblado, ya él estaba a Cíbola . . . Ansí que llegado que fue el negro Esteban a Cíbola, llegó cargado de grande número de turquesas que le habían dado y algunas mujeres hermosas que le habían dado y llevaban los indios que le acompañaban y le seguían de todo lo poblado que había pasado, los cuales en ir debajo de su amparo creían poder atravesar toda la tierra sin riesgo ninguno, pero como aquellas gentes de aquella tierra fuesen de mas razón que no los que seguían a el Esteban, aposentaronlo en una cierta eremita que tenían fuera del pueblo y los mas viejos y los que gobernaban oyeron sus razones y procuraron saber la causa de su venida en aquella tierra. Y bien informados por espacio de tres días, entraron en su consulta y por la noticia quel negro les dio como atrás venían dos hombres blancos, enviados por un gran señor, que eran entendidos en las cosas del Cielo. Y que aquellos los venían a industriar en las cosas divinas. Consideraron que debía ser espía o guía de algunas naciones que los querían ir a conquistar, porque les pareció desvarío decir que la tierra de donde venía era la gente blanca, siendo él negro y enviado por ellos, y fueron a él. Y como después de otras razones le pidiese turquesas y mujeres, parecioles cosa dura y determináronse a le matar y ansí lo hicieron, sin que matasen a nadie de los que con él iban. Y tomaron algunos muchachos y a los demás que serían obra de sesenta personas dejaron volver libres a sus tierras. (Castañeda, *Relación* 418–19)[6]

If students read these representations and analyze how each one molds Esteban's identity, character, and behavior to a different context and purpose, they can then return to Cabeza de Vaca's spare, though favorable, narration of Esteban's deeds to consider how sixteenth-century accounts by Spaniards both erase and mythologize the few Black participants in the Iberian expeditions. In this regard, Restall's "Myth" is an excellent framework for reading both *Naufragios* as a whole and Esteban within it.

Finally, while the voices of most participants of African descent in the Spanish expeditions of reconnaissance and conquest have been lost, reading one that has survived may allow students to imagine some of Esteban's knowledge, ability, and attitude toward his labor and leadership that is erased in *Naufragios*. One of the first Black conquistadors was Juan Garrido, whose voice, though mediated by the highly formulaic *relación* genre, can be heard in his own *probanza*.

I, Juan Garrido, black resident [*de color negro vecino*] of this city [Mexico], appear before Your Mercy and state that I am in need of making a *probanza* . . . , a report on how I served Your Majesty in the conquest and pacification of this New Spain, from the time when the Marqués del Valle [Cortés] entered it; and in his company I was present at all the invasions and conquests and pacifications which were carried out, . . . all of which I did at my own expense without being given either salary or allotment of natives [*repartimiento de indios*] or anything else. As I am married and a resident of this city, where I have always lived; and also as I went with the Marqués del Valle to discover the islands which are in that part of the southern sea [the Pacific] where there was much hunger and privation; and also as I went to discover and pacify the islands of . . . Puerto Rico; and also as I went on the pacification and conquest of the island of Cuba with the adelantado Diego Velázquez; in all these ways for thirty years have I served and continue to serve Your Majesty—for these reasons stated above do I petition Your Mercy. And also because I was the first to have the inspiration to sow [wheat] here in New Spain and to see if it took; I did this and experimented at my own expense. (qtd. in Restall, "Black Conquistadors" 171)

Yo, Juan Garrido, residente de color negro, vecino de esta ciudad [de México], me presento ante Su Merced y declaro que tengo la necesidad de hacer una probanza . . . , un reporte de cómo serví a Su Majestad en

> la conquista y pacificación de ésta Nueva España, del tiempo cuando el Marqués del Valle [Cortés] la llevó a cabo; en su compañía estuve presente en todas las invasiones y conquistas y pacificaciones que se llevaron a cabo, . . . todo lo hice a mis expensas sin recibir salario o repartimiento de indios, o alguna otra cosa. Soy casado y residente en esta ciudad, donde siempre he vivido; y también como fui a descubrir y pacificar las islas de . . . Puerto Rico; y también como fui a la pacificación y conquista de la isla de Cuba con el adelantado Diego Velázquez; en todas estas maneras por treinta y cinco años he servido y sigo sirviendo a Su Majestad, por estas razones me dirijo a Su Merced. También porque fui el primero en tener la inspiración de sembrar trigo aquí en la Nueva España y ver si crecía; esto lo hice a mis expensas. (Alegría 127)

The above representations illustrate the complexity of Esteban's identity: an enslaved, Black, and African person, but also a Spaniard, intermediary, communicator with the Native peoples of the Southwest, and conqueror.

Present and Future Meanings of Esteban

Let us return to our starting point, where Esteban's participation in the Spanish conquest has become for African Americans today a symbol of first presence in the southwestern United States. This meaning compels us to address the difficult question of African-Native relations. Scholarship is beginning to examine the history of these relationships, as in Restall's anthology *Beyond Black and Red*. If Esteban symbolizes a first African presence in the Southwest, what does he symbolize in the potential for interrelating the history-telling and representation by minority African American and Native communities?

In 1992, Diane Reyna from Taos Pueblo produced the documentary *Surviving Columbus*, in which the Acoma narrator Conroy Chino introduces Esteban with these words: "Ironically, the first white man to contact Pueblo people was Estevanico, a Black slave from Azemmour, Morocco" (00:18:36).[7] In incorporated archival footage dating back to 1990, the Zuni archaeologist Edmund Ladd explains that Esteban told the Zunis he represented powerful white men whom the Zunis would need to obey and that he likely pressured them for food, shelter, and gifts. Esteban's integration into Zuni oral tradition is evident in the words of the Zuni elder Mecalita Wystalucy. Esteban is the giant in Wystalucy's tale.

> The people who lived at the steaming springs had a giant who led them, who walked ahead of them as their guide. And the people from Hanlhipinnkya had the twin war gods as their leaders. The sun father knew that the giant could not be killed, so when they brought the weapons to the twin war gods, they pierced them with arrows, but the giant wouldn't die. Sun Father said, "his heart is in the gourd rattle. The gourd is his heart and if you destroy it, you will kill him, and your way will be cleared." The

younger war god stepped forward from the fighting and shot the gourd rattle. The giant fell, and all of his people ran away. They blew the conch shell and made the sound of war. (*Surviving* 00:20:24–22:10)

Fundamentally, for the Zuni, Esteban was a catalyst for the Spanish invasion. He sent symbolic messages that Fray Marcos de Niza interpreted to mean that he had found the seven cities of gold. This message ignited Spanish greed and brought Coronado and, later, Juan de Oñate and Don Diego de Vargas north from Mexico to subjugate the Pueblo peoples (*Surviving* 00:23:52).

The story of Esteban then and now allows students to examine the role of representation in the constructing and silencing of identity and to ask themselves how to confront the pain of erasure and colonization of three peoples—Hispanic or Latinx, African American, and Pueblo or Native—who share a national and regional space, where this history and its representations complicate questions of justice and decolonization.

NOTES

1. If Hayes's article depends on some assertions that are questioned by historians, it also provides more substance than most popular retellings of Esteban's travel.

2. When Esteban accompanied Marcos de Niza's 1539 expedition, he is thought to have reached the Zuni Pueblo, in what is now New Mexico, most likely at the now ruined village of Hawikuh, where he was killed.

3. The scholarship on the large-scale slave trade through the Middle Passage is plentiful. Starting points might include Klein and Vinson; Chira; and Vinson and Graves. The *Slave Voyages* database is also a tremendous teaching tool.

4. This perception is on display in Andrés de Claramonte's seventeenth-century play *Valiente negro de Flandes* (*The Valiant Black Man in Flanders*); see Claramonte y Corroy. For representations of Blackness and of well-known historical Black figures in early modern Spain, see Wright, who studies the Renaissance poet Juan Latino; Fikes, who sketches a biography of Juan de Pareja, the seventeenth-century painter of African ancestry who learned his art from Diego Velázquez; Jones, who examines the representation of Black speech in early modern Spanish theater; and Houchins and Molinero, who have edited the biography of the eighteenth-century Afro-Iberian religious woman Chicaba (Pan y Agua).

5. In oral traditions in New Mexico, this place has been identified with Hawikuh in Zuni, although Adorno and Pautz (2: 422) accept the scholarship that locates Esteban's death in northern Sonora.

6. I have modernized the spelling in the source.

7. In several instances, the 2020 rerelease cited in this volume uses different cuts of the footage included in the 1992 original.

Gender, Transgender, and Queer Inbetweenness in the *Relación*

Paola Uparela

It would not be wrong to assert that Álvar Núñez Cabeza de Vaca's *Relación* (*Account*) is a hypermasculine text: its exaltation of the writer's misfortunes and the hypostasis of the narrator-protagonist's heroism would certainly confirm this assertion. However, the *Relación* is exceptionally complex regarding gender representation. This essay covers ways to teach the *Relación* in classes on gender, transgender, and queer studies through an exploration of the following themes: the representation of women in the text; Cabeza de Vaca's performance of indigenous women's roles; the story of the cross-dressing figure referred to as Mala Cosa; the transgenderism and alternative sexual practices attributed to the indigenous men who do women's work, referred to as *amarionados*; and the warning from a Castilian woman that a Moorish woman had predicted the expedition's failure, a prophecy not revealed to the reader until the end of the *Relación*.[1]

The representation of women and trans subjectivities in the *Relación* merits pedagogical dialogue with students. A number of questions could guide the discussion: Where are the women in the *Relación*? What are the feminine roles Cabeza de Vaca took on? How might the ethnographies about the *amarionados* or Mala Cosa's transvestism or transgenderism tell us about those same transformations in Cabeza de Vaca? Should we study transgenderism as part of the inevitable processes of transculturation and performativity? What is the value of studying the Moorish woman's omen, given that women's voices are concealed by the masculine authorship and authority of the *Relación*? To respond to these and other questions, I propose a queering of Cabeza de Vaca's *Relación*. That is, following Daniel Marshall, Kevin Murphy, and Zeb Tortorici's proposal for queering the archive, I focus on those unstable and elusive instances of the narration that "become volatile under the pressure of the efforts we ask them to sustain" (1). This approach to the text sets up a pedagogical methodology, with examples to use in class, for reflection on how trans and queer experiences have been articulated within processes of colonialism and neocolonialism, gender inequality, and violence.

Women in the Relación

I begin by inviting students to examine descriptions of women and in-between subjectivities in the *Relación* (listed in the appendix). The objective here is for students to go back and reread the *Relación* while examining the list, analyzing the representation of indigenous women and contrasting these passages with those on the anomalous participation of Cabeza de Vaca and his companions, the *amarionados* and Mala Cosa, and the Moorish woman. Articles by Mariah Wade and by Carmen Gómez-Galisteo can serve as a point of departure.

Women's Clothing

Throughout the *Relación*, Cabeza de Vaca emphasizes the nudity of the Indians. Yet in the case of women, he mentions several types of clothing: woven mantles or cloaks, deerskins, cotton shirts, leather skirts, and clothes made of grasses, straw, and plant fibers. Given the stereotypical nudity of the Indians, these are a lot of clothing references! In chapter 6, when traveling toward the region known by the Indians then as Apalache, Cabeza de Vaca describes "small woven cloaks of poor quality with which the women partially covered their bodies" ("mantas de hilo pequeñas y no buenas con que las mugeres cubren algo de sus personas"; Adorno and Pautz, 1: 55; 54). In chapter 15, he says that the men of Malhado go nude, while the women "*cover part* of their bodies with a type of fiber that grows on trees. The young women cover themselves with deerskins" ("traen de sus cuerpos *algo cubierto* con una lana que en los árboles se cría. Las moças se cubren con unos cueros de venados"; 117; 116; my emphasis). In chapter 30, he notes that in the Rio Grande, "[t]he women wear deerskins, as do some of the men, notably the ones who are old and who are of no use in war" ("[l]as mugeres andan cubiertas con unos cueros de venado y algunos pocos de hombres, señaladamente los que son viejos que no sirven para la guerra"; 225; 224). And during his trip through northwestern Mexico, he observes that "[t]he women cover their *shameful parts* with grasses and straw" ("[l]as mugeres cubren sus *vergüenças* con hierva y paja"; 235; 234; ch. 32; my emphasis).

If the cloaks made of wool, grass, or straw were perceived as too short to cover the genitals, perhaps the women went around more exposed than covered. It is easy to imagine that when the weather was hot in Texas, women would go naked rather than impractically cover their vulvas with tiny cloaks. Similar descriptions can be found in texts by Christopher Columbus and Vaz de Caminha, wherein the genitals of indigenous women are nude or lightly covered by grass leaves or small pieces of cotton (Uparela, *Invaginaciones* 40–59). In these texts, the insistence on covering female genitals is suspicious, as it simultaneously implies a covering up of the European and androcentric gaze and the violence that this gaze inflicts (Uparela and Jáuregui 81–84; Jáuregui and Uparela 104, 112–16).

Cabeza de Vaca observes that the women of northwestern Mexico cover their bodies much more than those in other groups along the Gulf Coast: "Among these people we saw *the most decently clad women* we had ever seen in any part of the Indies. They wear some shirts of cotton that reach their knees and some half sleeves over them of folds of buckskin that touch the ground" ("Entre éstos vimos *las mugeres más honestamente tratadas* que a ninguna parte de Indias que huviéssemos visto. Traen unas camisas de algodón que llegan hasta las rodillas, y unas medias mangas ençima dellas de unas faldillas de cuero de venado sin pelo que tocan en el suelo"; Adorno and Pautz 1: 231; 230; ch. 31; my emphasis). Cabeza de Vaca describes shirts with sleeves and long skirts that reach the ground, made from clean, treated leather and worn with accessories such as belts and shoes. Notice that Cabeza de Vaca sets forth two general forms of dress for women: almost naked or covered from neck to foot. The former consists of covering the genitals with garments that Cabeza de Vaca finds small and insufficient. The latter form of dress is described in detail, including sizes, materials, and accessories; he associates this dress with female decency and good treatment. This connection can be studied in the *Relación* alongside other colonial texts in which we find descriptions of nude women associated with birth and innocence on the one hand and with libidinousness and a lack of modesty on the other (Uparela, *Invaginaciones* 47–59, 68–84).

Women's Work

Cabeza de Vaca offers detailed descriptions of the chores carried out by women from different indigenous groups he met on his journey, including hunting and fishing, collecting and preparing food, transporting water, gathering firewood, serving as trail guides, and communicating and mediating in conflicts (see appendix, table 1). In chapter 18, Cabeza de Vaca describes the work of Mariames women vis-à-vis that of men, who do not carry anything of weight:

> The women are very hardworking and endure a great deal, because of the twenty-four hours there are between day and night, they have only six of rest, and the rest of the night they spend in firing the ovens in order to dry those roots they eat. And from daybreak, they begin to dig and bring firewood and water to their homes, and put in order the other things of which they have need. (Adorno and Pautz 1: 141)

> Las mugeres son muy trabajadas y para mucho, porque de veinte y quatro oras que ay entre día y noche no tienen sino seis horas de descanso, y todo lo más de la noche passan en atizar sus hornos para secar aquellas raízes que comen. Y desque amanesçe comiençan a cavar y a traer leña y agua a sus casas, y dar orden en las otras cosas de que tienen neçessidad. (1: 140)

While the Mariames men do no heavy labor, the women spend eighteen hours a day pulling up and preparing roots to eat, firing up the ovens, and doing other chores. Cabeza de Vaca insists on the difference between the minimal duties of the men and the excessive labor of the women, who do chores that he himself has to carry out, as discussed below.

Breastfeeding

Chapter 24 includes descriptions of family and marital life among groups from Malhado to the Rio Grande. Cabeza de Vaca observes that the women do not typically sleep with their husbands for two years after getting pregnant, and he notes that these women are devoted to "nurturing their children, who suckle until they are twelve years old, at which time they are of an age that by themselves they know how to search for food" ("maman hasta que son de edad de doze años, que ya para entonçes están en edad que por sí saben buscar de comer";

Adorno and Pautz 1: 177; 176).[2] Cabeza de Vaca reports that the Indians would go without food for three or four days and that "they let their children suckle so that in times of hunger they [the children] would not die, since even if some should survive, they would end up sickly and of little strength" ("los dexavan mamar porque en los tiempos de hambre no moriessen, y que ya que algunos escapassen, saldrían muy delicados y de pocas fuerças"; 1: 179; 178). Cabeza de Vaca seems interested in these biopolitical matters of reproduction and food security (as were other colonial authors, such as Bartolomé de las Casas and Felipe Guaman Poma de Ayala), not only for the sake of ethnographic fascination but also because of the hunger he himself had suffered.[3]

Menstruation

Chapter 26 includes an ethnographic observation about menstruation and labor among the indigenous groups between Malhado and the Rio Grande: "when the women are *menstruating* they do not search for food except for themselves, because no other person will eat what she brings. In the time that thus I was among these people, I saw a wicked behavior, and it is that I saw one man married to another, and these are *effeminate, impotent men*" ("quando las mugeres están con su *costumbre* no buscan de comer más de para sí solas, porque ninguna otra persona come de lo que ella trae. En el tiempo que assí estava entre éstos, vi una diablura, y es que vi un hombre casado con otro, y éstos son unos *hombres amarionados impotentes*"; Adorno and Pautz 1: 191; 190; my emphasis). While at the beginning of this chapter, Cabeza de Vaca names the nations and languages he encountered from the island of the Malhado to the land of the Cuchendados, Rolena Adorno and Patrick Charles Pautz note that it is impossible to identify the group mentioned in the above-cited passage (1: 189n6). Sebastián de Covarrubias explains that women's menstruation "is called *costumbre*, because it is ordinary, and ... regular, ... occurring every month ... except for women who are pregnant" ("se llama *costumbre,* por ser ordinario, y ... regular, ... por ser cada mes ... excepto a las que se hacen preñadas"; 266).[4] The *costumbre* reduced the number of women working. At the same time, some men married each other and took on the tasks of women, as discussed below (see appendix, 1.5 and 3.6; see also Pupo-Walker, "*Naufragios*" 765n31). Students could reflect not only on the euphemistic lexicon ("costumbre") for menstruation used by Cabeza de Vaca but also on the social customs associated with labor, menstruation, and breastfeeding, then and now.

Going In Between; Becoming Women

Throughout the *Relación*, Cabeza de Vaca assumes at least four of the roles ascribed to indigenous women by performing arduous routine labor, communication between groups, mercantile exchange, and mediation in conflicts (see appendix, 1.1–1.4). As Gómez-Galisteo argues, "[w]orking in a job that a Native American woman would normally hold, [Cabeza de Vaca] could no longer be the epitome of masculinity" (11). The transition between cultures, in Cabeza de Vaca's case, often entails transvestism or transgenderism. The roles of Native women must not be disconnected from the positions assumed by Cabeza de Vaca and his companions. These Christians establish alliances that break with European categories of gender and filiation; they, as much as the indigenous women, are "going between," as Wade would put it.

Performing Women's Work

As a captive among indigenous groups, Cabeza de Vaca laments that he had to work with women through long, arduous days. In chapter 22, for example, he describes "very great ulcerations, which caused us very great distress on account of the large loads we carried" ("unos empeines muy grandes de que resçibíamos muy gran pena por razón de las muy grandes cargas que traíamos"; Adorno and Pautz 1: 173; 172). Still, Cabeza de Vaca does not relate his heavy labor to the work of the women. As Gómez-Galisteo points out, "[H]e did not embrace a new, female identity" (11), nor did he identify with the *amarionados* who also bore the burdens of women (see appendix, 1.5 and 3.7). But being among women and *amarionados* was probably quite convenient. Let's remember that the *Relación* is marked by constant food scarcity, to the point that the Spaniards were forced to eat horsemeat and even to resort to cannibalism, practices from which Cabeza de Vaca distances himself (Jáuregui, "Going Native" 184–88). Because of his place with women in the division of labor, Cabeza de Vaca has access to the fruits and roots that allow women and children to survive. I wonder if Cabeza de Vaca might have consumed milk from lactating women in this time of food shortages—the same milk that children would drink until puberty (see appendix, 7.3). We can at least say that he depended on a feminine economic order not to die of hunger.

Exchange of Goods

Cabeza de Vaca narrates how, after leaving Malhado, he assumes his new role as a merchant and gains mobility: "I had the freedom to go wherever I wanted, and I was not constrained in any way nor enslaved, and wherever I went they treated me well and gave me food out of want for my wares" ("tenía libertad para ir donde quería, y no era obligado a cosa alguna y no era esclavo, y dondequiera que iva me hazían buen tratamiento y me davan de comer por respeto de mis mercaderías"; Adorno and Pautz 1: 121; 120; ch. 16). Commerce is an activity for women in the groups with which Cabeza de Vaca lived on the coast of Texas (Gómez-Galisteo 11). As a merchant, Cabeza de Vaca does not mention recovering a masculine European identity; he talks about having the freedom to move, embracing fame, and recognizing his own strangeness and queerness: "I was very well known; when they saw me and I brought them the things they needed, they were greatly pleased. And those who did not know me desired and endeavored to see me because of my renown" ("entre ellos era muy conosçido; holgavan mucho quando me vían y les traía lo que avían menester. Y los que no me conosçían me procuravan y desseavan ver por mi fama"; Adorno and Pautz 1: 121, 123; 120, 122). Cabeza de Vaca is no longer an outsider, a captive, or a slave but rather a strange bearded man who, as Wade has pointed out, "uses his Otherness to seduce his native hosts. . . . As Other he can cross group boundaries" (336). Cabeza de Vaca discursively marks in his text the specific teleology of "going home" (Jáuregui, "Going Native" 179). However, he is advancing toward unknown lands and indigenous peoples among whom he, neither fully foreign nor Indianized, finds fame and mobility. Moreover, while Cabeza de Vaca says he is going home, throughout his journey from southwestern Texas to northwestern Mexico, he is going in the opposite direction, contrary to his stated intentions (chs. 28 and 30): Cabeza de Vaca enacts a queer displacement.

Communication, Translation, and Conflict Mediation

Among the Capoques and Han, in Malhado, the men were forbidden from communicating with the families of their wives, while the women were "at liberty to communicate and converse with their parents-in-law and relatives" ("Las mugeres tienen la libertad para comunicar y conversar con los suegros y parientes"; Adorno and Pautz 1: 111; 110; ch. 14). The women of southwestern Texas, like those of the Gulf Coast, whom Cabeza de Vaca describes earlier, "can mediate even when there is a war" ("contratar aunque aya guerra"; 1: 217; 216; ch. 30). Cabeza de Vaca and indigenous women share this job of mediating and communicating. As a go-between, Cabeza de Vaca achieves the liberation of his companions Andrés Dorantes, Alonso del Castillo Maldonado, and Esteban (ch. 17), and he negotiates between different groups. For example, traveling through northwestern Mexico, Cabeza de Vaca acts as a mediator and a protector of the natives when he meets Spaniards who are bent on enslaving Indians (1: 238–53; chs. 32–34). As a translator, toward the end of the *Relación*, Cabeza de Vaca claims that he has learned six indigenous languages and that he and his companions can communicate with all the groups—if not on their own, then with the assistance of indigenous translators or Esteban (1: 232–33; ch. 31). For example, before coming across signs of Christians, Esteban and Castillo are sent ahead to negotiate with the Indians from the next town, who are enemies of the Indians with whom Dorantes and Cabeza de Vaca are staying (chs. 30–32). Cabeza de Vaca and his companions serve as translators and intermediaries in situations of conflict among Indians and with Spaniards.

Messianism and Healing

According to Cabeza de Vaca, indigenous men have one wife, while indigenous healers or physicians can have two or three wives (Adorno and Pautz 1: 110–11; ch. 14). Cabeza de Vaca and his companions supposedly healed people, which is why at the end of their journey from Coahuila to northwestern Mexico they were followed by three or four thousand people (1: 212–13; ch. 29). What we do not know is whether, like the indigenous physicians, they had any wives; if they did,

Cabeza de Vaca makes no mention of it, perhaps because of his interlocutor (the emperor) and also because he was married to María Marmolejo since around 1520 (1: 359–60).

Cabeza de Vaca mentions several sudden births that seem enigmatic given the lack of references to sexual interactions or pregnancy: "It occurred many times that of the women who went with us some gave birth. And after giving birth they brought us the infants so that we could make the sign of the cross over them" ("Acontesçía muchas veces que de las mugeres que con nosotros ivan parían algunas. Y luego en nasçiendo, nos traían la criatura a que la santiguássemos"; 1: 230; 231; ch. 31). There are two important elements to this passage. First, the blessing of the newborn evokes baptismal traditions but even more so the possible presentation of the child to the presumptive father. Second, Cabeza de Vaca refers to the births with the verb *acontecer* in the imperfect tense, *acontesçía*, meaning that they would occur regularly. On the other hand, according to Covarrubias, *acontecer* is synonymous with *acaecer*: "things that happen randomly" ("las cosas que suceden acaso"; 32)—that is, "without thinking, or being warned" ("sin pensar, ni estar preuenido"; 34). Yet a birth does not happen randomly; the growth of the mother's belly, to give just one example, is a sign to anticipate the birth. This is a rather suspicious, if circumstantial, sign of *mestizaje*, a sign that the text glosses over and thereby reveals. While the Christians improvise their roles as *físicos* ("physicians"), they do not attend births; their role is limited to blessing the newborn babies.

Cabeza de Vaca indicates that he was pursued by a multitude of Indians, which prevented him from resting or sleeping (Adorno and Pautz 1: 230–31; ch. 31). He also complains that those who followed them were stealing from the towns and terrorizing their hosts. Even though he supposedly disagrees with this pillage and signals repeatedly in the text that he had authority over the Indians, he did not stop the looting (chs. 28–31; Jáuregui, *Espectros* 118). Let's direct our attention now to the comments on the claim that the Christian men were followed by indigenous women who had initially offered to serve them as guides (ch. 27). This instance of women following the Christians contrasts with the multiple instances in which indigenous women flee from the conquistadores in fear of abduction and rape.[5]

Cabeza de Vaca emphasizes his messianic and hagiographic experiences amid solitude and suffering, and when it comes to sexual matters, he prefers to talk about the practices of the indigenous people. He includes references to the polygamy of indigenous *físicos*, the implied sexual abstinence by women during and after pregnancy, the breastfeeding of prepubescent children, and the ceasing of work during menstruation. In chapter 26 Cabeza de Vaca comments briefly on sexual violence, enumerating the towns that he has visited from Malhado up the coast through the land of the Camoles and the people he calls "the fig ones" ("de los higos"; Adorno and Pautz 1: 187; 186). He refers to a ritual surrounding the preparation and consumption of an intoxicating beverage made from leaves that have been toasted and boiled (188–89). When it is time to drink, women "immediately stop without daring to move.... And if by chance one of them moves, *[the men] dishonor her* and beat her with sticks" ("se paran sin osarse mudar.... Y si acaso alguna dellas se mueve, *la deshonrran* y la dan de palos"; 1: 189; 188). "Dishonor" here is a euphemism for rape (189n3). The *Relación* implies that the Indians, not the conquistadores, are the ones who rape indigenous women.

Mala Cosa: Cross-Dressing, Sexual Transformation, and Hermaphroditism

In addition to Cabeza de Vaca's references to women, we have a brief history and commentaries on two subjects, Mala Cosa (ch. 22) and the *amarionados* (chs. 18 and 26), who seem to transit between genders. I propose addressing this topic in class by focusing on the ethnographies of the change of *hábitos* ("habits": clothes and roles); the description of sexual practices; the differences between transvestism or cross-dressing, transgenderism, sexual transformation, and hermaphroditism; and the challenges of studying representations of subjectivities with elusive, hybrid, or ambiguous identities.

Change of Habits, Change of Hides

Cabeza de Vaca narrates how the Avavares and Mariames told him the strange story of a subject that they call a *mala cosa* ("evil being"; Adorno and Pautz 1: 164–67; ch. 22): "many times when they danced, [Mala Cosa] appeared among them, sometimes in the costume of a woman, and other times dressed as a man" ("muchas vezes quando bailavan aparesçía entre ellos en hábito de muger unas vezes, y otras como hombre"; 167; 166). But what did a change of *hábitos* mean in Cabeza de Vaca's era? Gender, in sixteenth-century Europe, is defined by *hábitos*—that is, by the habitual form of dress and the carrying out of certain roles. Covarrubias explains that *ábito* "vulgarly stands in for the dress, and suit of each person" ("vulgarmente vale el vestido, y trage de cada uno"; 29) and he calls to mind the expression "the habit does not make the monk" ("el ábito no haze al monge"; 29), which suggests that *hábitos* could indeed be an identifying marker but not necessarily a reliable one. Although one could assume that *hábitos* should correspond to genital anatomy, this correspondence is rarely verified.[6]

Before assuming that the story of Mala Cosa presents a case of transvestism or transgenderism, it is important to identify the differences between women's and men's clothing according to the *Relación*. Across indigenous groups, Cabeza de Vaca insists on the nudity of the men—and of himself (chs. 1, 12, 13, 16, 21, 34)—versus the covering up of the women. This insistence could be due to a need to clarify that he did not cover himself up by wearing women's clothing, but on other occasions he mentions using hides and cloaks to keep warm (chs. 21, 22, 30). If the difference between men's and women's ways of dressing consisted of going naked or covering up, then Mala Cosa's and Cabeza de Vaca's so-called change of clothing would mean sometimes going naked and sometimes being clothed. For a European like Cabeza de Vaca, to wear indigenous clothing would not only give a transcultural appearance but would also be an ambiguous look that could signal transgenderism in the eyes of others.

Cabeza de Vaca did indeed use indigenous clothing made from deerskin to keep warm, and he shed his skin "like serpents . . . twice a year" ("a manera de serpientes . . . dos vezes en el año"; Adorno and Pautz 1: 171, 173; 170, 172). Changing hides literally denotes a change of skin (possibly due to sun exposure) but also a change of *hábitos* and a process of becoming other. For Wade, "Cabeza de Vaca literally sheds and regrows skin. . . . The practice of representing the Other gets under his skin. Once hybrid, he cannot return to a centered self" (333).

Sexual Transformation and Hermaphroditism

According to Adorno and Pautz, Mala Cosa corresponds to the Avavar version of the archaic, universal myth of the trickster (1: 167n2). As a trickster, Mala Cosa would be a subject of unstable nature, trans and inbetween: one who changes appearance with a change of clothing and travels between mythical-cosmic levels and between hurting and healing, good and evil (Pupo-Walker, "*Naufragios*" 764–65n30). Sabine Lang compiles information on at least forty-eight groups in which "[w]omen-men . . . were active as healers ('shamans'), medicine men, gravediggers, conveyors of oral traditions and songs, and nurses during war expeditions" (151). Mala Cosa could have been one of these "[w]omen-men," indigenous shamans with healing and magical abilities.

Mala Cosa's change of *hábitos* has inspired voyeuristic curiosity as well as the academic impulse to define the biological, mythical, and historical nature of this character. Adorno and Pautz see in Mala Cosa a case of "sexual transformation" (1: 167n2). In a similar vein, the change between feminine and masculine appearance leads critics to identify Mala Cosa as hermaphrodite (Glantz, "Cuerpo" 425; Maura 59). Bearing in mind that we are talking about a character in an indigenous narration, it is important to note, as Carlos Jáuregui does, that Mala Cosa's change of *hábitos* does not signify a sexual transformation or hermaphroditism, nor does it imply double, hybrid, or ambiguous genitals—it is barely even transvestism (*Espectros* 107–08). Although hermaphrodites are regularly associated with intersexuality, they were also understood in terms of change of *hábitos* and transgenderism. During the Renaissance, the Inquisition considered hermaphrodites to be prone to engaging in heretical practices, lustful acts, and sodomy (Sigal 103; Carpenter 148), a topic discussed below.[7]

We know very little about Mala Cosa's physical appearance: according to Cabeza de Vaca, the Indians "said that . . . he was small in body and that he had a beard, although they were never able to see [his/her/their] face clearly" ("dezían que . . . era pequeño de cuerpo, y que tenía barvas aunque nunca claramente le pudieran ver el rostro"; Adorno and Pautz 1: 167; 166; ch. 22). Cabeza de Vaca's text attaches a masculine gender to Mala Cosa, which authorizes the translation of Mala Cosa's "el rostro" as "his face." Nevertheless, Cabeza de Vaca talks about a bearded man who changes *hábitos*, a performance related to cross-dressing and transgenderism. So, by queering the archive to allow ambiguity and the multiple possibilities the original version denotes, we should be able to refer to Mala Cosa with various pronouns, including feminine, nonbinary, and nonsingular. However much we scrutinize the question of Mala Cosa's sex or genitalia, there is no mention of it in the *Relación*. Additionally, note that the Indians "were never able to see" Mala Cosa's beard (Adorno and Pautz 1: 167), the only trait mentioned that could be related to masculinity. Even more, if we attend to the imperfect subjunctive of the verb "to be able to see" ("aunque nunca claramente *le pudieran* ver el rostro"; Adorno and Pautz 166; my emphasis), this tense determines the impossibility of getting the evidence of Mala Cosa's identity not only in the past but in the future: the Indians talk about Mala Cosa's beard although they would have never been able to see his/her/their face clearly. There is something troubling in this story, for researchers as well as for students, related to the epistemological, political, and ethical problems of representing otherness, the impulse to classify, and anxiety surrounding the unclassifiable. Today it seems easy to speculate about the genital truth of Mala Cosa. I suggest instead that in classes instructors explore forms of "undiagnosing gender," following Judith Butler's proposal: to stop the authoritarian impulse to define gender as a "permanent phenomenon" and instead think of it "as a mode of becoming" (81).

The Sameness of the Other

Refuting associations with either the trickster myth or with hermaphrodites, Jáuregui proposes that Mala Cosa is above all a defamiliarized and spectral version of Cabeza de Vaca himself (*Espectros* 89–122). According to this reading, Mala Cosa would be a sort of alter ego (a bad shaman) of the mystic Christian (a good healer). Jáuregui shows how each point of the Mala Cosa story has its equivalent in Cabeza de Vaca's, a parallel that is both fascinating and unsettling to students. There is no other character that inspired more terror among the Indians than Cabeza de Vaca, as can be corroborated in at least ten chapters (chs. 12, 13, 17, 22, 23, 27, 28, 30, 31, 33); indeed, Cabeza de Vaca himself deserves to be called Mala Cosa or a "very strange thing" ("una cosa muy estraña"; Adorno and Pautz 1: 165; 164; Jáuregui, "Cabeza de Vaca" 434–40).

Adorno and Pautz translate "Mala Cosa" as "evil being" (1: 167; 166). The translation of *cosa* ("thing") as "being" and the capitalization of the words seem to be an attempt to contain this "very strange thing" as a specific identity with its own name: a feminine noun (*cosa*), represented by Cabeza de Vaca, as well as by scholars and translators, as a masculine thing. On the other hand, the surname *Cabeza de Vaca* ("cow's head"), which frequently strikes my students as odd, announces a transition between human and animal and between male and female, a transition associated with the trickster, a figure who, as we have seen above, has been connected to Mala Cosa but not directly to Cabeza de Vaca himself. Cabeza de Vaca and Mala Cosa evoke unstable identities: these characters are, using Butler's words, "that which we do not yet know how to name or that which sets . . . limits on all naming" (74). Both figures imply multiple possibilities: cross-dresser, Christian healer, indigenous shaman, transgender merchant, violent conquistador, and so on (Jáuregui, *Espectros* 89–122). Any singular definition ends up closing off the strangeness that resists identification with just one appearance or gender.

The opacity of Mala Cosa gets lost in Nicolás Echevarría's film *Cabeza de Vaca*, which represents the shaman as an evil being in the form of a dwarf with no arms. In the film, the character Mala Cosa is no longer the ambiguous anomalous subject in between genders but completely other. On the other hand, Theodor de Bry, in his 1590 illustration *The Conjurer*, offers a representation that is closer to the queerness of Cabeza de Vaca and Mala Cosa. According to Thomas Hariot, in the text that accompanies the illustration by De Bry, "the inhabitants" from Virginia "put great faith" in the conjurer's speech, "which often they find to be true" (De Bry and Hariot 57). In class, I invite my students to imagine either Mala Cosa or Cabeza de Vaca like De Bry's conjurer, running carelessly with their goodies in a leather sack tied to their waist.

Amarionados: *Transgenderism and Alternative Sexual Practices*

Cabeza de Vaca calls indigenous men who do the work of women and engage in alternative marital and sexual relations *amarionados* (chs. 18 and 26). Scholars have used disparaging labels, such as "sodomites" (Adorno and Pautz 2: 266; Roscoe 176), "homosexuals" (Lang 67; Roscoe 10), and "bardaches" (Adorno and Pautz 2: 269; Gómez-Galisteo 20; Roscoe 178–79), to refer to these individuals and have portrayed them as castrated or unable to procreate (Adorno and Pautz 2: 267; Lang 67). Here, students can critically explore the colonial associations of transgenderism with, on the one hand, homosexuality, and sexual practices that are considered sinful or diabolic, and, on the other hand, anatomical dysfunctionalities that are the product of castration or sexual impotence. It will also be important to discuss the differences between terms such as *homosexuality*, change of *hábitos*, *transvestism*, *sexual transformation*, and *nonreproductive sexual practices* (including sodomy).

In chapter 26, Cabeza de Vaca talks about the interruption of women's work during their *costumbre*, or menstrual period, and he goes on to describe the men who do the work of the women. We can infer that these men are *amarionados*. Cabeza de Vaca tells how on the coast of Texas he saw a "wicked behavior" ("una diablura"; Adorno and Pautz 1: 189, 191; 188, 190): "one man married to another, and these are effeminate, impotent men. And they go about covered like women, and they perform the tasks of women, and they do not use a bow, and they carry very great loads. And among these we saw many of them, thus unmanly as I say, and they are more muscular than other men and taller; they suffer very large loads" ("un hombre casado con otro, y éstos son unos hombres amarionados impotentes. Y andan tapados como mugeres y hazen offiçio de mugeres, y no tiran arco y llevan muy gran carga. Y entre éstos vimos muchos dellos así amarionados como digo, y son más membrudos que los otros hombres y más altos; sufren muy grandes cargas"; 1: 191; 190). This quotation contains several elements worthy of examination: the *amarionados* are described as effeminate, the whole scene is "wicked," these men marry each other, they take on feminine work, they do not go to war, they dress as women, they are taller and more muscular ("membrudos") than other men, and they are impotent.

Amarionado, translated by Adorno and Pautz as "effeminate" and "unmanly," and by Lang as "homosexual man" (67), is a relatively rare term for the period. In 1578, Alonzo López de Hinojosos described deviations in the gestation of a fetus that would result in an "*amarionado* man, who talks like a woman" ("hombre amarionado, que habla como muger"; fol. 169r). *Amarionado* alludes to a change of mannerisms or habits, as in *amanerado* ("mannered," which can mean "affected" but not necessarily "effeminate," whereas *amanerado* holds both meanings). *Amarionado* likewise corresponds to other terms used in Cabeza de Vaca's time, including slang or slurs such as *maricón* and *marimarica*, which Covarrubias defines as an "effeminate man, who is inclined to things pertaining to women" ("hombre afeminado, que se inclina a hazer cosas de muger"; 790). As a speculative queer etymology, instructors could mention the phonetic and morphological coincidence between *amarionado* and *Mariame*, the name of the ethnic group that Cabeza de Vaca lived with for a time; we might say that Cabeza de Vaca was *mariaming* in two senses: living between cultures when he was with the Mariame and working as the *amarionados* did, alongside women.

Cabeza de Vaca says he witnessed the "diablura" of male same-sex marriage. Covarrubias explains *diablura* as "mischief [*travesura*], and the bad action" ("la travesura, y el mal hecho"; 468); the mischief maker (*travieso*) is "restless and uneasy, [one] who does things that are reprehensible, almost transverse" ("el inquieto y desasosegado, que haze algunas cosas dignas de reprehensión, quasi transversus"; 976). The mischievous, "transverse" actions of the *amarionados* included marrying someone of the same sex, dressing like women, and doing women's work. Cabeza de Vaca is witness to relationships and alliances between men and between transgender subjects and women. The *amarionados* allow the labor force to increase, for not only did they carry heavy loads but they could even take on the work of women who were menstruating. Note that although Cabeza de Vaca refers to the *amarionados* as men ("hombre casado con otro"; "hombres amarionados"; "más membrudos que los otros hombres" [190]), he describes people who change their *hábitos* in the sense of both clothing and behavior. Just because the *amarionados* fulfill the roles of women, we cannot jump to the conclusion that their marriages were homosexual. Lang points out that the description of the feminine aspects of the *amarionados* "suggests that these were official marriages" (67). Although for Cabeza de Vaca they are, at first glance, men married to each other, according to his own descriptions, at least one of them would be an *amarionado*, so we may also be talking about transgender unions.

In addition to pointing out transgressions, *diablura* signals those sexual acts that were considered sinful, such as sodomy, known as the *pecado nefando* ("abominable sin"; Sigal; Tortorici et al.; Horswell). In this sense, *diablura* "suggests a range of meaning from prankish to satanic" (Cabeza de Vaca, *Narrative* 132n1). However, Cabeza de Vaca does not describe the sexual practices of the *amarionados*. Earlier, in chapter 18, he comments that some indigenous men "practice sodomy" ("pecado contra natura"; Adorno and Pautz 1: 141; 140), but he gives no details; we can infer that he refers to the *amarionados*, as he is in the midst of describing the work of women. Unlike Cabeza de Vaca, Gonzalo Fernández de Oviedo offers a detailed description of this practice among the inhabitants of Florida. He writes about a man "riding the other in the image of that abominable and unspeakable sin of Sodomy" ("cabalgando sobre el otro, en figura de aquel abominable y nefando pecado de sodomía"; qtd. in Torres Cendales 65). Oviedo's description corresponds to what Zeb Tortorici, Pete Sigal, and Neil Whitehead call "ethnopornography" (9). Oviedo further suggests that a change of *hábitos* is irremediably associated with anal sex. Those young men (*camayoas*) who engage in "that heinous crime" ("este maldito pecado"; *Sumario* 244) are dressed in *naguas* (skirts), or in women's clothing, and do women's chores. There is a colonial confusion between the sexual practice of anal penetration, a nonheteronormative sexual inclination, and a change of *hábitos*, transvestism, and transgenderism.

As in the representations of hermaphrodites, the *amarionados* described in the *Relación* are tall and muscular, with large extremities. Although one might think that their bodies would give them strength in war, Cabeza de Vaca clarifies that the *amarionados* do not use a bow, which could mean that they are not warriors. As in the myth of the Amazons, represented as warrior women who fulfilled both feminine and masculine roles, the *amarionados* are depicted as men who fulfilled women's roles. However, in contrast to the reproductive capacity of the Amazons, the *amarionados* are impotent. Just as we can find numerous colonial references that equate sodomy with sinful and demonic acts, it was also common to associate transvestism and transgenderism with dysfunctional bodies.[8] We have already seen how the doctor López de Hinojosos diagnoses an *amarionado* as the product of a fetal malformation that results in a man "who speaks like a woman" (169r). In 1615, Juan de Torquemada referred to the indigenous peoples of Florida who cross-dressed, practiced same-sex marriage between men, and engaged in proscribed sexual acts as "mariones impotentes" (427), which is practically quoted from Cabeza de Vaca. Adorno and Pautz, in a section called "Cabeza de Vaca's Account of Sodomy," explain that the impotent *amarionados* have been called eunuchs without any references to castration (2: 266–72). According to Lang, the impotence of the *amarionados* designates their "inability to procreate, without implying castration. Cabeza de Vaca obviously deduced—without closer examination—the infertility of the *amarionados* from their effeminacy, just as, for example, many of his contemporaries referred to women-men as hermaphrodites, although there are no indications that intersexuality was actually present" (67). Despite their apparently nonreproductive bodies, the *amarionados* did engage in several productive activities (i.e., chores) in alliance with women.

In the sixteenth century, transvestism, transgenderism, and nonreproductive sexual practices were generally rejected, and anal sex was emphatically condemned (Sigal 103). Núñez de Balboa, in what is known as "the first record of Spanish punishment of homosexuality on the American continent," in 1516 "recalled the presence of 'men dressed as women and practicing sodomy,' and he 'quickly threw some forty of these transvestites to the dogs . . .'" (Slater 49). As Adorno and Pautz suggest, it is difficult to believe that Cabeza de Vaca presents a "sympathetic view" of the sexual and marital practices of the Indians when he refers to the *amarionados* (2: 272). However, his view was more sympathetic than that of Oviedo and Bartolomé de Las Casas, who harshly and explicitly rejected these practices (Adorno and Pautz 2: 270–72).

Adorno and Pautz point out two lines of interpretation of Cabeza de Vaca's descriptions of the *amarionados*: "the application of the anthropological category of the berdache . . . to these same-sex unions" and "the application of the modern social category of homosexual" (2: 269). According to Gómez-Galisteo, the *amarionados* are not "feminized men"; they are "berdaches," a somehow derisive term replaced by "two spirits," "a third gender moving between the boundaries of man and spirits and also the boundaries of gender" (20; see also Roscoe 4, 12, 178–79). When identifying the *amarionados* as "two spirits" of the sixteenth century (first line of interpretation), instructors can bring in the work of the Native American artist and activist Demian DinéYazhi' and the collective RISE: Radical Indigenous Survivance and Empowerment. In one of its illustrations, RISE presents the famous 1877 photograph of Osh-Tisch and their wife. The photo is a close-up that is slightly out of focus; the background is a replicated negative image of a 1973 photograph by Marsha Johnson and Sylvia Rivera, founders of Street Transvestite Action Revolutionaries. The illustration is framed with the trans and decolonial maxim "Decolonize Your Luvvv," recognizing "Indigenous Queer & Trans cultures that were respected and honored prior to European-led Genocide, Heteropatriarchy, Religion, & Colonization" ("Bury My Art").

The second reading of the *amarionados*, according to Adorno and Pautz, characterizes them as being married in modern homosexual relationships. In fact, the *Relación* has been hailed by the LGBTQ+ community as one of the first documented instances of homosexual marriage (Pérez). However, this reading ignores the transgendered elements of the *amarionados*, who would cover their genitals like women do and perform women's work. It is important to keep in mind that gay marriage does not imply transgenderism or transvestism, just as a person who engages in anal sex does not necessarily identify as homosexual. The fact that there are very few references to the *amarionados* or the two spirits in Cabeza de Vaca's time does not mean that they were exceptional cases. As Will Roscoe provocatively suggests, America prior to colonization might have been "the queerest continent on the planet" (4). The *Relación* might be one of the first records of alternative sexual unions or of same-sex or transgender indigenous marriages. For class, I propose recognizing the role of Cabeza de Vaca among the women and his becoming an *amarionado*. Just as we can identify Mala Cosa with Cabeza de Vaca, following Jáuregui's *Espectros*, it is also possible to identify the *amarionados* with Cabeza de Vaca, recognizing that both performed women's roles and changed their *hábitos*.

Queering the Relación

Queering the archive implies disorganizing the text to allow for other readings. As Marshall, Murphy, and Tortorici state, "queer things cannot have straight histories" (1). I end this essay by commenting on the last chapter of the *Relación*, which takes us back to the beginning of the story. Cabeza de Vaca recounts the story of one of ten married women who did not disembark in Florida, a Castilian woman who warned Narváez about a prediction made by a Moorish woman before the expedition set sail for America (ch. 38; see appendix, 9.3): "a Moorish woman from Hornachos had told it to her (which account she had told us before we departed from Castile), and the entire voyage had occurred to us in the same manner" ("una mora de Hornachos se lo avía dicho [lo qual, antes que partiéssemos de Castilla, nos lo avían a nosotros dicho] y nos avía succedido todo el viage de la misma manera"; Adorno and Pautz 1: 275; 274). We learn only at the end of the *Relación* that Cabeza de Vaca's story had been foretold by one of the women who traveled with him.

The prophecy announced the failure of Narváez's expedition and warned of the minimal possibilities for survival: "if one of them were to come out, God would perform great miracles through him, but . . . she believed that those who escaped would be few or none at all" ("si alguno saliesse, que haría Dios por él muy grandes milagros, pero que creía que fuessen pocos los que escapassen o no ningunos"; 1: 273; 272). The prediction serves as a discursive device to make sense of the failure of the expedition: despite the warning, the Spaniards could not escape their unfortunate destiny. Cabeza de Vaca ends his *Relación* with this enigma, but instead of offering closure it sends us back to the beginning, creating the possibility of new readings. How do we explain, if not thanks to this fortunetelling, that as of chapter 4 Cabeza de Vaca "was certain and knew that he [Narváez] would not see the ships again nor the ships him" ("tenía por cierto y sabía que él [Narváez] no avía de ver más los navíos ni los navíos a él"; 1: 45; 44)?

Although the telos of Cabeza de Vaca's text is to return him to the land of the Christians, there are several moments in which the text betrays this purpose. The Moorish woman's prediction is one example. At the end of the *Relación*, as Cabeza de Vaca narrates his return to Spain in 1537, he includes the prediction, which was made at some point before June 1527. According to Pastor, the *Relación* has a circular structure that "starts when civilization is left behind" and concludes with "a return to civilization" (*Armature* 149–50). Echevarría's film represents this circularity in the scene in which Cabeza de Vaca tries to escape and runs until he is exhausted, only to realize that he has returned to the same place he had left. There he finds the circle that Mala Cosa's assistant has drawn in the sand around a tied lizard that, like Cabeza de Vaca, runs in circles (00:29:50–32:15). In the film, circularity is determined by witchcraft, while in the *Relación* we have the prediction of the Moorish woman, which we learn about only at the end of the text but which Narváez and Cabeza de Vaca had known about since the beginning of the expedition. The Moorish woman is a border figure who embodies a certain inbetweenness, like Cabeza de Vaca, and her prophecy—which came true—exceeds notions of historical truth, fiction, and superstition. The *Relación* has more of a spiral structure, triggered by a prophecy from which—using Pastor's words—"the action unfolds and multiplies" (*Armature* 150). Thus, through a queer reading of the *Relación*, we find that the narrator of such a masculine account turns out to be a mixture of feminine, trans, and eccentric voices.

The indigenous women, the transgender conquistadores, the *amarionados*, the fortune-telling Moorish woman, Mala Cosa, and all the other strange and queer characters in the *Relación* resist erasure and reappear in the text and scholarship as specters, as tenuous images that invoke the absent (Jáuregui, *Espectros* 37). We confront not only a hypermasculine text, strictly speaking, but also readings that insist on the hypermasculine cover-up of the numerous instances of transgender and queer betweenness in the *Relación*—nothing that a good class can't begin to unteach.

NOTES

This essay was translated by Juliet Lynd.

1. This research was supported by the Humanities Scholarship Enhancement Award from the College of Liberal Arts and Sciences, the UF Center for Latin American Studies, and the Department of Spanish and Portuguese Studies at the University of Florida.

2. In Posse's *El largo atardecer del caminante*, this episode is re-created with reference to "big-titted women" ("mujeres tetudas") and to a "[c]ow woman" ("[m]ujer-vaca"; 102).

3. For more on food, labor, and reproduction among the Indians, see Jáuregui and Solodkow; Uparela, "Multiplicarse."

4. Translations of quotations are by the author where not otherwise attributed.

5. Students can study related passages from Michele de Cuneo, Columbus, Las Casas, and Guaman Poma regarding sexual violence and terror (see Uparela, *Invaginaciones* 59–68, 76–80, 115–23, 180–82 and "Guaman Poma" 22–27).

6. Students can explore the cases of Catalina de Erauso, whose virginity was visually verified (Uparela, "'Yo llana estoy'"), and Eleno de Céspedes, who defied the social order by performing surgical interventions to his own genitals (Uparela, *Invaginaciones* 227–71).

7. For a comprehensive historical definition of the legal and theological term *sodomy*, which originated in the eleventh century and referred primarily to anal sex, believed to be the sin of Sodom and Gomorrah, see Jordan, who explores how sodomy was constructed as a category of moral and legal transgression during the Middle Ages, evolving through theological and ecclesiastical discourse. See Dinshaw for an analysis of how sodomy was used to enforce heteronormative sexual boundaries in later medieval legal codes.

8. The reference to impotent *amarionados* can be contrasted with descriptions of Indians' genitals; see Uparela, *Invaginaciones* 41, 190–91.

APPENDIX: REFERENCES TO WOMEN AND TRANS AND QUEER SUBJECTS IN THE *RELACIÓN*

All tables cite *Álvar Núñez Cabeza de Vaca: His Account, His Life, and the Expedition of Pánfilo de Narváez*, by Rolena Adorno and Patrick Charles Pautz.

Table 1. Women's Work

Reference	Chapter	Details
1.1	14	The women of Malhado carry out heavy labor, such as pulling up underwater roots to eat (1: 108–09).
1.2	18	The Mariames women work for eighteen hours and rest for six. They bring firewood and water to their homes, pull up roots, and dry them in ovens (140–41).
1.3	28	On the route to Pánuco, in northern Tamaulipas, women carry water (202–03).
1.4	29	The women who accompany Cabeza de Vaca across the Bahía River or its tributaries in northern Coahuila provide the Christians with sleeping mats and food, including prickly pears, spiders, and worms (210–13).
1.5	26	Among indigenous groups from Malhado to the Rio Grande region, some indigenous men do the work of women. Cabeza de Vaca calls them *amarionados* (190–91).

Table 2. Communication, Translation, and Conflict Mediation

Reference	Chapter	Details
2.1	14	In Malhado (among the Capoques and Han), women are free to communicate and converse with their parents-in-law and relatives (110–11).
2.2	24	Quevenes women intervene to resolve conflicts, although sometimes they are the ones who pick fights (182–83).
2.3	27	Along the Rio Grande, women serve as guides along the trails (192–93).
2.4	30	Women in southwestern Texas, like those of the Gulf Coast, serve as mediators in times of war. The Christians send two women, one of them a captive, to the next town to negotiate a treaty (216–17).

Table 3. Clothing

Reference	Chapter	Details
3.1	6	Women from Florida to Apalache use small woven cloaks to cover their bodies (54–55).
3.2	15	Women of Malhado use clothes made of plant fibers. The young women cover themselves with deerskins (116–17).
3.3	30	Women and a few older men wear deerskins in the Rio Grande region (224–25).
3.4	31	Women in northwestern Mexico are dressed in cotton shirts and full-length leather skirts (230–31).
3.5	32	In the zone of the town of Los Corazones, in northwestern Mexico, women cover their genitals with grasses and straw (234–35).
3.6	22	The Avavares tell Cabeza de Vaca the story of Mala Cosa, a character who appears in men's and women's clothing (164–67).
3.7	26	The *amarionados* cover their bodies the same way women do (188–91); see also "Women's work" and "Marriage and sexual relations."

Table 4. Festivals

Reference	Chapter	Details
4.1	26	Members of all the groups from Malhado to the Rio Grande get inebriated on a drink prepared with toasted leaves boiled in water. As soon as the drink is ready, women suspend all their activities (188–89).

Table 5. Marriage and Sexual Relations

Reference	Chapter	Details
5.1	14	Among the indigenous peoples of Malhado, physicians can have two or three wives, who maintain a harmonious relationship (110–11).
5.2	18	The Yaguazes, Mariames, and other neighboring groups do not marry their daughters to men from enemy tribes, so as to avoid increasing the population of the opposing group. They forbid endogamy and would rather kill a female relation than unite her with a relative or an enemy. As a result, they buy women from their rivals (136–39).
5.3	24	From Malhado to near the Rio Grande, a young man who is married and has not had children may remarry if he has disagreements with his wife (178–79).
5.4	18	Some of the Mariame men have same-sex relations (140–41).
5.5	26	The *amarionados* are, according to Cabeza de Vaca, men who marry other men (190–91); see also "Clothing."
5.6	38	Ten Castilian women stayed behind on the expedition boats off the coast of Florida; all of them were married, and once they saw that their husbands were not going to return to the boats, they married other survivors (272–75).

100   GENDER, TRANSGENDER, AND QUEER INBETWEENNESS

Table 6. Menstruation, Pregnancy, and Childbirth

REFERENCE	CHAPTER	DETAILS
6.1	24	From Malhado to near the Rio Grande, women do not sleep with their husbands for two years after they get pregnant (176–77).
6.2	26	Among the groups from Malhado to the land of the Cuchendados, menstruating women forage food only for themselves; the community does not eat anything gathered by a menstruating woman (188–89).
6.3	31	Some of the women who traveled with Cabeza de Vaca (from Coahuila to northwestern Mexico) gave birth; the Christians blessed the newborn babies (230–33). This may be a veiled reference to mixed-race children fathered by the conquistadores.

Table 7. Motherhood and Breastfeeding

REFERENCE	CHAPTER	DETAILS
7.1	14	Of the tribes observed by Cabeza de Vaca, the inhabitants of Malhado appear to treat their children the best. If a child dies, they mourn the death for a year (108–09).
7.2	18	According to Cabeza de Vaca, the Yguazes and Mariames do not love their children as much as other groups (140–41); see also "Superstitions."
7.3	24	From Malhado to near the Rio Grande, the women breastfeed their children until the age of twelve (176–77).

Table 8. Violence against Women

REFERENCE	CHAPTER	DETAILS
8.1	26	If any woman breaks the rules of the festival (see 4.1), she is beaten with sticks and raped (188–89).
8.2	30	While the Christians are in southwestern Texas, an indigenous woman is cruelly lacerated and murdered by other members of her community (218–19).

Table 9. Superstitions

REFERENCE	CHAPTER	DETAILS
9.1	18	Based on messages an indigenous woman claims to have received in her dreams, the Mariames order the death of Esquivel. According to Cabeza de Vaca, these women would even kill their children if these dream messages told them to do it (136–37).
9.2	26	Women must follow the rules of the ceremony in which the intoxicating beverage is prepared (see 4.1): they must halt their activities and not look at the pot in which the drink is concocted. If they disobey, everyone else pours out their drink because they believe it has been spoiled and may now be lethal (188–89).
9.3	38	A Castilian woman who traveled in the expedition warns Pánfilo de Narváez about the bad fortune foreseen by a Moorish woman from Hornachos before they set sail (272–75).

OTHER ACCOUNTS

The Southern Fiasco:
Law and Writing in *Comentarios*

Loreley El Jaber

In 1555, Álvar Núñez Cabeza de Vaca published *La relación y comentarios del governador Álvar Núñez Cabeça de Vaca, de lo acaescido en las dos jornadas que hizo a las Indias* (*Account and Commentaries of the Governor Álvar Núñez Cabeça de Vaca, regarding the Events of His Two Journeys to the Indies*). *Comentarios* presents Cabeza de Vaca as a dutiful governor and recounts his journey from the Spanish settlements on the coast of Brazil to Asunción in Paraguay and into parts of modern-day Argentina. He navigated the Paraná and Paraguay Rivers, facing resistance from indigenous tribes, difficult terrain, and internal settler conflicts.[1] However, his Río de la Plata experience had been a total fiasco. Accused of betraying the king, he was sent back to Spain in shackles with papers incriminating him. Written ten years after his return to Spain, *Comentarios* has a procedural and legal framework, given that it is a narrative response to the charges that weighed on Cabeza de Vaca for the eight years following his return.

Teaching *Comentarios* is no easy task. This is no grand story of adventure among "exotic" Indians or of travelers braving rough seas or battling strange beasts. Why, then, should *Comentarios* be taught? Precisely because of the questions that these differences elicit. If it does not relate a typical adventure story, then what does it tell? Is there, perhaps, another story of the Indies? As the last words of a man who feels unjustly dragged through the mud, a man who has lost everything, *Comentarios* confirms that there is still much to be said.

Comentarios could be taught in an undergraduate colonial Latin American survey and compared with *Naufragios* (*Shipwrecks*) and other early colonial accounts by Spanish conquistadores. The possibilities for a graduate course are many: for example, a cross-disciplinary approach with legal and colonial studies. However, the fact that *Comentarios* takes place in the Río de la Plata region, a peripheral territory in the Spanish conquest, tells another story altogether.

Teaching *Comentarios* means not only teaching texts on and about the edges of the Spanish Empire but also reconsidering the idea of "colonial failure" (Pastor, *Armature* 116–28) and placing it at the center of the discussion.

Yet again, what does *Comentarios* tell, given that as it lacks the motifs one would expect from a narrative of conquest? Cabeza de Vaca takes this question by the horns: when the lands one visits lack precious metals; when one's titles, ranks, and wealth are lost; and when one has shackles on one's feet, even then—or perhaps precisely then—one writes. This is the exciting adventure to address in class discussions: *Comentarios* is a grand story of failure and writing.[2]

Cabeza de Vaca and Río de la Plata

Comentarios was written not during the journey to Río de la Plata or upon the completion of the voyage but ten years after Cabeza de Vaca's return to Europe and a strenuous eight-year court battle. And that delay matters. After his experience in La Florida, Cabeza de Vaca returned to Spain, where he probably heard about the crisis that had unfolded in Río de la Plata after the death at sea of the adelantado Pedro de Mendoza. In 1537, Cabeza de Vaca requested that the Crown grant him the post of adelantado for La Florida, supported by a *probanza* ("account of merits and services") of his family's services to the king, dated 31 October 1537, in Jerez de la Frontera (Adorno and Pautz 1: 379). The emperor, however, had given the post to Hernando de Soto on 20 April, when Cabeza de Vaca was leaving Mexico (1: 381). In other words, his application for the job in La Florida arrived far too late. In this context, a leadership role in Río de la Plata seemed like a promising alternative, since there appeared to be plenty of opportunities to amass wealth (between 1530 and 1540, Spaniards viewed the discovery of these lands as a highly profitable enterprise).

The Spanish administration of the area was riddled with problems. When Governor Mendoza died, Juan de Ayolas was supposed to succeed him. After taking the post, however, Ayolas set out to find the mythical Sierra de la Plata,[3] leaving Domingo Martínez de Irala in charge. Ayolas's return took longer than expected. Irala waited in the port of Buenos Aires, but as the wait grew, hunger and constant attacks from local Indians forced him to abandon the port and head to Asunción. When Ayolas finally returned to Buenos Aires, he found the port deserted. Sensing their weakness, the natives attacked and killed Ayolas and his men.

After the deaths of Mendoza and Ayolas, it became imperative for someone to rescue the starving Spaniards, who were at the mercy of hostile Indians and on the verge of anarchy. A new adelantado had to be appointed, and Cabeza de Vaca seemed perfectly suited for the task. Thus, with the royal documents attesting to his assignment, Cabeza de Vaca made his journey to Asunción. He did not, however, receive a warm welcome: the royal officials and Domingo Martínez de Irala, who had continued to govern since Ayolas's departure in search of the Sierra de la Plata, were displeased at the sight of the newly appointed adelantado. The rivalry between Irala and Cabeza de Vaca is also crucial to the history of Río de la Plata during the mid–sixteenth century. They were certainly not struggling for control of gold or silver production. Unlike Mexico or Peru, there was no silver to be found in that area except in the name of the river Río de la Plata. Facing this absence of precious metals, the settlers devised a series of compensatory practices to profit from and exploit what little resources there were to be had (El Jaber, *País*). The encomienda (royal grant to exploit indigenous labor), the twenty-percent tax known as the royal fifth, the alliances and *cuñadazgo* ("family ties") with certain tribes, and the use and governance of the territory all reveal how these new colonial practices emerged to offset the lack of metals and were implemented by Irala and his followers.

However, Cabeza de Vaca saw these practices as flagrant abuses of the political, ideological, religious, and moral principles that defined the empire he represented as adelantado. This view distanced him from the other Spanish officials and the troops, who saw him as a threat to their interests, even though they had little to aspire to in such a dystopian territory. Cabeza de Vaca was eventually arrested, declared a traitor to the king, and sent back as a prisoner to Spain with documents outlining the charges and signed by all the Spanish residents of Asunción. Clearly, he was far from a popular leader. Upon his return to Spain, the outlook for Cabeza de Vaca was somber indeed.

During his governorship, a series of charges had been brought against him. On 20 February 1546, the prosecutor for the Council of the Indies at the royal court of Valladolid, Juan de Villalobos, filed thirty-four charges against Cabeza de Vaca, transcribed by José Rodríguez Carrión, mostly dealing with alleged abuses and the destruction of indigenous populations (Adorno and Pautz 1: 395–98). In addition, the adelantado Cabeza de Vaca was accused of putting his own interests over those of his fellow citizens by forbidding any type of trade involving Indians, confiscating property from the living and the dead without compensation, interfering in private contracts, hanging his own coat of arms instead of the king's, proclaiming himself king, interpreting royal tax regulations to his benefit, and prohibiting royal officials from communicating with the emperor (1: 396). Cabeza de Vaca filed his own depositions, charges against his enemies, and, later, appeals. The amount of legal documentation related to Cabeza de Vaca is thus immense.

Despite the evidence presented in his defense, on 18 March 1551, he was found guilty by the Council of the Indies, stripped of all titles, and sentenced to five years of military service in Oran (1: 398). He was also ordered to pay damages to anyone who had suffered losses during his governorship. Signed in Valladolid, the sentence included an additional clause stipulating "perpetual banishment from the Indies under pain of death" (1: 398). Although Cabeza de Vaca appealed, the sentence against him stood until 23 August 1552, when the council limited the ban from the Indies to Río de la Plata but upheld the rest of the sentence. In 1552, he continued fighting in court in order to recover his assets, almost all of which he had lost in Río de la Plata. Although Cabeza de Vaca's *Naufragios*, about his travel in La Florida, is commonly read as the story of a disaster, it is important to take a better look at Río de la Plata, where there was another ongoing disaster entangled with a series of political and legal disputes over power.

Law and Letters: Comentarios, a Counternarrative

Comentarios was published in 1555, three years after the end of Cabeza de Vaca's court battle over his rocky tenure at Río de la Plata. Between his return and the publication of *Comentarios* there is a large paper trail, including other *relaciones* ("accounts") that should be considered when teaching the textual corpus of this colonial venture. In fact, two *relaciones* presented by Cabeza de Vaca and his notary Pero Hernández upon their arrival in Spain in 1545 reveal that *Comentarios* is a rewriting of exculpatory narratives hastily drafted upon Cabeza de Vaca's return to Spain (see appendix).

Why did Cabeza de Vaca revisit these events a decade later, in 1555, after the most incriminatory charges had been already dropped? The reputation of the former adelantado had by then been restored, after a long legal battle of depositions, appeals, and testimonies, but his family name had not recovered its former glory. That is the aim of *Comentarios*: to regain what the court had failed to restore. It is also plausible that Cabeza de Vaca was reacting to the 1555 royal decree granting his former governorship to his archenemy, Irala.

Comentarios is the counternarrative to the writings and success of his enemies, a text that organizes the events that transpired in Río de la Plata but does so without the effervescence of Cabeza de Vaca's written testimony drafted a decade earlier in the heat of the moment. Cabeza de Vaca summoned his notary and recorded his version of the events that led to the legal battle lasting from 1545 to 1552, thus departing from the first-person narrative of his 1545 written testimony, *Relación general*.

Comentarios may be puzzling as a stand-alone text. I suggest examining it with *Naufragios* and the paper trail of Cabeza de Vaca's Southern Cone fiasco or at least sections thereof (see appendix). The first edition of *Comentarios* includes *Naufragios*. *Naufragios*, Cabeza de Vaca's narrative about his North American journey to La Florida, functions as a wider framework to his counternarrative about Río de la Plata in *Comentarios*. The survivor of the expedition to La Florida, the quasi-messiah from *Naufragios*, cannot be the same man who was branded a traitor and enemy. *Comentarios* (by way of Hernández) seeks to set the record straight, with the help of *Naufragios*. This is the exculpatory effect of publishing both texts in a single edition. And the voices of those who send Cabeza de Vaca off in shackles, tarnishing his name and leaving him destitute, come across as vindictive and nefarious. In this regard, *Comentarios* rests on a discursive framework that seeks to unveil an injustice not entirely recognized within the legal system, despite Cabeza de Vaca's good relations with the court, evidenced by the royal permit to publish the work and, especially, the dedication to the Infante Don Carlos that opens the text.

Cabeza de Vaca's Untarnished Honor

Comentarios presents Cabeza de Vaca as an honorable conquistador who comes to the rescue of the Southern Cone settlers and Indians.

Cabeza de Vaca to the Rescue

From the beginning of *Comentarios*, Cabeza de Vaca can be seen following the instructions laid out in the *capitulación*, or royal commission, for the governorship to aid the Spaniards stranded in Río de la Plata (Vas Mingo 362–66). The book clearly emphasizes that it is the king who commissions Cabeza de Vaca not only as adelantado but also as rescuer. The altruistic and humanitarian component to this mission is placed far above any expected personal gains, despite Cabeza de Vaca's significant investment in this colonial enterprise (the ducats and assets Cabeza de Vaca personally committed are listed in the *capitulación*; see appendix). The argument is that, although the journey was a failure for both the Crown and the governor, he did provide relief to the troubled settlers. Indeed, Cabeza de Vaca is portrayed right from the start as the individual who comes to the rescue of the Spaniards in Asunción. For example, chapter 3 describes Cabeza de Vaca's encounter with two Franciscan friars terrified that the local Indians might murder them. Before the meeting, "the governor, being well-informed of the case, sought to calm and pacify the Indians, and rescued the friars, and made peace with the Indians, and entrusted the friars to teach the Christian doctrine to the Indians of the land and that island" ("informado el gobernador del caso, procuró sosegar y pacificar los indios, y recogió los frailes, y puso paz entre ellos, y les encargó a los frailes que tuviesen cargo de doctrinar los indios de aquella tierra y isla"; *Comentarios* 103; ch. 3).[4] In the following chapter, similarly, new Christians fleeing the port of Buenos Aires to escape abuse by the Spaniards in Asunción seek out Cabeza de Vaca's help. The adelantado provides them with clothing and invites them to join his party. Moments like these lead up to Cabeza de Vaca's entry into Asunción, an arrival that all residents, in the notary's telling, saw as a great feat:

> [The captains and people of Asunción] came out with incredible joy and happiness, saying they had lost any hope that aid would arrive, because the road was so dangerous and difficult, and because no one had seen or heard of him [Cabeza de Vaca]. In addition, the port of Buenos Aires— their only hope of rescue—had been abandoned, and for that reason, the local Indians had dared to attack the Spaniards and kill them, emboldened by the fact that so much time had passed without any Spaniard coming to the province. The governor [Cabeza de Vaca] was overjoyed to see them [the Spaniards in Asunción] and he greeted them with great affection, explaining that he had come to their aid by order of His Majesty.

[Los capitanes y gentes de Asunción] salieron con tanto placer y alegría, que era cosa increíble, diciendo que jamás creyeron ni pensaron que pudieran ser socorridos, ansí por respecto de ser peligroso y tan dificultoso el camino, y no se haber hallado ni descubierto, ni tener ninguna noticia de él, como porque el puerto de Buenos Aires, por do tenían alguna esperanza de ser socorridos, lo habían despoblado, y que por esto los indios naturales habían tomado grande osadía y atrevimiento de los acometer para los matar, mayormente habiendo visto que había pasado tanto tiempo sin que acudiese ninguna gente española en la provincia. Y por consiguiente el gobernador se holgó con ellos, y les habló y recibió con mucho amor, haciéndoles saber cómo iba a les dar socorro por mandado de Su Majestad. (*Comentarios* 121; ch. 13)

A connection can be established between the rescue operations that Cabeza de Vaca heads in *Comentarios* and the chapters in which he leads Andrés Dorantes, Alonso del Castillo Maldonado, and Esteban out of captivity in *Naufragios* (chs. 17, 19, 20). The theme is a struggle for survival in which Cabeza de Vaca plays a leading role. Another well-known moment in *Naufragios* establishes a closer dialogue with *Comentarios*: after Pánfilo de Narváez abandons his responsibilities as commander and tells his subordinates that it's every man for himself, Cabeza de Vaca decides to take control, not only getting the raft safely to land but also saving the entire crew (ch. 10).

As Sylvia Molloy indicates, *Naufragios* goes a long way to argue that Cabeza de Vaca filled a power vacuum; in *Comentarios*, the adelantado's paperwork and actions have already placed him in a position of leadership. Likewise, as the previous quotations reveal, Cabeza de Vaca presents love as a pacification method in Río de la Plata, a way to iron out tensions between friars and Indians, advising them to remember and teach the Christian doctrine. Another important parallel is that after having gone naked in *Naufragios*, he is the one who clothes the mistreated Spaniards in *Comentarios*. Implicitly, Cabeza de Vaca acts as a messiah.

Cabeza de Vaca's assistance brings a singular type of heroism to the fore: he discovers that the port of Buenos Aires has been abandoned—that the Spaniards never responded to the letters asking for help from Asunción and the concrete danger of forging a path to Asunción—yet still he achieves his objective. The epic story of the deeds of the heroic, unjustly accused adelantado has clearly begun.

Restorer of the Law

Cabeza de Vaca's humanitarianism was not limited to his equals but also extended to the Indians mistreated by monks, royal officials, and common soldiers. In the *Relación general*, from 1545, he states:

These Spaniard Christians that I found in the province [of Asunción], particularly certain captains and officials of your Majesty and their friends, subjected the local Indians and their women and children to great indignities and cruelties, taking them by force with . . . their possessions, "caring" for them with lashes, and overworking them and forcing their parents and relatives to work for them by violent means and beatings, and never paying them for their work. In addition, they kill one another over the Indian women.

Estos cristianos españoles que hallé en esta provincia, y especialmente algunos capitanes y oficiales de Su Magestad é sus amigos, hazian grandes agravios é crueldades en los naturales y en sus mujeres é hijos tomandoselas por fuerça con . . . sus bienes, dándoles de açotes por celos y trabajos demasiados, y á sus padres y parientes haziéndolos venir á trabajar por fuerça y á palos, no les pagando sus trabajos, y demás desto se mataban unos á otros sobre los celos de las dichas indias. (28–29)

Upon his arrival in Asunción, Cabeza de Vaca is surprised by the lack of any legal, religious, or moral compass. As noted by José Rabasa, while Cabeza de Vaca is merely following the ordinances of 1526 in *Naufragios* (70), *Comentarios* reveals his knowledge of the new laws of 1542 regulating the treatment and exploitation of indigenous labor. Thus, not only does Cabeza de Vaca act in accordance with the Crown—as the text adamantly reiterates—he also defends his own order that the Indians be treated well: "Due to the great commotions and crimes against God and His Majesty, and for the sake of good governance and to bring peace on the land, I signed ordinances that favored the local Indians" ("por los desórdenes y desacatos tan grandes que se cometían en deservicio de Dios y de S.M. y por el buen gobierno y pacificación de la tierra, hice ordenanzas a favor de los naturales"; *Relación general* 29–30).

To impose order in Asunción, Cabeza de Vaca enacted a series of ordinances forbidding Spaniards from taking Indian women as concubines, charging debts owed to the king, forcing any Indians off their land (an ordinance that significantly reduced the available workforce), and selling, hiring, or trading free Indian men and women as slaves (*Comentarios*; chs. 15, 17, 18, 32; Gandía, *Indios* 32–34). These regulations underscore the imperialist morality that the adelantado faithfully represents. The portrayal of a man in Río de la Plata who was loyal to the law and to the religious and moral precepts of Christianity is fundamental to *Comentarios* because it provides further evidence against the accusations that he had mistreated Indians.

Cabeza de Vaca knows that respecting laws—or at least claiming to have done so—is of utmost importance. Thus, if there is violence, it must be "legal"; if there is war, it must be "just" (Rabasa 67). When the Spaniards advance on certain hostile tribes to demand obedience to the king, the adelantado reminds officers to "be especially careful to warn them once, twice, and three times, with great temperance" ("tuviesen especial cuidado de les hacer los apercibimientos una, dos y tres veces con toda templanza"; *Comentarios* 131; ch. 20), as established in the Requerimiento (War Ultimatum), an infamous legal text Cabeza de Vaca quotes time and again (see chs. 15, 20, 31). Cabeza de Vaca speaks, issues orders, and acts in accordance with the law; he also writes and puts together his story in keeping with the law. Given this state of affairs, the fact that he has been unjustly accused should be self-evident by now.

Irala versus Cabeza de Vaca

Working on *Comentarios* gives students the opportunity to examine a narrative that does more than recount events or describe indigenous customs: it lays out arguments, which makes it rhetorical. This feature of the text explains why *Comentarios* does not delve into the representation of the other. Ethnographic and anthropological data in *Comentarios* is scarce compared to other accounts of Río de la Plata. Indigenous customs are only described in relation to either their evangelization or the survival of the Spaniards. The military customs of the Agace (from the mouth of the Paraguay River; ch. 17) are directly related to Cabeza de Vaca's narrative of the party he sent to kill one of their rebellious chiefs. Likewise, nomadism is mentioned only as an obstacle to evangelization (ch. 22), cannibalism is described to justify conversion and conquest (ch. 26), and indigenous foodways are means to keep his men alive (ch. 8). Finally, the description in *Comentarios* of the indigenous custom of offering women as a token of peace and alliance building is used to highlight Cabeza de Vaca's tempered and chaste treatment of these women (chs. 43 and 73).

Comentarios sets out to convey once more, with the notary's help, what Cabeza de Vaca had argued for years before the Council of the Indies: neither the Indians nor the accused, Cabeza de Vaca, were responsible for Río de la Plata's descent into chaos, nor were they responsible for the region's straying away from church and Crown. Irala and his people are the real villains in this story:

> They [Irala and his men] cruelly tortured many other people to try to discover if there was a conspiracy to try to free the governor [Cabeza de Vaca] from prison . . . ; and many were torture and crippled by the injuries suffered in their legs and arms; and because [the phrase] *You will die for your king and for your law* had been written on the walls around the village, Domingo de Irala and his officers gathered testimonies to find out who had written it, swearing and threatening . . . that they would be punished.
>
> Dieron tormentos muy crueles a otras muchas personas para saber y descubrir si se daba orden y trataban entre ellos de sacar de la prisión al gobernador . . . ; y muchos quedaron lisiados de las piernas y brazos de los tormentos; y porque en algunas partes por las paredes del pueblo escribían letras que decían: *Por tu rey y por tu ley morirás*, los oficiales y Domingo de Irala y sus justicias hacían informaciones para saber quién lo había escrito, jurando y amenazando . . . que lo habían de castigar.
>
> (*Comentarios* 220; ch. 80)

Comentarios reveals the power struggle between Irala, chosen by Spanish officers and settlers in the conquered land,[5] and Cabeza de Vaca, appointed adelantado by royal decree. Yet what is also at stake here is the legal dispute between the geopolitical centralization undertaken by Cabeza de Vaca on behalf of the Crown and the lordly, peripheral aspirations of insubordinate conquistadores like Irala (Bauer 44).

Irala's supporters imprisoned Cabeza de Vaca and seized the legal papers establishing his governorship; they broke locks, burned legal papers kept by the notary Hernández, and drafted a slanderous libel signed by all the Asunción residents (ch. 75). In the face of these actions, all associated with the written word, Cabeza de Vaca asked his notary to draft a text in 1545, which was revisited and republished as *Comentarios* in 1555. The king was not aware that the former adelantado's allies had scrawled graffiti on the walls of Asunción, risking their lives to defend both Cabeza de Vaca and the king. *Comentarios* is Cabeza de Vaca's final public deposition for all who read it to bear witness to his innocence.

Tips on Teaching Comentarios

Although *Comentarios* consists of short chapters, most of which are less than five pages, the text is still a challenging one to teach. Yet its richness lies in the challenge it presents. Below are six themes that can be presented when teaching this text.

First, *Comentarios* and related texts weave multiple genres entangled at the intertextual, historical, and discursive levels: *capitulaciones* (public contracts between the Crown and the conquistadores), legal instruments and laws such as the Requerimiento and the Leyes Nuevas (New Laws), notary papers, graffiti, and libelous accusations, testimonies, and *probanzas*, among others. Tracing such a heterogeneous corpus allows students and scholars to see the colonial "lettered city" at work (Rama).

Second, the whole corpus on the Southern Cone fiasco could be approached as a courtroom drama. The instructor could divide students into two groups (supporters versus accusers of Cabeza de Vaca), each reading a selection of excerpts before the class discussion. For the supporters, I suggest chapters 75 and 80. Chapter 80 recounts the torture of Cabeza de Vaca's supporters and how they wrote graffiti on the walls of Asunción in support of their jailed adelantado. This little scene is appealing for the classroom because it sets up a parallel between the body and writing: Irala's followers imprison and confiscate the property of those who want to free Cabeza de Vaca from prison and those who dare scrawl their support on the village walls. How is this parallel constructed? What can be said when the same punishment is applied to such different offenses? What is the value of writing for those who take up the pen and those who condemn others for doing so?

For the accusers, I suggest reading chapters 74 and 75, which deal with Cabeza de Vaca's imprisonment and Irala's supporters' actions. Chapter 74 tells how Irala's officers head to the governor's house to steal deeds, legal papers, goods, clothing, wine, oil, and so on. How can this list be read? Why do the officers target the papers along with the various goods? Chapter 75 describes the drafting of the "slanderous libel" ("libelo infamatorio"; *Comentarios* 213) against Cabeza de Vaca and how people were convinced to sign. What arguments do his enemies offer? Why are they so effective? What role does loyalty to the king play in this conflict? What are the economic arguments and interests at play?

The third theme is the indigenous body and writing. Chapter 77 describes a naked Indian woman who secretly hands the imprisoned Cabeza de Vaca a message from his allies. This incredibly literary chapter presents a series of events and many teaching opportunities related not only to *Comentarios* and the colonial period but also to issues of race, gender, and power. There are obvious yet important questions to answer in class: How did the naked woman slip the letter into the jail? What did it say? Who sent it? What role does this document play in Cabeza de Vaca's legal saga? Also, what role does a scene like this (in which an indigenous woman uses her body to hide a message for the prisoner) play in a text as legalistic and argumentative as *Comentarios*?

The fourth theme concerns the Indians. Taking into account the role that the treatment of Indians plays in the legal case against Cabeza de Vaca and his alleged humanitarianism, I recommend reading and comparing certain important passages, like the chapter in which the adelantado prohibits Spaniards from buying or selling Indians (ch. 73). The chapters devoted to the Agace Indians—particularly the sections about Chief Aracaré, the main rebel in the story, who resists the conquerors and is finally hanged by Cabeza de Vaca—are especially relevant (chs. 33, 35, 37). This was not exactly what one would call a peaceful conquest. The way the Spaniards protect but also punish indigenous people is worth comparing in a discussion of Irala's actions after the adelantado's imprisonment. Forcing Indians off the land (ch. 78) and legalizing cannibalism (ch. 82) are two examples of tyrannical regulations that instill disorder and chaos. Irala is the incarnation of the disarray of the empire in *Comentarios*, just as Narváez was in *Naufragios*, though Irala has the continuous support of the soldiers, an achievement that eluded Narváez.

The fifth theme is the Spaniards and the others. One interesting activity for an undergraduate course is a compare-and-contrast exercise involving *Naufragios* and *Comentarios* (or excerpts from these texts) guided by the question of who the others are in each text. Chapter 12 of *Naufragios* is particularly insightful. There, a group of Indians from Malhado Island cry and sympathize with the fate of the starving Spaniards. Later, in chapter 22, Cabeza de Vaca and his companions are reduced to the condition of the Indians: naked and so hungry that they eat raw meat and hide "scrapings" ("raeduras"; 1: 173, 175; 172, 174). It is interesting to compare chapter 17 of *Comentarios*—which discusses peace with the Agace Indians—with those moments of infighting among the Spaniards in the same text. Incidents like the collection of debts from poor, hungry soldiers (ch. 18), the kidnapping of indigenous women (ch. 43), and Irala's betrayal of Cabeza de Vaca (ch. 74) in *Comentarios* all convey an idea of who the other is for Cabeza de Vaca. In both texts, otherness is depicted with unexpected twists, in a way that is anything but stereotypical or familiar.

The sixth theme concerns other narratives. The richness and complexity of this story can be better appreciated by comparing it to other texts, like the account by the German soldier Ulrich Schmidl, *The Conquest of the River Plate, 1535–1555*. Schmidl spent twenty years in the Río de la Plata region, and a good part of his chronicle deals with the period of Cabeza de Vaca's governorship. His story is special not only because of his subaltern position as a soldier, or because he is not Spanish, but also because, like almost all the other troops, Schmidl supported Irala. After students have read *Comentarios*, Schmidl's chapters 37 and 38 provide for a fruitful discussion (163–67).

These chapters describe the arrival of Hernando de Ribera (Schmidl's superior) in Asunción and the treatment his troops received from Cabeza de Vaca. Since the captain had traveled beyond the point that the governor had ordered, Cabeza de Vaca seized all goods obtained from Indians during the journey and imprisoned Ribera. When Cabeza de Vaca decided to hang Ribera, the soldiers mutinied and came to his defense. Schmidl characterizes Cabeza de Vaca as an arrogant leader guided by a "haughty head" ("orgullosa cabeza"; *Derrotero* 77; ch. 39), while *Comentarios* depicts his rule as measured and orderly. A comparative study could show students different ways of narrating the exercise of power, depending on one's locus of enunciation.

Comentarios emerges as the last defense of a man who, after two failed colonial ventures and a long legal battle, feels that justice has not yet been done and so takes his case before the court of history. The decision to retell what happened in Río de la Plata and to publish this story implies enormous confidence in the power of writing. In a nutshell, *Comentarios* chronicles the dispute between Cabeza de Vaca and Irala, but also Cabeza de Vaca's efforts to pacify the Indians and conquer the land. It casts Cabeza de Vaca not as the instigator of a fiasco but as a moral man, faithful to God, the king, and the law. *Comentarios* tries to clear the record and restore the good name of a conquistador who was never quite able to conquer anything.

NOTES

This essay was translated by Wendy Ann Gosselin, Carlos A. Jáuregui, and Luis Fernando Restrepo.

1. See fig. 2 in part 1 of this volume.

2. The foremost critical works on Cabeza de Vaca in Río de la Plata include Iglesia; Rabasa; Maura; Bauer; and El Jaber, *País*.

3. Sierra de la Plata was a mythical place much like El Dorado. In reports beginning in 1515, Guarani informants told Spanish treasure hunters that it was located deep

in the forests of Brazil, was ruled by a monarch known as the White King, and was rich with silver (Bane 133).

4. For class purposes, I recommend Cabeza de Vaca, *Naufragios y comentarios: Con dos cartas*. Baker Morrow's English version of this text is useful, although at times loosely translated; see Cabeza de Vaca, *South American Expeditions*. All translations of *Comentarios* not otherwise identified are by the translators of this essay.

5. When Ayolas undertook his journey to the Sierra de la Plata, he left Irala in his place. Ultimately, Irala held this post until Cabeza de Vaca arrived in 1539. After Cabeza de Vaca's arrest, the people chose Irala as governor, thus making him the first man in this territory to become leader by popular will; he served from 1544 to 1548 and then from 1549 until his death in 1556. In 1555, a *cédula real* ("royal decree") confirmed Irala in the post after several unsuccessful attempts by the Crown to designate a new adelantado (Gandía, *Indios* 31–96 and *Historia* 95–311).

APPENDIX: PAPER TRAIL OF THE RÍO DE LA PLATA FIASCO

1540

Contract with the Crown

18 March 1540. "Capitulación otorgada a Alvar Núñez Cabeza de Vaca para ir a conquistar y a socorrer a los españoles residentes en la provincia del Río de la Plata, dada en gobernación a Pedro de Mendoza ya difunto" ("Capitulation granted to Alvar Núñez Cabeza de Vaca to conquer and assist the Spaniards residing in the province of Río de la Plata, given under the governorship of the late Pedro de Mendoza"; Vas Mingo 362–66).

1545

Reports written upon Cabeza de Vaca's return from Río de la Plata

Cabeza de Vaca's report: *Relación general que yo, Álvar Núñez Cabeza de Vaca, Adelantado y Gobernador y Capitán general de la provincia del río de la Plata*... (*Account that I, Álvar Núñez Cabeza de Vaca, Adelantado and Governor and Captain General of the Province of Rio de la Plata*...; Serrano y Sanz 2: 1–98)

Pero Hernández's report: *Relación de las cosas sucedidas en el Río de la Plata* (*Account of the Events that Occurred in Rio de la Plata*; Serrano y Sanz 2: 307–58)

1546–52

Court battle

1546–47: Cabeza de Vaca indicted

20 February 1546: Juan de Villalobos, chief prosecutor of the Council of the Indies, files thirty-four charges against Cabeza de Vaca (transcribed by Rodríguez Carrión 101–06), forcing him to gather testimonies for his defense (Adorno and Pautz 1: 395–98).

1546–47: Exculpatory evidence and testimonies are gathered (Serrano y Sanz 2: 109–306; Adorno and Pautz 1: 397–98).

1551: Sentence and appeal
- 18 March: Cabeza de Vaca is found guilty (sentence documented in Irala and Quevedo 367–68; Rodríguez Carrión 149–50; translated with some omissions by Morris Bishop 285; Buckingham Smith 151–52n1). He appeals and requests commutation of prison sentence but is denied (Adorno and Pautz 1: 399).
- 22 November: The Court of Valladolid grants Cabeza de Vaca's petition to reopen his case and submit new evidence (Adorno and Pautz 1: 399).

1552: Sentence partially reversed by the Council of the Indies on 23 August (Irala and Quevedo 368–69; see also Adorno and Pautz 1: 399–400)

1555

Cabeza de Vaca's *Comentarios* published under the name of his ghostwriter and notary, Pero Hernández, in Valladolid with the revised 1542 *Naufragios: La relación y comentarios del governador Álvar Núñez Cabeça de Vaca, de lo acaescido en las dos jornadas que hizo a las Indias*

Colonial Reckoning: The Problem with Cabeza de Vaca

René Carrasco

Teaching Álvar Núñez Cabeza de Vaca's *Naufragios* (*Shipwrecks*), more often than not, results in an engaging class because of the work's versatile nature and singular characteristics. Unlike many colonial texts, *Naufragios* has a plot that loosely follows the Aristotelian dramaturgical tripartite structure.[1] There are identifiable, moderately complex characters that interact with each other while driving a plot that offers a compelling ending, in which triumph is achieved after the characters overcome disaster and considerable suffering. Moreover, the text can be categorized under various genres, having been read as a sort of hagiography, as an example of travel literature, and even at times as a distant offspring of the medieval chivalric romance. Given these particularities, it is safe to assume that this text will continue to appear in syllabi for a variety of courses for many years to come—a state of affairs that is not without its problems.

The main problem with *Naufragios* is that the text has seduced intellectuals and academics over the last hundred years into perpetuating oxymoronic ideas, paradoxical concepts, and pervasive aporias through its teaching. The narrative effectively conveys the sense not only that a "peaceful conquest" has taken place but that one is even possible. Moreover, the descriptions of alterity, the treatment otherness receives, and the language that names it have been fundamental in shaping a mythical, ontological, almost proto–magical realism. In fact, *Naufragios* has been so effective that it is often considered a foundational text of many genres, including Chicano and Latinx literature and Latin American semifictional narrative, just to name a few. In seducing its readers, the text has managed to present a mythicized colonial period as an inevitable, not always violent, and sometimes even noble process to which we, mestizo peoples of Latin America (note the sarcasm), owe our identity, culture, and existence. Unfortunately, *Naufragios* is often taught without a focus on the epistemic violence it deploys, rendering that violence invisible if not nonexistent.

In this essay, I address these prevalent notions and advocate for a contemporary approach to Cabeza de Vaca that centers on the problematic nature of *Naufragios* and exposes the epistemic violence it deploys. When statues of conquistadores continue to be toppled, and when there are increasing rumblings of a collective reckoning with the colonial question (Jáuregui, *Espectros* 27–31), it is time that we see the figures of the literary "darling conquistadores," as José Rabasa would call them, collapse under the pressure of history (29–30). It is perhaps more crucial than ever to continue teaching Cabeza de Vaca, but from a perspective that understands his work as a problem and not as a celebration.

Naufragios as an Instance of "Peaceful Conquest"

The central concept to be eliminated from the classroom is that of "peaceful conquest," dismantled by Rabasa (83). Conquest inherently involves one group's subjugation by another and carries a military connotation (see Covarrubias 349). Implying a peaceful subjugation is contradictory (Rabasa 32), revealing the paradoxical and violent nature of colonialism. Over time, the practice of interpreting and teaching *Naufragios* as an illustration of peaceful conquest, termed the "fallacy of the 'peaceful conquistador'" by Carlos Jáuregui (*Espectros* 91–94), has become common but can be avoided. Instructors should shift their focus from the text as an example to the concept itself, critically considering its rationale and limitations.

José Rabasa advises that when reading Cabeza de Vaca's *Naufragios*, we must consider the historical context, the author's circumstances during composition, the subtext, the author's goals in writing his *relación* ("account"), and other colonial texts highlighted as instances of peaceful conquest. Three supplementary texts can guide students in their reading.

Naufragios and the Southern Cone

Several texts detail the experiences and actions of Cabeza de Vaca in the Southern Cone, providing valuable insights into his role as a conquistador. *Relación general* provides a chronological account of events in the Río de la Plata region. *Comentarios*, dictated by Cabeza de Vaca to his amanuensis, Pero Hernández, serves both as a defense of his actions and a condemnation of Domingo Martínez de Irala. Finally, *Relación de las cosas sucedidas en el Río de la Plata*, written by Hernández, includes explicit descriptions of violence and sexual abuse against Guarani women to corroborate Cabeza de Vaca's account.

While Cabeza de Vaca's actions in North America, such as healing indigenous people and wandering naked, might be interpreted as benevolent or peaceful, his accounts of behavior in the Southern Cone challenge the notion of him as a peaceful conquistador. Instructors can highlight passages in *Relación general* where Cabeza de Vaca turns to war as a last resort after peaceful efforts fail. For instance, in section 39, he justifies war against the Guaycuru people as a legitimate last resort (Serrano y Sanz 6: 24–26). Similarly, instructors can address instances of sexual abuse and violence against Guarani women attributed to Irala in the section of *Relación de las cosas* titled "Vejaciones a las indias" ("Abuses against Indian Women"; Serrano y Sanz 6: 316–22 and 353–56). Finally, chapters 25 and 26 of *Comentarios* narrate a battle between Cabeza de Vaca's troops and indigenous forces, revealing a more aggressive side in subduing so-called hostile indigenous populations (Serrano y Sanz 5: 93–97).

This contrast between *Naufragios* and texts depicting Cabeza de Vaca as an adelantado in the Río de la Plata province illuminates the self-serving nature of the Spaniard's texts. It enhances students' understanding of colonial writing protocols and the inherent violence they entail, as does Rabasa's concept of "writing violence" as a negotiation, articulation, and justification of "certain regimes of terror" (72, 78). Additionally, recognizing Cabeza de Vaca's authorial motives unveils the legalistic subtext of *Naufragios*, facilitating a deeper interpretation. The *ordenanzas* of 1526 are crucial in this context.

Naufragios and the *Ordenanzas* of 1526

We must approach *Naufragios* as a text wherein the author aimed to demonstrate his compliance with the Spanish Crown's policies, particularly elucidated in a primary legal document of the era. This pedagogical approach aligns with Rabasa's interpretation. Briefly discussing the Ordenanzas sobre el buen tratamiento de los indios (Ordinances Regarding the Good Treatment of the Indians) could provide students with insights into the contextual backdrop of *Naufragios*. The *ordenanzas*, comprising twelve regulations, aimed to govern the behavior of Spanish expeditions and delineate the parameters for a proper conquest. These regulations were disseminated to conquistadores along with their *capitulaciones* ("contracts"). On the surface, the *ordenanzas* might appear to advocate for improved treatment of indigenous peoples, suggesting a corpus of law defending them from Spanish violence. However, a closer examination reveals the *ordenanzas*' paradoxical and "bizarre features," as characterized by Charles Gibson (13) in his description of the Requerimiento (War Ultimatum), another Spanish legal document informing the content of the *ordenanzas*. Beneath the colonial discourse of protection and affection for indigenous peoples lie the foundations of colonial "regimes of terror" (Rabasa 72–74).

In discussions of *Naufragios*, particularly the sections where Cabeza de Vaca provides seemingly innocuous ethnographic details about indigenous customs and practices, it is crucial to consider the information he is relaying to the Crown in the context of the *ordenanzas*. For instance, *ordenanza* 11 stipulates that if an encomienda, a form of indentured labor, could enhance the "*calidad* [quality], *condición* [condition], *y habilidad* [ability]" of indigenous individuals, it must be granted by the church representative (Rabasa 41). What precisely is meant by the quality, condition, and ability of indigenous people? How are these attributes assessed? According to Rabasa, "quality" and "ability" set criteria for anthropological evaluations of the most suitable methods for subjecting indigenous populations to the Crown's authority, including, if necessary, extermination. Furthermore, "reason" and "right" serve as both a rationale for warfare and a justification for its consequences, such as slavery and massacres (Rabasa 42). If we consider that the *ordenanzas*, along with the Requerimiento, prioritize religious conversion over political subjugation, it raises the question, Were religious documents that prioritized evangelization any different? While there are no definitive answers, a study of Bartolomé de las Casas's *De unico vocationis modo omnium gentium ad veram religionem* (*The Only Way*) is essential for formulating a response.

Naufragios and Las Casas's *De unico vocationis modo*

Las Casas emphasized the religious legitimacy of conquest, prioritizing evangelization over political and economic aspects. He advocated for love-based persuasion instead of coercion, envisioning conquistadores and clerics acting with compassion toward indigenous peoples. His 1537 work *De unico vocationis modo* can be viewed as a blueprint for the peaceful conversion or conquest model he attempted to implement in Verapaz, Guatemala, from 1537 to 1540, albeit with unsatisfactory results, according to Helen Parish's introduction to the work (Las Casas, *Only Way*, 36).

When teaching this text alongside *Naufragios*, instructors can compare Las Casas's condemnation of political subjugation of indigenous peoples to the Spanish Crown with the recognition of indigenous peoples as potential good vassals who could be converted to Christianity and made to provide free labor through the encomienda system. *De unico vocationis modo* delves into Las Casas's arguments against the injustice and illegality of wars against indigenous peoples (117–56) and his endorsement of restorative justice, particularly the concept of restitution to compensate indigenous peoples for injustices (158–71). Contrasting Las Casas's work with *Naufragios* highlights their respective impacts as texts. According to Rabasa, "*De unico vocationis modo* forced the Crown to revise the 1526 *Ordenanzas* in the New Laws ('Leyes Nuevas') of 1542, where the Crown outlaws all forms of slavery and calls for the dismantling of the *encomiendas*" (71). In contrast, *Naufragios* had minimal influence on laws or Spaniards' attitudes toward indigenous peoples. Thus, it is crucial to underscore the differences in the stances taken by Las Casas and Cabeza de Vaca on political subjection to the Crown and their interpretations of peaceful conquest. Las Casas critiqued the entire enterprise, advocating for a peaceful process of evangelization, while Cabeza de Vaca used the *ordenanzas* as a foundation for his narrative, not explicitly addressing political subjugation but presenting it as a given. These differences run deep.

Instructors should adapt these recommendations to their teaching contexts. In an undergraduate course where Cabeza de Vaca is discussed briefly, providing additional texts may not be feasible. Incorporating the perspective presented in this essay into the classroom allows instructors to "deconstruct the supposed originality of Cabeza de Vaca's critique of empire and advocacy for peaceful conquest," as Rabasa suggests. Incorporating this perspective also aligns with Rabasa's idea that we must recognize the coexistence of imperial and empathetic perspectives in Cabeza de Vaca's work in order to trace voices of resistance (83). Furthermore, it continues the process of unteaching Cabeza de Vaca as proposed by the editors of this volume, moving beyond the notion of peaceful conquest. The next challenge is dismantling the perception of Cabeza de Vaca as a precursor to the literary genre known as magical realism.

Naufragios *as an Instance of Proto–Magical Realism*

Assigning *Naufragios* in an introductory Latin American literature course can be a bold yet rewarding choice. Introducing a colonial-era text in these classes allows instructors to explore Latin American literary history beyond the usual focus on the twentieth century. By expanding the literary time line to include the colonial and pre-Hispanic periods, instructors can engage students in profound discussions about the essence of literature itself: What is literature? How is literature defined? Which texts qualify as such, and why? In the United States, *Naufragios* holds a significant place in this conversation, especially because of its alleged association with one of the most debated Latin American literary genres: magical realism (for a description of the genre, see González-Echevarría 109).

Roberto González-Echevarría points out that the first mention of magical realism in an academic context was in an essay written in 1955, titled "Magical Realism in Spanish American Fiction" (González-Echevarría 108), whose author, Ángel Flores, claimed that "since the Colonial Period but especially during the 1880s; the magical, writ large from the earliest—in the letters of Columbus, in the chroniclers, in the sagas of Cabeza de Vaca—entered the literary mainstream during Modernism" (Flores 189).

Since then, this hasty mention of Cabeza de Vaca, the only reference to him in Flores's essay, has marked him as a precursor of magical realism. What Flores initially labeled as the "amalgamation of realism and fantasy" he immediately rephrased into the formulation "realism and magic" (189), paving the way for the twentieth-century interpretation and, perhaps more important, the classification of Cabeza de Vaca's endeavors as magical, therefore forcing them into a relationship with magical realism. Subsequently, scholars like David Lagmanovich, Trinidad Barrera and Carmen de Mora Valcárcel, and Rolena Adorno (*De Guancane a Macondo*) have continued to explore this relationship.

Reading *Naufragios* as an example of proto–magical realism, however, presents several challenges. The most significant issue is the anachronistic tendency to impose a twentieth-century aesthetic category onto a sixteenth-century text. We do students a disservice when we use terms like *magical* in the classroom without providing the proper historical context in which such terms operated in the 1500s and then applying them as conceptual tools to understand Latin America's historical process and present-day situation. It is crucial to understand how categories of the supernatural functioned in the sixteenth century and to critically examine how and why they came to be related to Cabeza de Vaca's text as an example of proto–magical realism.[2]

A brief clarification of terms is a necessary point of departure. In discussing the literature of the fantastic, Tzvetan Todorov establishes a critical difference between that which we consider marvelous and that which is strange. The strange, he argues, can eventually be understood through reason and reflection (*Fantastic* 32, 35). On the other hand, the marvelous can never be explained without reference to the supernatural. While *Naufragios* could certainly be classified as marvelous because of the supernatural elements described in the narrative, it is essential to remember that, as Jacques Le Goff notes, medieval Western culture divided the concept of the supernatural into three domains: *mirabilis* (the "marvelous"), *magicus* (the "magical"), and *miraculosus* (the "miraculous"). *Mirabilis*, then, could reference the marvelous, which has pre-Christian origins, while *magicus* would encompass "lo sobrenatural maléfico, lo sobrenatural satánico" ("the supernatural evil, the supernatural satanic") and *miraculosus* "lo sobrenatural propiamente cristiano" ("the properly Christian supernatural") or "lo maravilloso cristiano" ("the Christian marvelous"; Le Goff, "Maravilloso" 13). In other words, within the medieval Christian framework, *mirabilis* described the marvelous as it was perceived in the world prior to the Middle Ages, where animals, beasts, and monsters were the main references. Over time, *magicus* became associated with dark magic inspired by demons and the devil himself—in opposition to so-called white magic, which was divine and almost godly. Meanwhile, *miraculosus* encompassed all elements of the *mirabilis* that were related to God and other religious elements.

There certainly are elements of the supernatural in Cabeza de Vaca's text. However, we must differentiate between them and understand how they operate in the logic of the sixteenth century, how they appear in the narrative, and what they achieve. Once instructors have done this, they can move on to the main instances in the text that have contributed to *Naufragios*'s reputation as a precursor of magical realism. Three episodes, in particular, can be instrumental when discussing Cabeza de Vaca's alleged association with that genre: first, the appearance of a burning bush and the series of healing instances it unleashes; second, the episode of Mala Cosa; and, third, the prophecy of the *mora de Hornachos* ("Moorish woman from Hornachos"), which foretells the story of the Narváez expedition. Each of these episodes can be discussed in terms of what concepts it has been associated with or categorized under and what influences said categorization has had in establishing any relationship between Cabeza de Vaca and magical realism.

A Burning Tree, Miraculous Healings, and a Resurrection

Clearly in the realm of the Christian *miraculosus*, or marvelous, the episode that leads to a series of healings portrayed as miracles takes place in chapter 21, when Cabeza de Vaca encounters a burning tree.[3] From this point on, Cabeza de Vaca abandons the narrative of disaster and captivity and focuses on his saint-like healing abilities, in this way crafting an image of himself as a divinely inspired hero with a remarkable proficiency for performing miracles. The most miraculous of the healings recounted by the Spaniard, however, takes place in chapter 22, when Cabeza de Vaca brings a dead Susola back to life. He recites a prayer next to the corpse, performs the *signum crucis* ("sign of the cross"), and then blows on the deceased. Later that night, Cabeza de Vaca is told that that man "had arisen revived and walked about and eaten" ("se avía levantado bueno y se avía paseado y comido"; Adorno and Pautz 1: 163; 162). Nonetheless, there is no certainty that the event took place. The author does not claim to have witnessed the resurrection, and the information is delivered to him by a third party, which would constitute hearsay in a court of law. It is possible, then, that the most miraculous of healings never took place.

The miracles performed by Cabeza de Vaca have generated a monumental bibliography that dates to the sixteenth century. There seems to be a consensus among critics about the fabricated nature of these events and the reasons for their inclusion in *Naufragios*. For some, Cabeza de Vaca's legacy as a *milagroso* ("agent of miracles") is a product not of the text itself but of interpretations from the sixteenth through the twentieth century (Lafaye). In contrast, others maintain that all hagiographic references as well as the evangelizing discourse employed by Cabeza de Vaca were not deliberate but were instead "recuperated and integrated" into the text as "expository and argumentative resources" because of their cultural relevance during the sixteenth century (Pupo-Walker, "Pesquisas" 522, 524). However, for Daniel Reff, Cabeza de Vaca's miracles were "more than a reflection of intertextuality" and instead "reflect[ed] the reality of life in New Spain following the Conquest" (118), in which indigenous people suffered from psychosomatic illnesses that the Spaniards "miraculously treated" (119), while Kun Jong Lee argues that the Spaniard intentionally crafted his miracle-filled narrative, and his own image, after Saint Paul to obtain funding for a new enterprise of conquest and colonization in America (242, 256–57). Jáuregui considers these miracles part of what he terms "messianic emplotment" ("Going Native" 186). Whether unintentional or deliberate, intertextual or part of a messianic self-representation, the miracles appear in the text and must be addressed.

Instructors can assign the passages from *Naufragios* referenced above and have an in-class conversation about the miraculous, the Christian marvelous, and the problematic association of these concepts with magical realism. To broaden the conversation, instructors could also discuss one of the most analyzed episodes of *Naufragios*: the tale of quite a strange thing.

Mala Cosa Affair

In the same chapter as the episode of the purported resurrection (ch. 22), Cabeza de Vaca recounts yet another tale that has become the object of many analyses and discussions among literary critics: the Mala Cosa affair. In broad strokes, the story is as follows: while staying with the Avavares, Cabeza de Vaca becomes aware of "something very strange" and is presented with the story of "a man they call an evil being" ("una cosa muy estraña ... un hombre que ellos llaman mala cosa"; Adorno and Pautz 1: 165; 164) who terrorized their towns, kidnapped people, and performed some sort of procedure that involved making incisions on peoples' bodies, pulling out and disposing of entrails, severing body parts, and then undoing everything, in this way healing people. Additionally, this "very strange" thing would appear during ceremonies and dances and perform feats that could, perhaps, be considered a display of supernatural abilities. This evil being never ate the food offered to him and claimed to have his dwelling place in a cleft in the ground. Cabeza de Vaca and his companions laughed at the story but then met people with scars on their body that, in the Spaniards' view, corroborated the tale. The Spaniards then proceeded to explain that the knowledge and worship of the Christian God would protect the Avavares and prevent this strange and evil thing from ever appearing again. This, according to Cabeza de Vaca, pleased the Avavares, who lost their fear (1: 168–69).

For Bauer, *Naufragios* "manifests a first step in the displacement of Western man's magic by God's miracles in the identification of 'magic' with Native American knowledge" (61). Of course, instructors would do well to familiarize themselves with other analyses, which, for example, interpret Mala Cosa as an iteration of the trickster figure that appears in indigenous tales throughout America (Adorno, *Polemics* 25–58), an instance of analogic narration of the unknown (Jáuregui, *Espectros* 49, 103–04, 121), a truth device that restores or strengthens the credibility of Christian miracles (Jáuregui, *Espectros* 98; Ahern, "Cross" 219–20), a fictional tale that complements Cabeza de Vaca's miraculous accounts (Pastor, *Armature* 238, 329), an evil figure that separates an indigenous cosmovision from its Christian counterpart by contrasting an evil healer with a good healer (Barrera 37; Spitta, *Between Two Waters* 326; Adorno, *De Guancane a Macondo* 50, 62–67), or even a mirror image of the Spanish conquistador (Jáuregui, *Espectros* 89–122).

Regardless of the interpretation that a particular instructor favors—and uses to frame the in-class discussion—it would be helpful to highlight the tale of Mala Cosa, considering the medieval dimensions of the supernatural and how it could have been subsumed under the title of magical realism or regarded as an early example of this sort of literature. Does Mala Cosa represent indigenous cosmovisions and epistemologies, as Adorno argues? Or is the story an indigenous attempt to explain the unknown, using the supernatural, with Mala Cosa being a version of Cabeza de Vaca himself, as Jáuregui suggests? Discussing this episode and its various interpretations can result in an interesting class. However, any conversation on *Naufragios* and its association with magical realism would be incomplete without the inclusion of the prophecy that frames the narrative as a whole: the *mora de Hornachos* omen.

Mora de Hornachos and the Prophecy

At the very end of the text, readers learn that the entire enterprise narrated in *Naufragios* is framed within a prophecy, that of the *mora de Hornachos*—the "Moorish woman" from Hornachos, in Badajoz, Extremadura—who predicted both the unfortunate events faced by the crew in Pánfilo de Narváez's expedition and the destiny of the few survivors. In chapter 38, as a sort of concluding tale, Cabeza de Vaca reveals an event that took place before the Narváez expedition, between the governor himself and a Muslim woman. According to Cabeza de Vaca, this woman warned Narváez that he should not go inland into Florida because "neither he nor any one of those who went with him would escape . . . , and that if one of them were to come out, God would perform great miracles through him" ("los que con él ivan, no saldrían de la tierra, y que si alguno saliesse, que haría Dios por él muy grandes milagros"; Adorno and Pautz 1: 273; 272).

How does this prophecy, uttered by a voice that is impossible to locate (Maura 170) and that foretells doom and miraculous exceptionality in the same breath, relate to the understanding of the supernatural? As a rhetorical device, the prophecy allows Cabeza de Vaca to frame his journey as a supernatural endeavor and to highlight the degree of adversity he had to face. It also strengthens his characterization of himself as a chosen one. However, what is the relationship of the prophecy, revealed at the end but having taken place at the beginning of the journey and uttered by a non-Christian woman, to the medieval concept of *mirabilis*? Could the prophecy be understood as a manifestation of the demon-inspired *magicus*? Does the prophecy legitimize Cabeza de Vaca's claim that his journey was divine and, therefore, part of the *miraculosus*? Or should this prophecy be read as yet another rhetorical tool in Cabeza de Vaca's arsenal to help further his case for recognition as a divinely chosen leader and hero? An in-class conversation about this episode could be enlightening when discussing the alleged place of *Naufragios* as a precursor to magical realism.

That *Naufragios* continues to be read as a text that contains episodes of miracles, marvelous events, and elements of the supernatural that may ultimately be considered magical is not the problem. Problems arise when we, as professors, are not able to differentiate between the use of categories like *magicus*, *mirabilis*, and *miraculosus* as they appeared in the sixteenth century and the use of equivalent terms in the twentieth century. Without understanding these semantic differences, we cannot account for how the concept of the marvelous evolved from one time period to another: How did the Christian marvelous (*miraculosus*) in the sixteenth-century *Naufragios* become the surrealist marvelous or the magical realism of the twentieth century, and to what effect? When we fail to recognize these shifts in conceptions, we risk suggesting, as Flores did, that these conceptions are rooted in the environment in which the narrative unfolds. This perspective displaces the focus from the text's historical contexts and internal rhetoric to the environment, leading to the characterization of the American continent as inherently magical and its people as possessing magical cultural practices. This displacement has contributed to the notion that magical realism as a literary current emerged in America rather than in Europe.

Today, what is magical about Latin America? A key to answering this question is, perhaps unwillingly, provided by González-Echevarría when he describes the motive behind the work of Alejo Carpentier, one of the most celebrated authors associated with magical realism, as the search "for the marvelous buried beneath the surface of Latin American consciousness, where African drums still beat and Indian amulets still rule; in depths where Europe is only a vague memory of a future still to come" (123). This quotation suggests that the concept of the magical arises from the unique cultural and historical contexts of

Latin America, drawing from indigenous and African traditions. However, categorizing these diverse epistemologies as magical risks creating a hierarchy of knowledge that privileges Western rationalist perspectives. This framing implies that Western perspectives are the standard of rationality, while other ways of knowing are seen as exotic or lesser. As instructors, we must be aware of this problematic analysis and avoid its perpetuation at all costs.

Colonial Reckoning

As instructors continue to teach *Naufragios*, it is important for them to recognize the increasingly complex colonial order that it reveals and that has not been superseded. The problem with Cabeza de Vaca is the problem of the ongoing colonial question (Jáuregui, *Espectros* 27–31) and the civilizing project that it spawned, the history of our civilization, the heroes it has celebrated, the events it recognizes, and the processes it recounts. As we as a society continue our collective reckoning with the colonial past, the figures of the colonial literary canon, like the colonial statues that adorn modern cities and parks, must be analyzed critically and, eventually, toppled. But a metaphoric toppling of colonial literary figures is achieved not by censoring or silencing the texts from the period but through a critical approach, a Benjaminian reading against the grain (257) or a Rabasan unteaching process that evidences the epistemic violence inherent in those texts.

NOTES

1. Although far from being a novel, Cabeza de Vaca's text does display novelesque elements, according to critics like Pastor (*Discursos*); Pupo-Walker ("Pesquisas"); Dowling; Lewis; and Lagmanovich.

2. The term *magical realism* was first deployed by the German art critic Franz Roh in 1925, and its use was encouraged by André Breton in a manifesto where "the *marvelous*" is proclaimed as "an aesthetic category and even a way of life" (González-Echevarría 109). In Latin America, the term appeared first in the 1940s, "when it had already been forgotten in Europe" (109), and again in the 1950s, as critics rushed to find the roots of the novels that fueled the Boom movement and in an attempt to "justify their experimental nature" (111). Most of these critics interpreted Latin America as a land that oozed magical realism from its pores and that was, a priori, a fertile ground for the development of a literature that embraced this ostensibly autochthonous trait.

3. While out on a food-gathering expedition, Cabeza de Vaca wanders off by himself and has to spend the night alone in the wilderness. He is saved because he "found a tree aflame, and warmed by its fire I endured the cold that night" ("hallé un árbol ardiendo, y al fuego dél passé aquel frío aquella noche"; Adorno and Pautz 1: 157; 156; ch. 21).

CABEZA DE VACA ACROSS DISCIPLINES

Early Spanish Expeditions in La Florida and the Archaeology of Conquest

George Sabo III and Jeffrey M. Mitchem

The accident-plagued journey of Álvar Núñez Cabeza de Vaca and his three companions produced written accounts with fascinating information on North American landscapes, environments, and indigenous communities. Yet the veracity of this information has been a matter of considerable debate from the times it was disseminated in both manuscript and printed versions. As such, the accounts of the Pánfilo de Narváez expedition join with documents produced by other early-to-mid-sixteenth-century Spanish expeditions—including those led by Juan Ponce de León, Lucas Vázquez de Ayllón, Hernando de Soto, Tristán de Luna y Arellano, and Juan Pardo—in generating tantalizing but questionable descriptions of the natural and cultural features of a poorly defined territory generally referred to as La Florida.

These accounts are complex intertextual historical artifacts. There is a common need for readings of virtually all accounts of that era, as well as later travel accounts, to evaluate specific textual passages with respect to a variety of factors, including identification of the circumstances under which observations were made, the observer's identity and understanding of what was witnessed, motivation for reporting that information, and the audience for whom the passage was written. We are thus interested not only in the veracity of written accounts but also in the dynamic interplay between early Spanish observations and the sixteenth-century cultural frameworks that shaped written descriptions of North American landscapes. In some instances, material evidence collected from archaeological sites can be linked to recorded events, providing an important source of evidence germane to both of these concerns and offering the prospect of more reliable assessments of historical accounts.

In exploring this interplay between cultural frames and observational perspectives, we acknowledge several well-known material records that contribute to the understanding of what and how travel information was presented by sixteenth-century Spanish writers. Several essays in this volume address these issues in greater detail, but in brief, many conquistadores—including Cabeza de Vaca—wrote from the perspective of cultural frameworks that embraced early modern worldviews, driven by the search for wealth, power, and the saving of souls, even as perceptions concerning the humanity of indigenous communities remained uncertain and clouded by unfamiliarity with their cultural beliefs and practices and their environments. As a result, many early modern texts project an overriding sense of bewilderment (as discussed in Greenblatt; Pagden, *Fall*; Todorov, *Conquest*). Our task in examining these texts is thus driven, in part, by a need to recognize where elements of confusion intrude and assess those elements against alternative sources of information—including archaeological data—that provide contexts for more accurate reconstruction of the events that gave rise to bewildered assessments and associated decision-making.

If there was ever a historical episode in which archaeology might offer a better understanding of texts and the cultural perspectives on which they are based, the Narváez expedition surely qualifies. Even so, we face a problem owing to the scanty nature of the archaeological record: there is very little direct material evidence of the Narváez entrada, and even that evidence must be interpreted cautiously because of the absence of any clear associations of artifacts with specific activities or events. In this essay, we offer a general overview of the kinds of archaeological evidence generated by these early expeditions, review some examples of how that evidence has been assessed thus far, and summarize what we have and have not been able to say about early Spanish explorations in La Florida. Our primary focus then moves to the coastal and interior regions of southeastern North America, where we have the best archaeological information to place alongside expedition records. Doing so enables us to offer summary conclusions on what further archaeological study may contribute to our understanding of the Narváez entrada.

The Archaeology of Entradas

Let's summarize a few basic points that derive from research to date on the topic of early Spanish entradas (Mathers; Mathers et al.; Milanich and Milbrath; D. Thomas). First, it is possible to identify a series of artifacts—including beads, brass harness bells, and metal tools, weapons, and other personal items—that are diagnostic of this era. It is important to recognize that diagnostic artifacts tend to discriminate only between earlier (before 1560) and later (after 1560) periods, so it is often difficult to use these items to identify specific expeditions that took place within close time frames, especially if they followed overlapping travel routes, as is the case with the Narváez and Hernando de Soto entradas and Cabeza de Vaca's uncertain route to the West (Smith, "European Materials" and "Chronology"; Little; Mitchem, "Initial Spanish-Indian Contact" and "Artifacts").

For the earlier, pre-1560 period, which is of primary concern here, the diagnostic artifacts include Nueva Cádiz beads, faceted chevron beads, striped olive-shaped beads in various colors, brass harness bells, coins, and a limited variety of metal tools, implements, and weapons. Nueva Cádiz beads are elongated tube beads with a square cross section and are opaque blue in color; these have been found only on contact-era sites from before 1550 (Deagan 163; Smith and Good 10–11; Mitchem, "Initial Spanish-Indian Contact" 52 and "Artifacts" 102). Faceted chevron beads are another type of drawn tube bead with layers of different-colored glass; they are oblong in shape but have ground facets. Chevron beads with blue, white, red, and green layers with a pale green inner layer have been found at several pre-1560s archaeological sites across the Southeast, some of which can be associated with the Soto entrada (Smith and Good 46–50; Mitchem "Contact" 52–56; "Artifacts" 107). Brass harness bells were brought to the New World by early Spanish and later French explorers and colonists (Brown, "Historic Trade Bells"). One variety, known as Clarksdale bells, are also associated with pre-1560s archaeological sites. These feature two hemispheres joined at the equator with a square flange, a wide loop attached through a slot in the upper hemisphere and soldered onto the interior surface, and two holes connected by a slit in the lower hemisphere (I. Brown, "Bells" 204). According to Jeffrey Brain (129–30), beads and bells constituted the primary set of goods presented to indigenous groups by Spanish conquistadores. Other items found at archaeological sites dating to this period include coins; knives, scissors, chisels, and other tools made of iron; and sundry beads, disks, pendants, bracelets, and other objects fashioned from brass, copper, silver, and (more rarely) gold.

Next, ongoing studies suggest that archaeological materials may be the product of different circumstances. Single or small groups of objects lost or discarded along the way are sometimes identified but are virtually impossible to link with specific events or entradas. In other words, these isolated finds identify little more than the presence, possibly only somewhere in the vicinity rather than at the find spot, of early sixteenth-century Spaniards. More concentrated artifact scatters and related features (e.g., the remains of cooking fires) associated with travel camps offer a means to confirm inferred travel routes, but very few of those kinds of sites have been discovered in the Southeast—perhaps because of their ephemeral nature—and none have been linked so far with the Narváez entrada prior to its final encampment at the Bay of Horses along the Florida Gulf Coast (chs. 8 and 9 in Cabeza de Vaca's *Naufragios*).

Finally, we do have documentary information for locations—typically at or adjacent to Native American villages—where expeditionary forces camped for weeks or months during the winter seasons. One example is Soto's 1539 winter camp at the Native town of Anhaica in the Apalachee region located in modern Tallahassee, Florida (Ewen and Hann). Soto's forces remained at this location for five months, a comparatively extensive amount of time. Excavations at that site produced artifacts providing reasonably good attribution to the Soto entrada, supported in part by the presence of bones from pigs that Soto brought along, in contrast to the porcine-free travels of Narváez and Cabeza de Vaca through the same province.[1] Beyond anchoring the Soto expedition at Anhaica during the winter of 1539, these finds offered little information about the Apalachee Indians; inferences were limited to a tighter chronological frame for locally produced ceramics and the conclusion that the Apalachee community did, in fact, persist several decades after the encounter with the Soto expedition with little evidence of outward change (110–11). But these examples are rare, and the sites of other important interactions between early Spanish conquerors and Native Americans remain elusive. One example is Mabila, thought to be located in central Alabama, where Soto's forces engaged in an extensive battle with warriors allied to a powerful leader named Tascalusa (for more information, see Knight). Since the Narváez entrada spent only two months trekking through Florida, from the time of its landing to its arrival at the Bay of Horses, sites of long-term, intensive occupation will not be part of the archaeological record attributed to them.

Much earlier scholarship examining the material traces of early Spanish exploration in La Florida focused on the topic of reconstructing travel routes and identifying Native communities at which significant events took place (e.g., Swanton). The relationship between travel routes and Native community locations is complicated not only by geographic ambiguities inherent in the accounts but also by the fact that names ascribed to indigenous communities in the sixteenth century bore little, if any, relation to the names of better-known tribes of the seventeenth century and thereafter. More recent studies, begun during the 1980s by Charles Hudson and his colleagues, have brought refined methods of textual examination to the assessment of those accounts, adding to a larger and better understood body of archaeological information. This approach enabled more accurate reconstructions of the social geography of the sixteenth-century Southeast (Hudson, *Juan Pardo* and *Knights*; Hudson and Tesser; Ethridge and Hudson). These studies pave the way for examination of related topics, including indigenous actions in response to Europeans, from which we glean at least some elements of Native perspectives.

For example, assemblages of metal artifacts from the Stark Farm site in northwestern Mississippi, many of which can be ascribed to the Soto entrada, bear evidence of intentional modification and use wear consistent with incorporation into indigenous technologies for accomplishing day-to-day tasks (Boudreaux et al., "Early Contact Period"; Legg et al.). In this case, it becomes clear that the acquisition, modification, and use of European tools and raw materials by indigenous communities were organized around principles of adaptation and persistence rather than abrupt and negative change. In a survey of the archaeological contexts in which sixteenth-century artifacts have been excavated across the Southeast, Marvin Smith and David Hally have been able to infer a series of mechanisms by which indigenous communities acquired those objects, including Spanish gifting of select items to indigenous leaders, barter, trophy taking in battle, theft, and scavenging at abandoned Spanish encampments (209). These inferences provide useful hints about indigenous agency in the context of first encounters with Europeans and also point to the role of preexisting indigenous trade and exchange systems in distributing European goods far beyond the places of initial acquisition (Worth; cf. Rodning). Smith and Hally also suggest that, in addition to being incorporated within mundane technological systems, goods acquired from Spanish conquistadores sometimes became incorporated into indigenous cultural frameworks as prestige goods, as emblems of leadership institutions or status and identity projections, and as objects to be celebrated with reference to their life histories and acquired symbolic values (209–13). While these studies are only beginning to deepen our understanding of indigenous perspectives on, and responses to, encounters with Europeans, they suggest considerable prospects for future study. But, as Dennis Blanton convincingly argues, new insights developed along these lines will only be possible when we are able to evaluate artifact assemblages (rather than isolated objects) derived from carefully excavated and well-understood archaeological contexts (100).

Despite the advances reflected in these and other recent studies, the archaeological record of early Spanish entradas in the Southeast remains problematic. As mentioned, it is often difficult to link diagnostic artifacts with specific expeditions. It is even more difficult to link archaeological evidence to specific events, though one exception is reflected in evidence—in the form of a radiocarbon-dated post remnant—for a wooden cross erected on a mound by members of the Soto expedition at the principal town of Casqui, now preserved as Parkin Archeological State Park in eastern Arkansas. And we are only beginning to explore the better-contextualized artifact assemblages that provide more robust indications of indigenous responses to European exploration and its aftermath (see, e.g., some of the ongoing studies reported in Boudreaux et al., *Contact*).[2] Even so, current investigations of Native American and European contact and interaction that have been stimulated by the works of Hudson and his collaborators have brought many advances in our knowledge. Even if our understanding of microscale, event-specific interactions requires much additional scrutiny, there is now a much better understanding of larger-scale topics—including the geographic distribution and cultural variability of indigenous communities, processes of cultural transformation that led ultimately to the emergence of well-documented tribes and nations of the seventeenth century and thereafter, and the multilayered agency of indigenous communities in catalyzing those transformations (Ethridge, "Differential Responses"). It is from this cautionary but hopeful vantage that we turn now to the question of what archaeology can tell us about the colonial misadventures of Cabeza de Vaca and his companions.

The Archaeology of Narváez and Cabeza de Vaca in La Florida

To guide our review of archaeological evidence associated with the Narváez entrada and Cabeza de Vaca's journey, we examine the overland portion of the trek from the landing and disembarkation on the Florida coast to the party's return to the coast two months later, where the Spaniards built five rafts at the Bay of Horses (chs. 3 to 9 in Cabeza de Vaca's *Naufragios*) for the anticipated journey along the coast to the target destination of Santisteban del Puerto, near the mouth of the Pánuco River along the Mexican coast. We find the "Commentary on the Narváez Expedition Accounts" provided in volume 2 of Rolena Adorno and Patrick Charles Pautz's work *Álvar Núñez Cabeza de Vaca* to be the most useful source for this review (2: 43–142).

In return for more than two decades of service in the Indies (though not without controversy; see Adorno and Pautz 2: 3–16), Emperor Charles V in 1526 granted Narváez a contract to explore and colonize lands in La Florida extending eastward from the Río de las Palmas to the Florida Peninsula. He was awarded the titles of adelantado of those lands but was to personally bear the cost of the expedition. Cabeza de Vaca was appointed second in command as *alguacil mayor* (chief law enforcement official) and treasurer. In keeping with Spanish colonization agendas, Narváez's hope was to conquer La Florida and administer its colonization, and Narváez expected to amass great wealth and political power (see also Marrinan et al.).

When the ships carrying Narváez and his forces sighted land along the west coast of the Florida Peninsula, the expedition leaders actually thought they were sailing along the Mexican coast, somewhere in the vicinity of the Pánuco and Las Palmas rivers, on the opposite side of the Gulf of Mexico from where they actually had sailed (Adorno and Pautz 2: 75). While it is fascinating, on the one hand, to contemplate how completely lost Narváez and his pilot found themselves, on the other hand, this circumstance portends how we must approach the accounts of their subsequent actions. That is, the motivations prompting crucial decisions were often, if not always, based on the interplay between misinformation and fanciful imagination. What can archaeology tell us about the consequences of those perilous calculations?

Anchoring on 14 April 1528 at the "mouth of a bay" ("boca de una baía"; 1: 33; 32; ch. 2), where a nearby Indian village could be seen, Narváez established his first base camp. Examination of adjacent stretches of the coast led to the discovery of another, nearby bay to which the camp was moved. The landing site remains uncertain, but somewhere in Tampa Bay along the west coast of the Florida Peninsula is perhaps most likely given the travel distance, the bifurcated configuration of Tampa Bay, and the circumstance that artifacts of pre-1560 Spanish origin—including both Nueva Cádiz and faceted chevron beads and Clarksdale bells—have been found at three sites (Weeki Wachee, Ruth Smith, and Tatham Mounds) north of Tampa Bay, the direction in which the land expedition eventually proceeded (2: 77–83; Mitchem, "Artifacts").

From the Spaniards' base camp, initial explorations around the bay advanced tentatively, as expedition members began to comprehend the uncertainty of their location. This puzzlement, compounded by the absence of any signs of nearby Spanish settlements, gave rise to a series of questionable decisions that included dispatching one of the ships to search for the Pánuco River while the other ships remained offshore. Rather than waiting for the ship to return, Narváez continued his land exploration ever farther into uncharted territory, never again to see his ships. Consideration of interactions with indigenous villagers suggests a framework for understanding Narváez's fateful decision.

As soon as they landed, Narváez wasted little time attempting to engage with the local Indians. These interactions were constrained, though, by lack of an ability to converse in ways permitting accurate exchange of information. Attempts to inquire about the presence of other Spaniards, where gold or food might be found, and similar topics proved frustrating. This convinced Cabeza de Vaca, at least, of the perils of further travel under such circumstances (ch. 4). It is likely that gifting or bartering involving Spanish goods took place, but on balance these encounters left Cabeza de Vaca with the impression that the Spaniards were considered unwelcome by the local inhabitants (Adorno and Pautz 2: 85–86). These encounters also suggest the creation of, at best, an ephemeral archaeological signature marking the outset of the Narváez entrada. But the Spaniards were soon to discover something considerably more profound.

At one Native village visited during these early forays around the bay, Narváez and his men found several shipping crates from Castile (ch. 4). These contained dead bodies—the identities of which could not be determined—covered with painted deerskins. But pieces of linen cloth and plumes of European origin were also discovered in the village—which, after the Spaniards' uncertain questioning of the villagers, were attributed to another province, located farther to the north, called Apalachee (or Apalachen). Narváez took from this exchange two inferences: first, that they must indeed be close to the Río Pánuco and, second, that the Indians' identification of Apalachee as the source of Spanish goods could only be in reference to yet another fabled indigenous city filled with gold (Adorno and Pautz 2: 89–94). This sealed the decision to plunge headlong into the Florida wilderness, in search of a Native town comparable to Tenochtitlan, the sprawling Mexica city conquered only a decade earlier by Hernán Cortés, who at that time held Narváez in prison. What delicious revenge this would be for Narváez!

By this point, the expedition had divided into two groups: the overland contingent, led by Narváez and Cabeza de Vaca, and the ships left along the coast, which now had moved on in search of the Río de las Palmas. While the overland contingent, comprising about three hundred men, struck off in search of an indigenous city offering the prospect of great wealth, the maritime contingent focused on the more practical matter of determining exactly where in the Gulf of Mexico they had arrived.[3]

Heading off in a northerly direction, Narváez and Cabeza de Vaca led their group for two weeks through lands where they encountered no Indians and found very little food. Crossing a river—considered by modern scholars to be the Withlacoochee—they arrived at an Indian village where they camped for a few days. Believing the river to be either the Pánuco or Las Palmas, Cabeza de Vaca led a group to its mouth, hoping to locate their awaiting ships but discovering instead waters too shallow to serve as a harbor. Continuing, the Spaniards soon met an Indian named Dulchanchellin, to whom they presented "beads and bells and other items of exchange" ("cuentas y caxcaveles y otros rescates"; 1: 51, 50; ch. 5). Thought to belong to a group that was a rival of the Apalachee, Dulchanchellin and a few of his warriors led the Spaniards on to another river, probably the Suwannee. Upon crossing that river, Narváez and Cabeza de Vaca entered the province of Apalachee and discovered a town consisting of some forty houses and abundant quantities of maize. Modern scholars believe this to be the village of Ivitachuco, visited eleven years later by the Soto expedition (Marrinan 74). The Spaniards remained at that location for nearly a month.

What can we say about the archaeology of the Narváez entrada from its departure at Tampa Bay to its arrival at Apalachee province? Believing that it was moving in the direction of the Las Palmas and Pánuco Rivers and knowing that Spanish settlements had been established a short distance upstream from the rivers' mouth, Narváez and Cabeza de Vaca led their men along a route tracking not very far from the coast, thus avoiding contact with the more densely settled interior regions of the Florida Peninsula. The Spaniards typically overnighted at locations where no gifting of goods or bartering with Indians was documented and where we can therefore anticipate the creation of only ephemeral material traces associated with the march and the camps. None, so far, have been found. The few days spent at the Indian village just beyond their first river crossing could have produced more pronounced evidence, but such has not been found by modern archaeologists. The archaeology of this part of the expedition remains as hazy as Narváez's and Cabeza de Vaca's understanding of their developing circumstances.

During their stay in the Apalachee village, tensions built and culminated in the killing of a Mexican Indian, named Don Pedro, brought along by one of the Spanish friars. This prompted a decision to depart and follow a nearby river flowing south toward the coast (ch. 7), which is thought to be the Saint Marks River. The route led the Narváez party nine days later to a village named Aute (chs. 7 and 8), which Jeffrey Mitchem suggests was located along the Wakulla River at the Work Place archaeological site (Mitchem, "Artifacts" 101).

The St. Marks National Wildlife Refuge Cemetery is located a short distance downstream from the Work Place site. Plundered by local relic hunters, the St. Marks cemetery yielded impressive quantities of silver disc beads as well as other perforated discs made of brass, gold, and silver; brass Clarksdale bells; and glass beads including striped olive-shaped beads, faceted chevron beads, and Nueva Cádiz beads (Mitchem, "Artifacts" 101–02). The St. Marks site may have served as the burial grounds for local villages including Aute, and the nearby Marsh Island Mound—which also yielded an array of European artifacts—might have had a similar function. The burial contexts that produced most of these artifacts suggest that the use of the cemetery extended over a long period, and furthermore it cannot be ruled out that some of these materials could have been salvaged by the Indians from offshore shipwrecks rather than being acquired through direct interaction with Spaniards. Even so, these materials constitute the best evidence for the presence of Narváez expedition members (Marrinan et al. 76–77; Mitchem, "Artifacts" 101; Mitchem "Initial Spanish-Indian Contact").

At Aute, the Spaniards suffered attacks by the Indians as well as illness, which affected many men, including Narváez. Departing that location, the group made a one-day journey to a coastal bay that had been discovered by an exploratory party sent out from the main group. At this point in the entrada, no wealthy indigenous cities had been discovered, and no valuables had been seized. No ships awaited the group just offshore. And, now two months into the expedition, uncertainty as to the group's whereabouts remained. As a consequence of these circumstances, priorities shifted from conquest and colonization to survival and escape. A member of the contingent who was a carpenter suggested that the group build rafts for sailing along the coast, and over the next two months the survivors constructed five rafts, sufficient to transport the remaining men and their supplies (ch. 8). During this interval, the expedition members survived on rations of horsemeat, generating a scatter of skeletal remains, after which that portion of the coast came to be known as the Bay of Horses. Maize seized at Aute was ground using stone mortars and saved for provisioning the rafts.

Beyond the Bay of Horses

The raft voyage itself left very little material evidence. When the raft commanded by Téllez and Peñalosa made for the shoreline, Camones Indians killed the crew and then collected all their possessions for trade with interior neighbors. The distribution of such materials along that section of the Texas coast thus reflects indigenous exchange networks rather than the presence of Spanish survivors (Adorno and Pautz 2: 183–84).

On the other hand, Cabeza de Vaca and his companions did engage in occasional trade with various Indian communities along the Texas coast to acquire food or other necessities as they slowly made their way in the direction of the Pánuco River. Cabeza de Vaca tells us that he became a merchant while living among the Charruco Indians after leaving Malhado Island (ch. 16). The goods traded included raw materials or finished goods that constituted the material culture of the indigenous inhabitants of the region. Some items obtained along the coast had value among interior communities, including mussel shells and mollusk or whelk shells. Interior materials valued by coastal groups included animal hides, chert or flint, and mineral pigments. Deer hair spun into thread, cordage, or decorative tassels incorporated into a wide range of woven items also appeared in the inventory of the Spaniard's trade goods assemblages. All these items reflect indigenous production and activity systems.

Cabeza de Vaca also incorporated a variety of ritualized performances into his behavioral repertoire. Surely these developed over time to correspond to indigenous religious belief and practices related to a range of outcomes, including healing and ritual interaction with the spirit world. These activities appear to have abetted the Spaniards' abilities to survive long episodes of captivity, as well as passage from one indigenous community to the next, by conferring on the conquistadores an aura as powerful beings. To the extent that these performances might have incorporated a material component, it is again likely if not certain that any such items would have represented indigenous ritual apparatus.

In sum, any material component reflecting the journey by Cabeza de Vaca and his companions from the Malhado landing to the Río Petatlán in Sinaloa six years later, where they were met by Diego de Alcaraz, will be difficult to detect archaeologically, despite the fascinating events that unfolded during this time, as examined elsewhere in this volume.

This brief review of archaeological sites and materials attributable to the Narváez entrada and Cabeza de Vaca's journey indicates, above all, that very little archaeological evidence can be linked to their travels. And of the extant evidence, almost none possesses a contextual association with specific events presented in the documentary record. Even so, a few projections can be made.

Cabeza de Vaca's account suggests that it may be worthwhile to consider a dichotomous framework for organizing and assessing new archaeological evidence. First is the portion of the entrada extending from the Tampa Bay disembarkation to Aute, during which the expedition members' actions were motivated by cultural frameworks reflecting principles of exploration and conquest. A subsequent episode of misfortune at Aute compelled the Spaniards to flee toward the coast. At this point, the cultural framework for decision-making shifted to one embracing principles of retreat and survival. If sufficient evidence accrues, it may be interesting and useful to compare the archaeology of exploration to the archaeology of survival. And in this case, the archaeology of exploration is furthermore complicated by the recognition that much of the day-to-day decision-making was based on imagined projections of a successful conquest of a wealthy indigenous community. In contrast to those expectations and to the realities experienced by many other exploratory adventures, Cabeza de Vaca's journey to the West offers no prospect of studying the archaeology of conquest.

Another topic for future investigation concerns the nature of the Spaniards' interactions with indigenous communities. There is presently very little to go on, but the textual record of interactions with indigenous people at Tampa Bay, the Withlacoochee River, Apalachee, and Aute suggests interesting prospects for the discovery of additional archaeological evidence. Studies of the much richer archaeological records associated with the Soto and Pardo expeditions document a wide range of Spanish and Native American interactions and responses (e.g., Hudson, *Knights*; Ethridge, *From Chicaza*). Responses by Indians interacting with Soto's forces ranged from peaceful accommodation and attempts to win Spanish alliance in support of indigenous objectives, to avoidance and other efforts to minimize interaction, to outright resistance to Spanish incursions, resulting in episodes of pitched warfare. As evidenced in the examples summarized in this essay, the results of these interactions for indigenous communities ranged from benign to transformative to destructive; in contrast, the Spaniards' experiences ranged from being barely tolerated to facing outright hostility and resistance. As future investigations expand our understanding of the archaeology of the Narváez expedition, it will be interesting to develop such comparisons with other expeditionary examples.

NOTES

1. In outfitting his expedition while in Cuba, Soto assembled horses for transportation, pigs for food, and dogs as a weapon against the Indians. Domestic animals are reservoirs for a variety of pathogens that can affect humans, and of the animals Soto brought to La Florida the pigs were most likely to transmit diseases to Indians, including anthrax, brucellosis, leptospirosis, tuberculosis, trichinosis, and taeniasis and cysticercosis (Ramenofsky and Galloway).

2. Especially relevant are the contribution by Boudreaux and colleagues on early contact-era archaeological sites in northeast Mississippi (*Contact*), Blanton's comparative study of sixteenth-century artifact assemblages in the Southeast, Worth's insightful review of the materiality of sixteenth-century Spanish presence in Florida and its implications for indigenous socioeconomic systems, Gougeon's reconstruction of the structure and organization of indigenous Gulf Coast communities relative to their interactions with Spanish conquistadores, the examination by Shreve and colleagues of the persistence of indigenous agency in eastern Tennessee, and Ethridge's comparative assessment of differential responses to Europeans across the Southeast ("Differential Responses").

3. Goodwin documents what happened to the group that remained on the ships ("De lo que sucedió").

North American Space in the *Relación*

Vanina M. Teglia

This essay examines the representation of geographic space in Cabeza de Vaca's *Relación* and the elusive map of North America that it contains. Although the lack of geographic details and the absence of any overarching organization in the text means that it resists any reliable mapping of the lands traversed by the author, the geographic information provided was what legitimized his text as a valuable one for the Conquest. Indeed, the *Relación* is still read today in history, literature, geography, anthropology, and other areas as one of the first Spanish chronicles of the Indies, referring to North America. Hence, this analysis proves valuable for elucidating the possible meanings of its geographic references. First, this essay situates the *Relación* within the genre of travel literature, the narrative axis of which privileges space over time. Cabeza de Vaca's text, however, like many maps of the American mainland from the period, offers only a vague representation of the inland territory. Second, I explore four issues related to geography and space in the *Relación* that provide for rich discussion in the classroom: first, how the men in Pánfilo de Narváez's expedition miscalculated their course and ended up in La Florida as their first stop, even though the king had ordered it to be the last; second, the extent to which the travelers interpreted the inland through a combination of their European imaginaries—rooted in the archives of myth and religion—and the indigenous perspectives they encountered in their journey; third, the connection between the reversal of the survivors' subalternity in the Native communities and the unexpected deviation from the intended route to Mexico; and, finally, the question as to why the geographic descriptions of North America in the *Relación* are so imprecise.

Students typically love maps, and they recognize the places on them, much more so than events listed on time lines. It is difficult to imagine, for example, a poster of a historical time line hanging on the wall of a student's room, yet maps are a common decoration. In my experience teaching Latin American literature to students at the University of Buenos Aires since 2007, I have come to the conclusion that reading Cabeza de Vaca's *Relación* centers on identifying the geographic spaces traversed by the four survivors, despite how scarce the geographic references in the text may be. This is why the editors of recent published editions of the work have included hypothetical maps of the survivors' route from Tampa Bay to what today is northern Mexico. Moreover, in my 2013 edition of the text, I found it necessary to devote almost half the critical prologue to analyzing the description of space in the text and the geographic references, both literal and allegorical (Cabeza de Vaca, *Naufragios* [Teglia]). In the second volume of their monumental edition of the *Relación*, Rolena Adorno and Patrick Charles Pautz have made an enormous effort to annotate geographic references based on educated guesses. To complement this effort, in this essay, I trace the subjective and cultural (European and indigenous) perceptions of space contained in the *Relación*, including the validating function that spatial references had in travel writings of the time.

In texts by conquistadores, such as the *Relación*, there was a broad geographic curiosity that was no doubt linked to the emergent knowledge of the American continent and to the spaces of the *plus ultra*.[1] This general epistemological concern for space in the royal institutions of Spain led officials to place cartography and geography at the center of their agenda—so much so that travel writing, which proliferated throughout the period of European expansion, was marked by the syntax of the path[2] and privileged the representation of space over the narration of experiences organized by time. The chronotope of the path is the dominant element in the travel narratives of sixteenth-century transatlantic voyages. I have yet to see any text or document from the Indies, other than Christopher Columbus's *Diario* (*Journal*) as summarized by Bartolomé de las Casas (*Historia de las Indias* 1: 182–374; chs. 35–86), in which geographic references are subordinated to the temporal organization of the story. This means that these texts split and weave their narrative episodes according to their geographic points of reference, whether or not these spatial anchorings have any basis in the physical space in which they are, so to speak, grounded.

All this means that university students will be able to approach the plot of the *Relación* and differentiate its narrative parts only if they first manage to identify the spaces to which the narrative refers. Cabeza de Vaca's *Relación* is exemplary of the ways in which sixteenth-century chronicles subordinate their temporality to the spatial axis, and the story moves through the following places: Sanlúcar de Barrameda, Santo Domingo, Cuba, Florida, Tampa Bay, Aute (the land of the Apalache), Malhado Island (Galveston Bay), areas near the Colorado River or the Rio Grande (Río Bravo), the Llano River, the Uto-Aztecan territories, Sinaloa, Culiacán, Mexico, Veracruz, Havana, the Azores, and Lisbon.[3] However, there are three issues linked to space that differentiate the *Relación* from the rest of the chronicles of the Indies: first, the Spaniards head inland and venture far from the coasts; second, there is no reference to any significant indigenous city inland; and, third, the text—though often assumed to be geographically authoritative—is imprecise when identifying the places visited by the survivors.

A great part of Western travel writing, including sixteenth-century chronicles of the Indies, tells stories about maritime and fluvial travel. Conquistadores sailed along coastlines and navigated great rivers, founding cities along the shores. This is true of the chronicles referring to the islands of the Antilles; the coasts of Central America, Brazil, Peru, and California; the basins of the Amazon, the Mississippi, the Paraná, and other rivers; and the Strait of Magellan. That is to say, the chronicles of the Indies create a sort of portolano chart, which describes the movement of ships from port to port. Other chronicles, by contrast, relate the experience of traveling to great pre-Columbian cities. Examples include the journeys of Hernán Cortés and the conquest of the Incan Empire and the territories of Nueva Granada. In the case of the *Relación*, however, we find the narration of a journey inland through a space described as deserted and infertile and lacking any large indigenous settlements.

Despite the centrality of the theme of geography in the organization of the *Relación*, its descriptions do not permit a clear identification of the places to which they refer (Adorno and Pautz 2: 38). After the Narváez expedition's brief stops in Hispaniola and Cuba, and upon its arrival in Florida, the first stop in Tierra Firme (Mainland) territory, the issue of geography starts to get murky. Geographic observations repeat the same vague features for different places—for example, "thick woods" ("espresso monte"; 1: 55; 54; ch. 6), a place where there were "forty houses" ("quarenta casas"; 1: 55; 54; ch. 6; 207; 206; ch. 29), a scarcely described bay, and so on.[4] The same can be said about indigenous groups inhabiting these lands: the people and their customs are described in vague terms and never clearly identified.[5] Adding to this geographic uncertainty, Miruelo, the master pilot in charge of guiding Narváez's expedition along the Florida Peninsula, becomes disoriented near Tampa Bay, marking the beginning of the widespread geographic confusion that will lead the Spaniards to failure as they become lost conquerors in terra incognita.

Although there was scant knowledge of American geography in Europe, early transatlantic travel and the conquest of the Americas can be characterized as a moment of glory for cartography and for the chroniclers, conquistadores, and captains who were sent to the West Indies and who drew maps or commissioned them. Yet any map derived from the *Relación* would be incomplete, its statements about space would be no more than conjectures, and it would prove unable to guide and inform the user. Thus, in the classroom, it is useful for students to observe—or, better yet, draw—maps that represent North America in a hypothetical way. Students can be referred to beautiful maps easily accessible on the Internet:

Pietro Martire d'Anghiera. *Map of the Caribbean Area*. [1511], Sidney R. Knafel Map Collection, Phillips Academy, Andover, Massachusetts. *Digital Commonwealth*, ark.digitalcommonwealth.org/ark:/50959/hq37vv30f.

Diogo Ribero. *Carta vniversal en que se contiene todo lo que del Mundo se a descubi[erto] fasta aora. Die beiden ältesten General-Karten von Amerika: Ausgeführt in den Jahren 1527 und 1529 auf Befehl Kaiser Karl's V,* Klassik Stiftung Weimar, 1860. *Herzogin Anna Amalia Bibliothek*, nbn-resolving.org/urn:nbn:de:gbv:32-1-10012566072.

Giovanni Battista Ramusio. *La carta universale della terra ferma e Isole delle Indie occidental*. 1534, John Carter Brown Library Map Collection, Brown U, Providence, Rhode Island. *The JCB Library*, jcb.lunaimaging.com/luna/servlet/s/z2c578.

Battista Agnese. *Atlas*. 1544. *Biblioteca Digital Hispánica*, bdh.bne.es/bnesearch/detalle/bdh0000023260.

Sébastian Cabot. *Mapamundi.* 1544. *Bibliothèque Nationale de France*, gallica.bnf.fr/ark:/12148/btv1b55011003p.

Girolamo Ruscelli. *Nueva Hispania Tabula Nova.* 1561, Libraries Special Collections, U of Texas, Arlington. *UTA Libraries*, libguides.uta.edu/ld.php?content_id=931789.

Diego Gutiérrez, *Americae sive quartae orbis partis nova et exactissima descriptio*.1562, Lessing J. Rosenwald Collection, Library of Congress, Washington, DC. *Library of Congress*, lccn.loc.gov/map49000970.

Diogo Homem. *Atlas Universal.* 1565, National Library of Russia, St. Petersburg. *Instituto Geográfico Nacional*, www.ign.es/web/catalogo-cartoteca/resources/html/031683.html.

This is a useful sample of European cartographic knowledge about Central and North America and their rivers, coasts, vegetation, fertile lands, and animals. Despite Europe's great interest in exploring and exploiting the overseas territories, these maps evidence the general lack of European knowledge about America, a contributing factor to the disorientation of the survivors of Narváez's party. The conquistadores were misinformed and lost even before they set foot in Florida. For example, they believed that the distances in the Gulf of Mexico were shorter than they actually are, and therefore they miscalculated the time it would take to reach Pánuco (today Tampico). When examining these maps, students will surely be interested in their representations of mythical creatures and fantastical elements along with ethnographic, natural, and topographic representations. Gutiérrez's 1562 map is exemplary in this respect, in that it includes sea monsters resembling whales, apes, sea horses, mermaids, flying fish, snake-like rivers, Indians with bows and arrows, cannibals, giants, and even Neptune himself in the Atlantic Ocean. Cartography—and in this case teratological cartography—can pedagogically illustrate the fantastical geography of the *Relación* as well as the interpretations of events marked by mythological and biblical symbolism, as discussed below.

Now that we have differentiated the *Relación* from other chronicles of the Indies, let's focus on four issues that are linked to geographic and spatial aspects of the work and that can be discussed in the classroom. As discussed in the sections below, scholars have worked on these questions, but the biogeography of the *Relación* remains elusive. Instructors can ask undergraduate and graduate students to discuss these topics, contrasting textual descriptions, information, and maps obtained from updated digital platforms as well as their own travel experiences.

"Small" Miscalculations

The first issue is why Narváez's expedition went to Florida instead of to the Río de las Palmas (now Soto la Marina River) as had been anticipated by the capitulation or contract with the Crown (*capitulación*).[6] The Río de las Palmas and its banks, closer to Nueva España (Mexico), were better known to conquerors and colonizers than Florida was. Because of the overwhelming number of storms that occurred in the northern region of the Gulf of Mexico at that time, as the text succinctly states (Adorno and Pautz 1: 26–33; chs. 1–2), the party sought refuge by heading to Havana but then ended up in Florida, probably involuntarily. There are several interpretations that could suggest why the final itinerary was the reverse of what was expected, since the text is not clear on this point.

Adorno and Pautz interpret the episode as a deviation from the course, due to storms and hurricanes, which Narváez's men thought they could correct. However, doing so was ultimately impossible considering the master pilot's miscalculations. Adorno and Pautz infer that, after approximately fifty days of travel, the crew must have believed that on 12 April 1528 they had indeed reached the west side of the Gulf of Mexico near the mouths of the Río Pánuco and the Río de las Palmas (2: 71, 73–75). Although Cabeza de Vaca's text does not mention this miscalculation or the corresponding disorientation, this was presumably the reason the Spaniards were trying to reach the Pánuco as if it were around the corner and adjacent to the Florida Peninsula.

Sylvia Molloy also interprets the arrival in Florida as unexpected for Narváez's party. But she focuses instead on the fact that the itinerary of Cabeza de Vaca's text is the reverse of the royal mandate: that is, the group traveled from an unknown and peripheral place to a place that was already part of Christendom (429). Although neither Molloy nor other scholars of the *Relación* explicitly dwell on the possibility that this unexpected direction was the result of disobedience on the part of Narváez, I propose that the text does allow for such a reading. The text attests to Narváez's recklessness, alleging his rampant lack of responsibility, disloyalty, refusal to immediately resume the itinerary anticipated by the *capitulación*, and the resulting failure of the expedition. Or so argues Cabeza de Vaca; none of the other witnesses to the debate about disembarking in Florida lived to tell the story. Narváez's incompetence and betrayal can be seen in the shipwrecks in the Gulf of Mexico; in the decision to search for the land of Apalache once it was known that the group was not on the Río de las Palmas; in the captain's decision to abandon his crew between the mouth of the Mississippi River and Galveston Bay, leaving them to their fate; and in his earlier failure, back in Castille, to listen to the warnings of a Moorish woman from Hornachos who had allegedly predicted the fate of the expedition before Narváez and his men set sail.

At the same time, and returning to Molloy's reading, the notion of *revés* ("backward" or "upside down") is at the core of the text and allows Cabeza de Vaca to arrange all the wrong and disloyal decisions of the man who had been his captain into a paradoxical but consistent plot. It is clear that throughout this journey the crew was at the mercy of the unknown geography and had no sense of where they were. Moreover, after Narváez relinquished his command, near the mouth of the Mississippi, the party also lost its captain.

American Geography with European-Indian Baggage

The second issue linked to space that often puzzles editors and longtime researchers of Cabeza de Vaca (such as Barrera López, Pupo-Walker, and Adorno and Pautz, among others) even to this day concerns certain comments about Florida in chapter 7 that the 1555 Valladolid edition titles "Of the character of the land" ("De la manera que es la tierra"; Adorno and Pautz 1: 57; 56). This is the only chapter in this edition that has a title specifically referring to space and, metonymically, to nature. In this section, more than in others, the narrator describes the geographic features of the land and its fauna. The chapter is found in the text immediately after the crew's disappointment at not finding the land of Apalache, which the Indians near the western coast of the Florida Peninsula had described as a city of infinite wealth. Cabeza de Vaca was referring to La Florida as a geographic entity that stretched from Tampa to Galveston, Texas, and beyond. This is a teaching opportunity to explore the meaning of *La Florida* in the sixteenth century vis-à-vis the state of Florida today. In this section of the *Relación*, the narrator describes traveling the Floridian Peninsula all the way to the southern edge of the Appalachian Mountains, where he and his men were between mid-April and September 1528.

In this section, there is a comment that perplexes editors and critics: "In that region it is very cold" ("Por allí la tierra es muy fría"; 1: 57; 56; ch. 7), which does not at all coincide with typical weather conditions of the area in the middle of the Caribbean summer (Cabeza de Vaca, *Naufragios* [Teglia] 81n43; Adorno and Pautz 2: 135–36). Furthermore, it is surprising how hungry the travelers were in that fertile and plentiful region. Indeed, the narrator follows up one such comment about hunger with a description of the abundance of the land and the variety of species there: "There are many good pastures for grazing cattle. There are birds of many types" ("Tiene muy buenos pastos para ganados. Ay aves de muchas maneras"; 1: 57; 56). All this makes Molloy think that the geographic information provided in the *Relación* "shifts" ("traslada"; my trans.; 432) along with the changes Cabeza de Vaca undergoes in different cultural contexts: from being a subordinate in Narváez's expedition to a captive of the Indians, from a self-described slave to a merchant, and, later, as a leading shaman among indigenous communities. Space and nature, in this way, are vital extensions of the different identities assumed by the protagonist.

Moreover, the description of space usually accompanies, in a coded way, the moods described by the narrator. The descriptions of fertility and abundance in the Florida Peninsula correspond to the optimistic search for the riches of Apalache, but the narrator figuratively frames the characters in poverty and coldness once they become disillusioned by this failed quest. Paying attention in the classroom to these striking, unsettling representations of the landscape sheds light on another important issue: in the sixteenth century, narratives described space with a variety of codes and rhetorical devices that were not always realistic and that were related to medieval and Renaissance discourses. For example, according to the theory of the antipodes, the traveler would have found the world upside down when moving away from home. and in those distant regions would find soulless beings, monsters and unfamiliar landscapes. In other myths, the symbols and allegories were Christian. In narratives with biblical intertextual references, desert spaces and fertile spaces are used to metaphorically frame the states of the characters. The symbolic meaning of every space (in Christian texts) enables a moral and allegorical reading of each episode of Cabeza de Vaca's *Relación*.

The instructor can introduce the analysis of the codification of space: its cultural and rhetorical traditions, the effects of literal and symbolic readings, and, most important, the ways in which these codifying practices change throughout history. In this way, when Cabeza de Vaca's narrative refers to the sea, the forest or jungle, and the desert, students can first notice and then research the evident codifications coming from various traditions. Many of them were medieval traditions transformed in the fifteenth and sixteenth centuries by the narratives of the transatlantic voyages. In understanding the figuration of North American and Caribbean places alluded to in the *Relación*, it would be necessary to observe how certain Spanish, and more broadly Western, medieval and modern topographical codifications collided with particular American and indigenous beliefs.

As far back as the *Aeneid*, representations of episodes at sea have tended to resort to the topoi of shipwrecks: the cries and confusion of the passengers, the pounding of the waves at night, the rumbling of thunder, the cargo falling overboard, the feelings of horror as well as compassion in those onboard, the misery of their tormented bodies, and their solace and resignation (Herrero-Massari 206). For students, as for anyone, these clichés are clearly recognizable. Literary and popular culture provide many examples of shipwrecks and captains relinquishing their duties and abandoning their crew and passengers just as Narváez did on the Galveston coast. Literary productions from the nineteenth century onward, as well as well-known television series and movies, cling to topoi of shipwrecks, pirates, and tsunamis.[7]

In the sixteenth century, setting sail on the high seas was considered a most risky venture. A century earlier, it appeared in one of the typologies of madness in Sebastian Brandt's 1494 *The Ship of Fools*. The classic trope of fortune usually appears associated with danger at sea, and Cabeza de Vaca mentions it in the *proemio* ("foreword") of the *Relación* (Adorno and Pautz 1: 16–17). Images of capsized boats and ships in the text were well-known allegories of reversals of fortune. This is why the Byzantine or Greek novel considered travel by sea and shipwreck as evidence of the stoicism and courage of the hero. Elsewhere, I have examined the intertextuality of this novelistic genre in the *Relación* in elements such as navigation as a source of adventure, narrative interpolation, the effect of intrigue, the absence of sexual references, the perfection and prudence of the characters, captivity, the transformation of the destiny of the protagonists, and venturing into unknown regions (Cabeza de Vaca, *Naufragios* [Teglia] 38–42).

The forest, for its part, appears in the *Relación* as fantastical. It is mentioned right before the travelers' arrival in Apalache and is only described and alluded to in the text through the words of the Indians. Among the dangers of the lush forest, there were *flechero* ("bellicose") Indians who besieged the Spaniards, swamps that were difficult to cross, and surprisingly giant trees that, felled to the ground probably by hurricanes, hindered the Spaniards on their journey. There, even the Native peoples looked like giants. Jacques Le Goff, among others, has described how, for the medieval knight, the forest represented a natural border, a no-man's-land replete with bandits and wild animals (*Civilización* 187). North American traditions symbolically transferred these Judeo-Christian attributes from the spaces of the forest and jungle to desolate spaces such as Alaska, the frontier regions between countries, and the internal border areas adjacent to Indian spaces, such as those in the Far West as well as Patagonia in South America.

Finally, the representation of the desert in the *Relación* is clearly codified by biblical allegories. Once the survivors have garnered fame and security as shamans, Cabeza de Vaca gets lost on his own and lives through an epiphanic episode in which he sees a burning tree. In the text, this symbolic moment reveals to him his upcoming salvation: the recovery of his life among Christians. The hagiography genre typically includes episodes narrated with the trope of characters wandering through deserts, a metaphor of the search for salvation. In this vein, the *Relación* narrates the final journey of the four survivors of Narváez's expedition through a metaphorical desert, drawing on tropes of the struggles of Christian pilgrims as well as the physical suffering and moral integrity of hermits. The instructor can point out that these tropes can also be found in apocalyptic literature, including films and television series, in which the main character—a kind of redeeming messiah—struggles along solitary and destructive paths because destiny has chosen that person to save their people.[8]

The indigenous conceptions of space that the text manages to capture deserve special mention. On the island of Cuba, in the midst of the hurricane that bore down on the expedition in the port of La Trinidad, Cabeza de Vaca narrates the areito of the natives that lasted all night until the storm stopped: "Walking along in this way we heard all night long, . . . much noise and a great clamor of voices, and the loud sounds of bells and flutes and tambourines and other instruments, all of which continued until the morning when the storm ceased" ("Andando en esto oímos toda la noche, . . . mucho estruendo y grande ruido de bozes, y gran sonido de cascaveles y de flautas y tamborinos y otros instrumentos que duraron hasta la mañana que la tormenta çessó"; Adorno and Pautz 1: 29; 28; ch. 1). Magical control of meteorological phenomena was probably a matter that interested the Caribbean Native peoples. These areitos, as reported by the chronicler, could be a stereotypical reference to indigenous magic and pagan customs and even to sorcery (suggesting that the indigenous peoples could have summoned the storm). The ritual caught the attention of Cabeza de Vaca, who describes it without knowing its meaning but intuits that it has something to do with living with nature in the New World.

In Florida, still under Narváez, the expedition went in search of the city of Apalache, after Native people living near Tampa Bay informed the Spaniards about riches nearby: "In addition, we found samples of gold. By means of signs we asked the Indians where those things had come from. They indicated to us by gestures that very far away from there there was a province called Apalachen, in which there was much gold" ("Hallamos también muestras de oro. Por señas preguntamos a los indios de adónde avían avido aquellas cosas. Señaláronnos que muy lexos de allí avía una provincia que se dezía Apalachen, en la qual avía mucho"; 1: 39; 38; ch. 4). Western and European mythical discourses informed the desire for the cities of gold. Moreover, the conquest of México-Tenochtitlan, only seven years prior, encouraged similar expectations in other conquistadores of encountering fantastically wealthy cities. Narváez was a direct competitor of Cortés's. While Indians most likely used their imagination to conjure up the rich land of Apalache to divert the conquistadores away from their own communities, it is possible to trace indigenous myths and practices in the descriptions included in Cabeza de Vaca's text. In contrast to Apalache, the rich land of the *tunas* (prickly pears) appears later in the narrative when the Mariame Indians—who probably lived near what today is called Matagorda Bay in Texas—refer to it in similar terms: "The best season that these people have is when they eat the prickly pears, because then they are not hungry, and they spend all their time dancing and eating them, night and day" ("El mejor tiempo que éstos tienen es quando comen las tunas, porque estonçes no tienen hambre y todo el tiempo se les pasa en bailar, y comen dellas de noche y de día"; 1: 143; 142; ch. 18). This indirect indigenous account of the place of the prickly pears is hyperbolic and fantastical, evocative of paradise. Later, Cabeza de Vaca reveals the real condition of the land: not bountiful at all and a far cry from that rosy picture painted by the indigenous people. Indeed, the narrator states that the prickly pears were not so abundant or of as high quality as the Mariames had suggested and that the fruit was available for just a few months of the year. However, and most important, the Native peoples' description shows how food-gathering cycles determined the seasonal movement of those groups. Further, it is evident that these indigenous food sites gave rise to mythical Indian ideas and to collective feelings in the communities, noted by Cabeza de Vaca as well as his shipmates and referred to in the *Relación*.

Wait! Where Were These Christians Going?

The third issue regarding the geographic interest of the *Relación* concerns the last part of the four survivors' journey. When they managed to escape from the Mariames (the prickly pear eaters), they began a rather accelerated two-year journey until they reached the land of Christians. Although there is no description of marine accidents nor are there any attempts to embark on self-made rafts to escape as they had done in Florida, the itinerary follows the shoreline until they turn inland. It is evident when the survivors are along the coast because the narrator describes not tall mountains but only a few sporadic and low hills and because they crossed wide rivers that were probably the deltas where the rivers flow into the sea. All this time, and even after crossing the river that was "as wide as that of Seville" ("tan ancho como el de Sevilla"; Adorno and Pautz 1: 195; 194; ch. 27), probably the Colorado River or the Rio Grande. These four Christians had already made a name for themselves as *físicos*—healers or shamans—among the Indians (1: 152, 154, 156). The path that the survivors took during their time with the Mariames and the Yguazes was, in part, negotiated with the different peoples they encountered. On repeated occasions, the indigenous people reportedly resisted being abandoned, which they demonstrated by means of prayers and cries, particularly when the four Christians went through the process of shamanization and, while still enslaved, when they were taken in by the Indian peoples to do their healing. Finally, the four managed to escape by taking advantage of the authority they asserted among the Indians and with the help of the women who trafficked products between indigenous communities in the region and who were able to act as guides for the survivors.

Once the four travelers could get away, they went inland, westward across the mountains. This is a turning point in the route as well as in the story: the survivors altered their path while they managed to completely escape from their situation of subalternity vis-à-vis the Native communities. Readers can venture different explanations for this change of direction. Adorno and Pautz, who have tried to unravel the route of the four survivors, point out that Cabeza de Vaca's narrative turns the men's struggle for survival into their search for the Pacific Ocean: "he naturalizes the choice of itinerary as though it had been planned all along: the only way to go was west, and the only way to arrive at the west was by going north" (2: 288–89).

The *Relación* succinctly explains that the four travelers decided to cross the mountains (Sierra de Pamoranes, in northern Tamaulipas) rather than continue along the coast to reach the Pánuco River because "[a]ll the people of the coast [Quevenes] are very bad" ("[t]oda la gente della es muy mala"; 1: 201; 200). Likewise, they chose not to climb the mountains, "at the near end of the sierras ("estavan a la punta de las sierras"), to the hilltop villages as their indigenous companion suggested, "because this was off our route" ("por ser fuera de nuestro camino"). Instead, as stated, they headed across the land to meet "better" people and Native communities: "because the people farther inland are of a better disposition and they treated us better, and we considered it certain that we would find the land more populated and with better means of sustenance" ("porque la gente [Avavares] que está más metida adentro es más bien acondicionada, y tratávanos mejor y teníamos por cierto que hallaríamos la tierra más poblada y de mejores mantenimientos"; 1: 200; 199).These are the main motivations the survivors put forward to justify their decision to go inland. However, these three motives seem insufficient to justify such a detour and the abandonment of the Pánuco as a destination. Moreover, whether the Indians of the coast were bad or rude does not seem to have been a problem up until this point, since the four travelers had succeeded in establishing great authority over the Indians they had encountered thus far.

I am more persuaded by another explanation that Cabeza de Vaca offers, albeit in a cryptic manner, about the westward turn of the journey. He states that they made this decision in order to "give an account and description of the land" ("dar nuevas y relación de la tierra"; 1: 201; 200) and, thus, to serve the king. The problem is that later on the text does not really offer a description of this region as it had promised. This seems to be an explanation after the fact, and we can infer that the truth was silenced under a euphemistic interpretation, as often happens throughout Cabeza de Vaca's *Relación*. Carlos Jáuregui suggests that at this point in the journey they became bandits and were profiting by using their shamanistic roles and power to inspire terror, and so the telos of the journey changed accordingly. It seems that the survivors took advantage of their fame and power not only as healers among the indigenous peoples but also as figures of authority to solve disputes or discord between tribes, and the idea of returning promptly to the Pánuco River and Christian lands was abandoned. It was only after they encountered Christians that there was a new turn toward going home. So, after the fact and under the questionable light of the narrative, the *Relación* turns a group of renegades and ransackers into a group of honest conquistadores returning to civilization (Jáuregui, "Going Native"; Adorno and Pautz 1: 202–05). In this deceitful way, the narrative that Cabeza de Vaca offers from the moment the survivors moved far away from the coast until they entered conquered territory in Nueva Galicia is clearly one of apparent triumph and dominance over the indigenous communities—a triumph that may be read toward the end of the *Relación*.

Lost in Geography

The fourth issue concerning space in the *Relación* touches on all the aforementioned issues. Readers may wonder why the text does not strive to offer geographic precision. Obviously, Cabeza de Vaca was not thinking about our students, who often find that this vague geography compounds the confusion created by the temporal organization of the narrative. For example, no precise description identifies the river that separates the region inhabited by the Mariames from that of the Avavares. We can deduce that it is a wide river or wide tributary of a main river because of the difficulties suffered by the four travelers when crossing it: it is probably the Colorado River or the Rio Grande, as explained earlier.

The same vagueness can be found in a large number of other geographic references in the *Relación*. Adorno and Pautz have made a great effort at examining previous discussions that have tried to identify the sites to which the chronicle alludes (Cabeza de Vaca, *Narrative* 5–12). When the text refers to lands that were already known from previous expeditions and that had been mapped, the narrator uses precise language because he has the Spanish names to identify the sites. Nevertheless, once the travelers abandon the ships and head inland, the text loses its onomastic and differentiating geographic capacity, and it also fails to include the Indian proper nouns. Because of all the topographical imprecision, many editions of the *Relación* include maps that offer hypothetical visualizations of the route covered by the expedition over the course of a decade (e.g., Cabeza de Vaca, *Naufragios y comentarios* [Ferrando], *Castaways*, and *Naufragios* [Teglia]; Adorno and Pautz). The *Relación* is abundant in silences, and the geography is one of the aspects most affected by the lacunae in the text.

Despite the happy ending that Cabeza de Vaca declares on the final pages of the *Relación*, I consider the text to be an unsuccessful or, at least, unconvincing, negotiated effort to control people, geography, and measurements of time and space in the New World. Following the *ordenanzas* of 1526, geography was central to the strengthening of the authority or validity of a text. This is why Cabeza de Vaca states in the *proemio* that since the expedition itself had been so wretched and disastrous he could only bring to the Crown an account of all that he had observed and learned in the nine years he had walked lost and naked through the land (see Adorno and Pautz 1: 18–19).

In conclusion, despite the intentions declared in the *proemio*, the *Relación* neither authoritatively informs its readers about the geography of the New World, clearly differentiates any American provinces, nor aptly describes the lay of the land. The *Relación* includes proto-ethnographic references to pre-Columbian North American Indian ways of living, yet rarely does it provide precise measurements of the distances between landmarks, cities, and peoples encountered. Although the descriptions of the bison and North American marsupials are among the most attractive descriptions known of these animals, explanations of the flora and fauna are rather brief, in contrast, for example, to the narrative about the suffering the travelers endured in their efforts to survive. This account of the travelers' suffering amid the natural and human spaces they encountered is paradoxically the most precise and vital geographic report among the other sixteenth-century attempts to explore, conquer, and map the region.

NOTES

Translated by Juliet Lynd and Vanina M. Teglia.

1. *Plus ultra*, meaning "further beyond," was the motto of Charles V, Holy Roman Emperor and King of Spain and symbolized his ambition for empire expansion.

2. Colombi points out that the chronotope of the path is the backbone of travel narratives, as characters are always "on the road" (304, 305).

3. See fig. 1 in part 1 of this volume.

4. Some examples in the *Relación* are "very great woods" ("un monte muy grande"; Adorno and Pautz 1: 175; 174; ch. 23), "very great forests" ("muy grandes montes"; 1: 53; 52; ch. 5), "very thick woods" ("muy espesso monte"; 1: 55; 54; ch. 6), and "dense woods" ("espesura de montes"; 1: 59; 58; ch. 7).

5. For example: "All the Indians we had seen from Florida to here are archers, and as they are of large build and go about naked, from a distance they appear to be giants" ("Quantos indios vimos desde la Florida aquí todos son flecheros, y como son crescidos de cuerpo y andan desnudos, desde lexos paresçen gigantes"; Adorno and Pautz 1: 63; 62; ch. 7). For a similar instance, see 138; 139; ch. 18.

6. The contract between the Spanish Crown and Narváez (11 December 1526) twice repeats the phrase "From the Río de las Palmas to the cape of Florida" ("Del río de las Palmas hasta el cabo de la Florida"; *CDI* 22: 224–25; my trans.). Likewise, after the foreword the *Relación* addresses the Crown mandate and quotes the places in the same order (Adorno and Pautz 1: 23; ch. 1).

7. See, e.g., *Moby-Dick* (Melville), *Relato de un náufrago* (*Story of a Shipwrecked Sailor*; García Marquez), *Vingt mille lieues sous les mers* (*Twenty Thousand Leagues under the Sea*; Verne), *The Blue Lagoon*, *Titanic*, *Cast Away*, the *Pirates of the Caribbean* films, *Life of Pi*, and *The Impossible*, to name a few.

8. The films *Star Wars*, *Terminator*, *The Matrix*, and *I Am Legend*; the TV series *Westworld* and *Dark*; and the novels *1984*, *Fahrenheit 451*, and *The Handmaid's Tale* are just a few of the more well-known narratives that can be read as actualized versions of hagiographies.

Food Studies and *Naufragios*

Mariselle Meléndez

For the cultural historian Massimo Montanari, "food is culture" because a person, "while able to eat anything, . . . does not in fact eat everything but rather *chooses* his own food" for economic, nutritional, or symbolic reasons (xi). Montanari's point is that those who are able to choose do so by making decisions based on necessity, convenience, or taste. For those who do not have a choice of what to eat, or who have nothing to eat at all, their food insecurity and hunger tell a story about the role food plays in the cultural and power relations that affect those in need. In fact, the history of famine since pre-Columbian times teaches us about the strategies of survival that cultures have adopted in order to confront the threat of food insecurity and hunger.[1]

When the Spanish arrived in the Americas, the new environment and their daily contact with indigenous societies transformed the manner in which they thought about food. For indigenous societies in colonial Latin America, food represented an integral part of daily interactions and religious beliefs. Enslaved Africans who arrived in Spanish America in the early sixteenth century experienced changes in their diets as a result of interactions with Europeans and indigenous societies, and they contributed to the transformation of other groups' food consumption. Furthermore, as producers of food, African and indigenous groups who were forced to work the lands through the systems of encomienda, *mita* ("forced labor draft"), and enslaved labor played a key role in transforming food consumption at a global scale (Restall and Lane 140–41). This transformation, commonly known as the Columbian Exchange and described by John Schwartz as the "great food migration," affected societies on both sides of the Atlantic and across the Pacific, broadening menus and transforming cultures at the expense of indigenous and African labor (58). This exchange was accompanied by what Mathew Restall and Kris Lane refer to as an "environmental conquest" facilitated by "the spread of Old World plants and animals" with devastating consequences to Native American populations and their lands that are still palpable in Latin America today (118).

This essay provides useful strategies on how to teach Álvar Núñez Cabeza de Vaca's *Naufragios* through the lens of food studies. *Naufragios* (*Shipwrecks*) lends itself to a productive discussion on the relationship between food, culture, and society in the sixteenth century. Food studies is an interdisciplinary approach that uses food as a "powerful lens of analysis" to approach issues of migration, diaspora, globalization, nationalism, race and ethnicity, gender identity, taste perception, culinary tourism, social justice, and human rights, among others (Counihan and Van Esterik 2). This approach provides theoretical tools to critically analyze "the role of food in history and culture" and how food works as a "means of communication" (10) and as "an index of power relations" (11). I underline the interconnectedness between food and the environment in the geographic areas that Cabeza de Vaca traveled through on his way from what is today Florida to the Southwest of the United States. When we read *Naufragios* through food, we better understand the articulation of social hierarchies, identity constructions, cultural distinctions, and power that are so present in the text. The essay devotes attention to how leitmotifs found in *Naufragios* such as food, hunger, survival, and harsh terrain are relevant to understanding how some areas of the Southwest are still perceived today. Instructors can teach students how Native Americans engaged in food production and consumption by mastering the ecology in which they lived. In sum, *Naufragios* lends itself well to an examination of how food works as a mechanism of social interaction and the role that nature plays in human beings' ability to confront a foreign environment with the ultimate goal of survival.

The overall learning objectives of a class on food and culture in Spanish America are as follows: acquire the critical tools necessary to formulate informed readings of colonial Spanish American texts, learn key theoretical terminology in the field of food studies that will facilitate the analysis of primary texts, understand how the relationship between food and culture was transformed through contact between different cultures, and comprehend how pre-Columbian and early modern views and conceptions of food still influence Latin American society today. In my experience teaching a class on this subject for the past few years, *Naufragios* is a fascinating text to discuss, and students enjoy learning about the United States's colonial past.

Cabeza de Vaca's relationship with food was determined by the route that the conquistador was forced to take in the Southeast and Southwest. Through Florida, parts of Alabama, Mississippi, Texas, and northern Mexico, Cabeza the Vaca and his companions encountered a diverse terrain along with diverse groups of people that forced them to adapt to extreme circumstances. It must be clear that this adaptation did not erase Cabeza de Vaca's own sense of superiority over the indigenous people he encountered. In his prologue, addressed to Charles V, he emphasizes that all those eight years that he was "lost and almost naked" ("perdido y en cueros"), he learned about the diversity of lands and animals along with "the diverse customs of many and barbarous peoples with whom I conversed and lived" ("las diversas costumbres de muchas y muy bárbaras naçiones con quien conversé y viví"; Adorno and Pautz 1: 19; 18). From the moment he reached the west coast of Florida as part of Pánfilo de Narváez's failed expedition to his ultimate arrival in Culiacán, the scarcity of food became a constant preoccupation. Diet change became one of the most salient consequences of Cabeza de Vaca's venture into new terrains and one through which cultural values and preferences can be understood.

For instructors approaching *Naufragios* in an advanced undergraduate culture or literature course, it is important to discuss the historical and cultural context that surrounded the failed expedition to La Florida and the subsequent series of unfortunate events. Who organized the expedition? Who was in charge?

And why La Florida? The study by Rolena Adorno and Patrick Charles Pautz in their bilingual three-volume edition (1: 293–412) can help students contextualize the account. Vanina Teglia's introduction to her edition of *Naufragios* can complement these other resources well (Cabeza de Vaca, *Naufragios* [Teglia] 10–110). Of course, the understanding is that in a general course about colonial Spanish America, instructors should first assign a broader historical context for the sixteenth-century Spanish conquests and their aftermaths. I find Restall and Lane's work extremely helpful in understanding what they refer to as "Before the Great Encounter" (1–46) and "The Long Conquest" (47–128).

Once the historical and cultural background has been covered, students should visually understand the territories that encompassed the expedition, the shipwreck, and the journey of survival. A productive point of discussion is for the instructor to present early modern maps of what was known as La Florida in the sixteenth century and of the northern frontier of New Spain so students can gather an idea of the trajectory that Cabeza de Vaca and the other survivors followed. Maps such as Diego Gutiérrez's "Americae sive quartae orbis partis nova et exactissima descriptio," from 1562, and Abraham Ortelius's "La Florida," from his 1584 edition of *Theatrum Orbis Terrarum*, can be very helpful. In the case of Gutiérrez's map, it is the "only sheet map printed during the sixteenth century that is known to have been derived from Spanish sources" (Padrón 70n18).[2] It is also known that Ortelius followed Gutiérrez's map closely in creating his own. Both maps were based on the accounts of Spanish sources who participated in Hernando de Soto's expedition, and De Soto himself depended on indigenous informants whom he forced through violence to share their routes (Strang 29). As Cameron Strang contends, survivors of De Soto's expedition provided geographic details to the institutional center of Spanish cosmography, the Casa de Contratación in Seville. The royal cosmographer Juan López de Velasco incorporated the so-called De Soto map—which included reports from the Lucas Vázquez de Ayllón, Narváez, and De Soto entradas—as "part of his effort to construct a more complete map of the world by synthesizing data from throughout the Spanish Empire" (Strang 29).

It is also believed that De Soto's knowledge of Florida prior to his departure from Spain in 1538 was based on the maps drawn by Diogo Ribeiro and Alonso de Chaves (both royal cosmographers of the Spanish Crown), which depicted the coastal configuration of Florida (Weddle 220).[3] Other maps of this area can be found at the *Old Florida Maps* website, hosted by the University of Miami Libraries (scholar.library.miami.edu/floridamaps/). To help students understand the trajectory, instructors should show a current map illustrating Cabeza de Vaca's route. Adorno and Pautz's edition includes a detailed map of the journey through Florida, Mississippi, and Alabama. To complement their understanding of the route, students can access the web page "Route of Cabeza de Vaca," which offers a very good re-creation of the route on a map of today's Texas. Of course, all these routing maps are speculative to some degree: the conquistadores did not map their journey, and there have been major changes in the geography since then, as noted by Adorno and Pautz (1: xv–xvi; Cabeza de Vaca, *Naufragios* [Teglia] 22–23).

It is important for instructors to complement these sources with the map on the *Tribal Directory* website, which were published online to promote the importance of Native American societies in the history of the United States. The site offers a map of the country divided into tribal regions. Each region named below the map links to a list of all the indigenous groups that inhabited and still inhabit each region, including the ones who inhabited the regions where Cabeza de Vaca traveled ("North American Tribal Regions"). The website *Native Land* offers an interactive map (native-land.ca). Again, the identifications of these indigenous groups should be taken cautiously since they are based on accounts that date a century or more after Cabeza de Vaca's journey. The diversity of the terrain and of the people made encounters with indigenous groups challenging for the Spaniards. Given that students may not have traveled to these areas, this visual material enables them to understand their geographic and ethnic diversity.

Audiovisual materials can also offer a productive platform to visualize the terrain that Cabeza de Vaca and his comrades covered as part of their journey. Instructors can show the movie *Cabeza de Vaca*, directed by Nicolás Echevarría, and they can ask students to consider how the director recreates Cabeza de Vaca's journey and in particular the topic of food and survival. The movie occasionally treats food as a leitmotif of the journey: some scenes imagine the environment in which Cabeza de Vaca and his companions were forced to find alternative sources of food, such as roots.[4] Students can also discuss why the topic of hunger and the types of food the Spaniards had to eat are not as present in the film as they could have been. After all, Cabeza de Vaca's written account offers specific information about the dietary changes that he had to make to survive. The PBS documentary television series *Conquistadors* can also be used to complement students' visual understanding of the journey by showing students how the terrain of Cabeza de Vaca's journey looks today, so they can better understand the challenges that nature posed to the Spanish survivors.[5] Students can refer to the website *Conquistadors* that accompanies this documentary (www.pbs.org/conquistadors/). The short video "The Incredible Journey of Cabeza de Vaca (1527–1536)" is also helpful in visually reconstructing the geography in *Naufragios*. The goal is for instructors to emphasize that in the Southeast and Southwest of the United States, nature, geography, and the environment did not give way to an ecosystem that facilitated an extensive agricultural system. The challenges that the environment posed made local indigenous groups "masters of adaptation," turning them also into mobile societies whose survival skills were deeply rooted in observation, experience, and knowledge of seasonal changes (Restall and Lane 15). After all, what made Cabeza de Vaca's journey more unbearable for him was the fact that he and the rest of the Spaniards were unable to control nature as a commodity.

Discussion can then be organized along the main topics associated with food: environment and ecology, dietary practices of the indigenous people, the

Spaniards' dietary transformations, including resorting to cannibalism, and hunger. These topics are all intertwined with issues of power and knowledge. For the first topic, the aim is to discuss those passages in which Cabeza de Vaca describes the land, nature, and the environment and their impact on food availability. Cabeza de Vaca underlines in the first chapter, after the shipwreck off the coast of Cuba, what will be a leitmotif in the rest of his account: the lack of food and the impact on the Spaniards' survival. Cabeza de Vaca states, "Thus we found ourselves for some days in great hardship and necessity because the town's provisions and stores had been lost, along with some cattle. The land was left in such a state that it was a great pity to see it, the trees fallen, the woods destroyed, all stripped of leaves and grass" ("assí estuvimos algunos días con mucho trabajo y necessidad porque la provisión y mantenimientos que el pueblo tenía se perdieron y algunos ganados. La tierra quedó tal que era gran lástima vella: caídos los árboles, quemados los montes, todos sin hojas ni yervas"; Adorno and Pautz 1: 31; 30; ch. 1). This quotation underlines how they were at the mercy of the environment and those who mastered it in order to survive. In class, I have students discuss how this preoccupation becomes more prevalent in La Florida, as the journey progresses; Cabeza de Vaca describes the land "as unpopulated and as poor" ("despoblada y tan pobre"; 1: 41; 40; ch. 4) and "so strange and so poor" ("tan estraña y tan mala"; 1: 67, 69; 66, 68; ch. 8). The environment and indigenous resistance will dictate the failed conquistadores' lack of access to food.

A great part of the discussion of *Naufragios* centers on the dietary practices of indigenous groups. This topic is important as Cabeza de Vaca and his companions had no choice but to eat what the indigenous people had to offer or what in several instances the Spaniards stole from them. Cabeza de Vaca offers a broad description of the indigenous people in those lands. In chapter 18, when referring to the Yguazes, he offers an extensive list of food this group consumed and how they consumed it. According to Cabeza de Vaca, Yguazes ate deer meat, corn, beans, squash, fish, a variety of roots including cattails, clams, types of nuts, cactus (tunas), ants, worms, lizards, salamanders, snakes, spiders, and even a powder prepared by grinding parts of fish and snakes. It would be important at this point to go over the dietary and medicinal aspects of the foods that indigenous people consumed. The goal is to problematize the idea, suggested by Cabeza de Vaca, that hunger and desperation also led indigenous people in these territories, including the Yguazes, to eat a bone powder from fish and snakes and even deer excrement, which Cabeza de Vaca viewed as unacceptable types of food (1: 141, 143; 140, 142). As he states in chapter 18, "they satisfy their hunger two or three times a year at as great a cost as I have said. And for having lived through it, I can affirm that no hardship endured in the world equals this one" ("satisfazen su hambre dos o tres vezes en el año a tan grande costa como he dicho"; 1: 145; 144).

From the European perspective, these dietary habits were insufficient and led to hunger and pain. Although there was never an abundance of food, these traditional Native foods, which sometimes are referred to as "wild," were high in protein, fiber, and nutrients and were indeed enough to survive on (Pratesi).

Furthermore, as Gregorio Saldarriaga argues in a recent essay published in Climent-Espino and Gómez-Bravo's volume, "it became acceptable for Spaniards to consume foods that were only taxonomically suitable for the indigenous peoples when those foods were framed within a consumption structure that made them acceptable" (93). What did not fit within these parameters of acceptability was conceived by Cabeza de Vaca as wild. A good example is when Cabeza de Vaca eats bison meat, thinking that bison are cows: "Cows sometimes range as far as here, and three times I have seen and eaten of them. And it seems to me they are about the size of those of Spain" ("Alcançan aquí vacas y yo las he visto tres vezes y comido dellas. Y parésçeme que serán del tamaño de las de España"; Adorno and Pautz 1: 147; 146; ch. 18). Eating what he thought were cows was more acceptable than eating horses, a point that he underlines in chapter 12: "although the horses were killed during the time the rafts were being constructed, I could never eat of them" ("porque aunque se matraron los cavallos entretanto que las barcas se hazían, yo nunca pude comer de ellos"; 1: 99; 98).

Chapter 18 is extremely important also because Cabeza de Vaca goes on to describe cooking techniques performed by Yguaze men and women. He adds that Yguaze women are very hardworking, only resting six hours a day, as they spend much of the night "firing their ovens in order to dry those roots they eat. And from daybreak, they begin to dig and bring firewood and water to their homes, and put in order things of which they have need" ("atizar sus hornos para secar aquellas raíces que comen. Y desque amanesçe, comiençan a cavar y a traer leña y agua a sus casas, y dar orden en las otras cosas que tienen neçessidad"; 1: 141; 140). He also goes into detail on the diverse ways the Yguaze Indians prepare and make use of the prickly pears, which involves a drying process, a preparation of the pear's juice, after which they eat the fruit and extract the juice, and then "they grind the skins and make a powder of them" ("las cáxcaras dellas muélenlas y hazénlas polvo"; Adorno and Pautz 1: 143; 142). Grinding was a cooking technique used by other indigenous groups as well. When the Spaniards arrived in Apalache, Cabeza de Vaca mentioned that "[t]hey had many vessels for grinding maize" ("[t]enían muchos vasos para moler maíz"; 1: 55; 54; ch. 6).

Cooking ingenuity is also underlined in chapter 27, after Cabeza de Vaca leaves the Arbadao Indians to go with the Cuchendados Indians, he describes how the latter prepared for the Spaniards a mesquite mixture made of a fruit similar to Spanish carobs. This food was made in a pit in the ground; the preparation involved grinding the fruit and pouring water into the pit. The juice, served in a vessel in the form of a two handled-basket, was consumed as part of a banquet at the end of which, according to Cabeza de Vaca, the Indians had "swollen bellies from the earth and water they have drunk" ("las barrigas muy grandes de la tierra y agua que an bevido"; 1: 193; 192). Cabeza de Vaca seems on one hand to dismiss the Native technique of cooking in pits by stating that the end result was the consumption of high amounts of earth and water, but on the other hand, he acknowledges earlier in *Naufragios* that the technique served to make the fruit "sweet and good to eat" ("dulçe y bueno de comer"; 1: 191; 190).

Cabeza de Vaca describes how, in addition to cooking in pits, indigenous peoples in the area where the Rio Grande meets the Río Conchos in Coahuila, Mexico, used a unique method for cooking inside gourds. They placed hot rocks at the bottom of the gourds to generate heat, boiling the water and cooking the food within the gourds. Cabeza de Vaca frames this description with the premise that these indigenous groups lacked pots ("no alcançan ollas"; 1: 226; ch. 29); however, perhaps unconsciously, he highlights their ingenuity in using gourds to achieve the boiling technique.

For students to gain insight into how Cabeza de Vaca perceived the dietary habits of indigenous peoples—habits he considered different from European norms—it is instructive to focus on chapters 17 and 18 of his account. In these chapters, Cabeza de Vaca elaborates on the collection, preparation, and consumption of tunas, or prickly pears. According to his observations while living with the Quevenes, this fruit was a staple in their diet for three months of the year. He mentions two types of tunas—"vermillion and black" ("bermejas y negras"; 1: 129; 128; ch. 17)—and all the parts of the cactus they consumed including the buds. In the following chapter, and now describing the customs of the Mariames, he highlights that "the best season that these people have is when they eat the prickly pears" ("el mejor tiempo que éstos tienen es cuando comen las tunas"; 1: 143; 142; ch. 18) as the pears satisfied their hunger. This quotation can serve as a great opportunity to discuss the dietary and medicinal benefits of cactus, so students understand why it was so venerated by indigenous people, as Cabeza de Vaca notes, and how it is still consumed. Instructors can show different resources, such as Lizzie Streit's "Prickly Pear: Nutrition, Benefits, Recipes, and More," that spell out the benefits of eating prickly pears as well as other parts of the cactus.

The seasonal practice of cultivating food in extreme climates was foreign to Cabeza de Vaca but not to the indigenous people of these areas. He observes with some bafflement how because of the terrain the local people had to survive on the same limited foods for a certain extent of time. As Lois Ellen Frank suggests, this entailed a "variety of subsistence adaptations" based on the nature of the land (*Native American Cooking* 18).[6] In chapter 17, Cabeza de Vaca complains that two of the indigenous groups he encountered in what is today Texas, known as Yguazes and Mariames, ate only nuts for two consecutive months a year, grinding them "without eating any other thing. And even this they do not have every year, because the trees bear fruit one year but not the next" ("sin comer otra cosa, y aun esto no lo tienen todos los años, porque acuden uno, y otro no"; Adorno and Pautz 1: 127; 126). Because of these environmental challenges, indigenous people learned to be very active at different times of the year.

An important quotation for instructors to discuss with students regarding the seasonal harvesting of food is Cabeza de Vaca's comment in chapter 22 when he talks about the Avavares:

> All these people did not know how to calculate the seasons either by the sun or by the moon, nor do they have reckoning of the months and years,

> but they understand and know the differences between the times when the fruit comes to mature and when the fish die and the stars appear, in the observance of which they are very skilled and well practiced.   (1: 169)
>
> Toda esta gente no conosçían los tiempos por el Sol ni la Luna, ni tienen cuenta del mes del año, y más entienden las differençias de los tiempos cuando las frutas vienen a madurar, y en tiempo que muere el pescado y el aparecer de las estrellas, en que son muy diestros y ejercitados.   (1: 168)

After reviewing this quotation, students can engage in group discussion about the interconnectedness of harvesting food and the notion of time for these Native societies. Nature dictated their relationship with food. Instructors can inform students that the cholla buds of a saguaro cactus have to be seventy years old before they will produce fruit. As Mary Paganelli Voto points out, this is one reason why, even today, in desert areas "some things are just meant to be in small quantities" (qtd. in Pratesi). This fact ties into Cabeza de Vaca's observation that for Native American groups, the availability of food guided their understanding of the seasons.

Physical and dietary transformations form a third significant theme worth discussing. Cabeza de Vaca acknowledges that during their journey he and his companions accepted food that they were not familiar with. They did this out of necessity. For example, in chapter 21, when he was with the Avavares Indians, he indicates that in exchange for the Spaniards' curing some sick people, the Avavares brought them "many prickly pears and a piece of venison, a thing that we could not identify" ("truxeron muchas tunas y un pedaço de carne de venado, cosa que no sabíamos qué cosa era"; Adorno and Pautz 1: 155; 154). His willingness to eat this piece of meat despite his inability to identify it underlines his inconsistent attitude toward unfamiliar foods. This is noteworthy because early in the account, when he and his fellow Spaniards were in Florida, they had readily accepted venison from the indigenous people they encountered there. However, the most difficult adaptation that some Spaniards made was to eat the meat of their horses and dogs and, at least in two instances, human flesh. In chapter 5, Cabeza de Vaca recounts a grim episode following the death of Juan Velazquez, who drowned in a river because he did not know how to swim. Driven by extreme hunger, they were forced to eat Velazquez's dead horse to survive (1: 62–63). In several other passages, such as in chapter 8, the Spaniards were forced to eat their horses. It is important for students to consider why Cabeza de Vaca, despite repeatedly expressing his extreme hunger, refused to eat horse meat. This decision underscores the aforementioned notion of what was considered acceptable food. However, he does admit in chapter 23, when he was with the Arbadao Indians, that he and the other Spaniards had to eat dogs. Cabeza de Vaca never explains why he refused to eat dead horses, but we can extrapolate that he viewed horses within the Spanish tradition of nobility and royalty and that eating them was repugnant to someone of his social status.

An important theme to discuss along with this is the one of cannibalism. In chapter 14, Cabeza de Vaca describes the first scene of cannibalism at Malhado Island within the context of extreme conditions and hunger that led a group of Spaniards into what they believed was the quintessential form of barbarism: "five men who were in Xamho on the coast came to such dire need that they ate one another until one remained, who because he was alone, had no one to eat him" ("Y cinco christianos que estavan en Xamho en la costa llegaron a tal estremo que se comieron los unos a los otros hasta que quedó uno, que por ser solo, no huvo quien lo comiesse"; 1: 105, 107; 104, 106). Another episode of cannibalism has to do with a story narrated by Figueroa to Andrés Dorantes and Alonso del Castillo Maldonado about Hernando de Esquivel, the last survivor of Narvaez's party after the governor's raft was lost at sea. After Pantoja, Narvaez's lieutenant, was killed by his men, the group descended into chaos and cannibalism. People started dying of hunger, and the survivors ate the dead until Esquivel became the sole survivor (1: 130–37; chs. 17 and 18).[7] Instructors can ask what these scenes of cannibalism tell us about the famine among the Spaniards and how the issue of food scarcity is perceived by Cabeza de Vaca. How does the Spaniards' turn to cannibalism compare with the ability of indigenous people to master their environment and survive in those lands? Why does Cabeza de Vaca approach Spanish cannibalism with ambivalence (Jáuregui, "Going Native" 177)?

Regarding the fourth topic, hunger, it is crucial to explore its impact on the physical transformation of the Spaniards. After all, Cabeza de Vaca sought to visually convey this transformation to the Spanish king from the beginning of his account, in the prologue. In chapter 21, Cabeza de Vaca emphasizes the extreme hunger that he and his companions experienced while with the Avavares (Adorno and Pautz 1: 154, 155). The discussion can focus on the scenes where Cabeza de Vaca recounts how the physical transformation of the Spaniards astonished other conquistadores and the indigenous peoples alike. For example, when Cabeza de Vaca and companions arrived at Malhado Island in a dire condition, the Indians took pity on them. They were so thin that, in Cabeza de Vaca's words, "with little difficulty our bones could be counted, appeared like the figure of death itself" ("con poca dificultad nos podían contar los huessos, estávamos hechos propia figura de la muerte"; 1: 99; 98; ch. 12). Here, before proceeding with the analysis it would be helpful for instructors to show visuals of how death was represented in iconography in early modern times—which was in the form of skeletons. The Spaniards' situation was so extreme that when the indigenous people of the island (Capoques and Han) encountered the Spaniards they were frightened: "But when they saw us in this manner and dressed so differently from the first time, and in such strange state, they were so frightened that they withdrew" ("mas cuando ellos nos vieron así en tan diferente hábito del primero y en manera tan estraña, espantáronse tanto que se bolvieron atrás"; 1: 99; 98; ch. 12). This passage is an excellent starting point for students to discuss why Cabeza de Vaca thought it necessary to visually convey to the king the physical transformation they had undergone.

In chapter 13 Cabeza de Vaca writes that he and his companions were so physically transformed that the other Spaniards could not even recognize them as fellow countrymen. Dorantes and Castillo reunited with Cabeza de Vaca and other survivors in Malhado: "Upon encountering us, they received a great fright to see us in the condition we were in. And it gave them great sorrow" ("[S]e espantaron mucho de vernos de la manera en que estávamos. Y resçibieron muy gran pena"; 1: 103; 102). In chapter 19, Cabeza de Vaca says that he lived a "very bad life" ("muy mala vida"; 1: 147, 146) because of hunger and mistreatment by the Indians. Students can discuss how he rhetorically uses his physical suffering to appeal to the king for a reward.

I like to close my class discussion of *Naufragios* by reading about indigenous foods of the Southwest as they are today. The goal of this comparative discussion is to show that for centuries indigenous people of the Southwest have managed to preserve many Native food sources, even as culinary customs and recipes have undergone various transformations. I assign Gwen Pratesi's article "Indigenous Foods of the Southwest—Original Native American Cuisine" and the episode "The Original Americans" of the television show *Taste the Nation*, hosted by Padma Lakshmi. In different ways, these sources chronicle the culinary practices of Native American people and chefs in the Southwest today. We start by examining the epigraph to Pratesi's article, a quotation of Chief Luther Standing Bear of the Oglala band of Sioux: "We did not think of the great open plains, the beautiful rolling hills, and the winding streams with tangled growth, as 'wild.' Only to the white man was nature a 'wilderness' and only to him was the land 'infested' with 'wild' animals and 'savage' people. To us it was tame. Earth was bountiful and we were surrounded with blessings of the Great Mystery." Focusing on this quotation prompts students to discuss how indigenous and Western views of nature differ and how this difference can be related to Cabeza de Vaca's account.

Instructors can enrich this discussion by including academic sources about traditional indigenous foodways, from cultivation practices and crop types to food patterns and cooking techniques that are tailored to the landscape. Enrique Salmón's *Eating the Landscape* offers a useful environmental perspective on the indigenous foodways of the southwestern United States and northwestern Mexico. He focuses on Amerindian farmers and their stories about land and food. The stories he collects demonstrate how for example, Ak-Chin, Hopi, and O'odham farmers even today rely on environmentally conscious cultivation practices developed centuries ago (11). Salmón adds, "[T]he scattered O'odham devised the perfect conspiracy by timing the planting of their crops, the wild crafting of desert foods, and the final harvesting with the desert seasons, thereby keeping efforts to maintain the human-landscape cycles to a comfortable minimum" (84). While Chief Luther Standing Bear speaks to the importance of recognizing the land as an integrated system, Cabeza de Vaca's narrative often overlooks or misunderstands this indigenous wisdom. These different perspectives on land and food can inform not only understandings of Cabeza de Vaca's account but also our problematic relation with nature today.

To deepen students' understanding of indigenous perspectives, instructors can include selections from Frank's book *Foods of the Southwest Indian Nations*. This resource offers testimonies from elders of various Indian nations about the symbiotic relationship between the land and its people. Those views differ across regions of the Southwest, but all of them show unique adaptations with considerable pedagogical potential. These adaptations, in turn, have resulted in different cooking techniques and protocols that are still practiced. As Frank adds, today Southwestern peoples and their nations practice "varying farming and planting techniques that have been handed down from generation to generation to suit the environments in which they live," and sometimes they incorporate "contemporary ingredients and utensils" (*Foods* 20, 21).

Reading these contemporary sources enables students to understand the differences and points of incompatibility between early modern indigenous views of the land and the views narrated by Cabeza de Vaca. Students can also discuss how the relationship of Native Americans in the Southwest with nature has survived years of conquest, colonization, racism, and marginalization. As a further layer to this discussion, students can examine how the use of traditional ingredients and cooking techniques has persisted despite the imposition of unhealthy diets on indigenous communities following their displacement to reservations in the 1800s.[8] Students can address how Native American chefs such as Janos Wilder and Joshua Johnson are championing the inclusion of wild Native American ingredients in their menus. Their efforts help preserve and elevate these traditional cuisines.

"The Original Americans" can help students understand the connections between the Southwest where Cabeza de Vaca traveled, including the eating practices he witnessed and adopted, and the culinary practices that exist today in the region. One important point made by a Native American activist in this episode is that "food is plentiful if you know how to find it" (00:05:40–43). However, it's essential to consider the obvious material conditions of scarcity. Students can examine the significance of this message of knowledge and abundance compared to experiences of poverty and food insecurity. Students can examine the significance of these messages of abundance and scarcity, especially in contrast to Cabeza de Vaca's frequent complaints in his account that the food the Spanish conquistadores found was never enough. Another point of discussion could be the insights from local Native American chefs and food activists shared in their interview with Padma. They emphasize that food has always provided a connection to the earth and suggest that it can be a pathway to achieving food sovereignty. These statements could prompt a discussion on Cabeza de Vaca's failure to appreciate seasonal food consumption based on cultivation patterns. Cabeza de Vaca's inability to connect nature and food along with his portrayal of the New World as a land of scarcity reveals not just the predatory mentality of the conquistadores. It also sheds light on contemporary society's tendency to view nature only in terms of material consumption.

Although indigenous groups most likely endured hunger, they also learned how to subsist within the limitations that the environment offered them by taking advantage of seasonal crops and eating less. For contemporary indigenous groups, the cultivation and consumption of ancestral, local foods connects with their ancestors. Food is not just sustenance but also part of their identities and a means of learning about their past, and this is an important topic to take into consideration when discussing *Naufragios*. The following three activities can be integrated into the course when teaching *Naufragios*:

> Critical reflection. Students select a current news article that relates to food topics discussed in *Naufragios* and write a two-page essay explaining connections they find between the news article and the content of the primary text.
>
> Field study activity. Students virtually or physically visit a restaurant where Native American food is served and write an essay responding to these questions: What names does the restaurant use to describe the dishes? What ingredients are predominant? What connections do students find between the ingredients used and the social geography of the region? What do the decorations of the restaurant and the restaurant's name convey about the authenticity of the food? Finally, what does the menu tell about the culture represented by these foods?
>
> Class presentation. Students prepare group presentations on the cuisine of one particular Native American group from the regions that Cabeza de Vaca traveled in.

To conclude, teaching *Naufragios* from the critical angle of food studies illuminates the crucial role that food played in Cabeza de Vaca's narration of his journey. What Cabeza de Vaca ate and did not eat became an integral part of his identity and that of his companions. Food serves as a vehicle for students to understand these cultural identities forged out of desperation in foreign lands. Additionally, food studies can help students recognize how Native American in these territories acquired and managed food through their mastery of the surrounding environment.

NOTES

1. For a historical discussion of food and famine at a global scale, see Anderson 209–34.
2. See the Gutiérrez map in Padron 70 and in the digital repository of the Library of Congress at www.loc.gov/item/map49000970. The Othelius map is widely available online and can be consulted at www.loc.gov/item/84696980/.

3. Diogo Ribero and Alonso de Chaves worked in the Casa de Contratación in Seville in charge of the secret master maps known as "royal register" ("padrón real"; Weddle 220).

4. The consumption of hallucinogens is another leitmotif that the film explores.

5. For another point of view about this documentary, see Luis Fernando Restrepo's essay in this volume.

6. According to Frank, "some Peoples cultivated only limited crops, deriving most of their food from wild plant and animal resources. Other groups engaged in irrigation agriculture supplemented by hunting and gathering. Settlement patterns were and are equally diverse" (*Native American Cooking* 18).

7. For a thorough discussion of these passages regarding cannibalism from a different critical angle, see Jáuregui, "Going Native."

8. The food that the government provided to Native Americans on these reservations largely consisted of white flour, white sugar, powdered milk, and lard (Pratesi). This shift in dietary habits has contributed to the health problems such as diabetes and obesity that are so prevalent among Native American populations today (Venkat Narayan).

HISPANIC LITERATURES, BORDER STUDIES, AND DIGITAL HUMANITIES

Between Land and Sea: The *Relación* as New World Literature

Ralph Bauer

In his 1991 historical drama *Cabeza de Vaca*, the Mexican filmmaker Nicolás Echevarría presents a scene in which the eponymous protagonist, following the wreck of his raft off the Texas coast and his capture by local Indians, makes an attempt to escape from his captors, a Native shaman and his dwarflike companion.[1] As Álvar Núñez Cabeza de Vaca runs in what appears to be a straight line along the coast, the shaman stakes a pole into the ground and ties to it a small lizard that begins to run around the pole in ever smaller circles. Eventually, Cabeza de Vaca's flight ends against his will; like the lizard, he has made a complete circle. Realizing that he has come under the spell of the shaman's magic, Cabeza de Vaca tries to reassure himself of his identity as a Christian conqueror by naming things in the Castilian language and by reciting a popular medieval ballad about the so-called *Reconquista*, the Christian reconquest of the Iberian Peninsula from the Moors ("Romance de Abenamar"). After having gradually reverted to a fetal position during his mental breakdown, the protagonist emerges from this experience reborn as a powerful healer who, during his journey across the North American continent, synthesizes the spiritual efficacy of European Christianity with elements of Native American shamanism and as the first cultural mestizo of what would become the Mexican nation-state.[2]

To be clear, Echevarría's film is not a cinematic version of Cabeza de Vaca's account of the Pánfilo de Narváez expedition; rather, it tells a strongly fictionalized story that seems intended to reinterpret the meaning of Cabeza de Vaca's journey against the meaning constructed by his own account. Nevertheless, I find the film useful in the classroom because it opens a window to many themes and topoi that are omnipresent in the literature of the European discovery and conquest of America, including Cabeza de Vaca's *Relación* (*Account*). These themes and topoi include the narrative deployment of the Spanish medieval chivalric tradition as it took shape over the eight hundred years of the *Reconquista*; the literary allegory of the shipwreck motif as it derived from the classical and medieval epic tradition; and the ideas of reform, renovation, and rebirth of the European subject in the New World. The literary history of these themes and topoi begins with the travel writings of Christopher Columbus and extends well beyond the literature of discovery and conquest in the early modern period into the literary histories of the Americas up to the present day.

This essay outlines a strategy for teaching Cabeza de Vaca's famous account of his epic journey by focusing on the interplay between two metafictional devices in the text: conquest and shipwreck. In what follows, I trace the enduring rhetorical power of this dialectic between so-called landed narratives of conquest (which solidify cultural identities) and narratives of the sea (which unsettle cultural identities) in the *Relación*. I begin by placing the narrative's breakdown of the chivalric code that the *crónicas de indias* (chronicles of the Indies) inherited from the medieval romances of chivalry in the historical context of the so-called New Laws of 1542, which stripped the conquerors of the neofeudal privileges afforded by the encomienda and that inspired the conquerors' self-image and aspirations in the New World. In the second part of the essay, I explore the shipwreck motif as an allegory of renovation in the context of the epic literary tradition, drawing attention to the close connections between political argument and rhetorical form in the *Relación*. I believe that this analysis can be useful to the instructor of this text in several contexts of various literary historical scope. First, the *Relación* can be understood as a story about a failed conquest that yet achieved considerable literary notoriety in the sixteenth century and that intervenes in the literature about the rights of conquest—what Rolena Adorno has called "the polemics of possession" raging in the Spanish Empire during the sixteenth century. This large and diverse body of literature encompasses the letters of Christopher Columbus and Hernán Cortés, the lectures of Francisco de Vitoria, and the historical narratives of Bartolomé de las Casas and Bernal Díaz del Castillo, among many others. Second, the *Relación* can be understood as a story about the protagonist's breakdown of his Old World (Spanish) identity, his reformation, and his emergence as a new man; in this vein the story connects to texts well beyond the immediate context of the sixteenth-century conquest that might collectively be called New World literature. The history of this literature requires a hemispheric and translinguistic approach, incorporating texts from Portuguese, French, and English literature that attempt to come to terms with the meaning of America for the history of modernity, from John Winthrop's famous sermon "A Model of Christian Charity" to J. Hector St. John de Crèvecoeur's late-eighteenth-century *Letters from an American Farmer*. Finally, through its generic and discursive inversions (the story begins in the mold of a chronicle of conquest aborted by shipwreck, then transforms into an epic story of wandering and finally into a protoscientific description of cultural and social practices), the *Relación* may be seen as an important text in the history of world literature that may fruitfully be brought into conversation not only with influential classical and modern verse epics from diverse traditions (from Homer's *Odyssey* or the *Ramayana* to Derek Walcott's *Omeros*) but also with the modern anti-epic or prose epic that emerged during the second part of the sixteenth century in Western culture with the picaresque (e.g., *Lazarillo de Tormes* and Carlos de Sigüenza y Góngora's *Infortunios de Alonso Ramírez*) and that developed into the modern novel, from Cervantes's *Don Quixote* to James Joyce's *Ulysses*.

Cabeza de Vaca and the Renewal of Empire

The *Relación* begins in the vein of a chronicle of discovery and conquest: "On the seventeenth day of the month of June 1527, Governor Pánfilo de Narváez, with the authority and mandate of Your Majesty, departed from the port of Sanlúcar de Barrameda to conquer and govern the provinces that are found from the Río de las Palmas to the cape of *Florida*, which are on the mainland" ("A diez y siete días del mes de junio de mil y quinientos y veinte y siete partió del puerto de Sanct Lúcar de Barrameda el gobernador Pámphilo de Narváez con poder y mandado de Vuestra Majestad para conquistar y governar las provincias que están desde el Río de las Palmas hasta el cabo de la Florida, las quales son en tierra firme"; Adorno and Pautz 1: 23; 22; ch. 1). But what begins so auspiciously as the would-be conquest of lands believed to hold fabulous riches, the mythic Fountain of Youth, and the legendary Seven Cities of Cíbola soon takes disastrous turns once the conquerors landed near Tampa Bay on 14 April 1528. The project of conquest comes to a screeching halt as the Spanish hidalgos are transformed, first into abject shipwreck survivors and captives traveling humbly, naked, and on foot, and then into merchants as well as powerful healers and missionaries.

As Adorno has explained, Cabeza de Vaca's self-transformation in his narrative can be understood as an attempt to redefine the Spanish imperial project from that of a militant conquest by means of arms—familiar, for example, from Cortés's letters about the conquest of Mexico—to that of a "peaceful conquest" as advocated by Las Casas and adopted as official policy and mandate by the Hapsburg monarchy ("Peaceful"; see also *Polemics* 267, 299). The emergence of this imperial mandate for a "peaceful conquest" must, however, be understood within the historical-political context of imperial consolidation and renewal. The early expeditions of discovery and conquest had largely been private enterprises, encouraged by the Crown with grants of political and economic privileges, a tradition that harked back to the seigniorial rule of the Middle Ages and especially the *Reconquista*. The practice of awarding an encomienda (a grant of Native tribute labor) to the conquerors of American lands had its legal foundation in the medieval *Libri Feudorum* (*Books of Feudal Codes*), which had codified the contractual relationship of "obligations and rights" between the emperor and the feudal lords, in which the latter expected royal favors in exchange for loyalty and military service (Haring 75; see also Adorno, *Polemics* 148–71). However, as early as the Catholic Monarchs' dealings with Columbus, the Crown, while realizing its dependency on private initiative in the overseas conquests, had been wary of the conquerors' quasi-feudal privileges and did not miss an opportunity to reappropriate administrative authority over the American territories. Gradually, the Crown abandoned its earlier hands-off policy and "undertook to recover sovereignty in its overseas territories" by revoking many of the privileges conceded earlier; consequently, Clarence Henry Haring writes, the conquistadores and their descendants found themselves "debarred from all high posts of administration by the old aristocracies of the metropolis," thus accentuating the "tendencies to centralization and uniformity" (76). In 1524—three years before the embarkation of the Narváez expedition—the Crown had established the Royal Council of Indies, located in Seville, to oversee all government activity in the Americas. A year later, the Crown issued the Ordenanzas sobre el buen tratamiento de los Indios (Ordinances for the Good Treatment of the Indians), tacitly targeted at the American conquerors in its implication that the Indians were not currently receiving "good treatment." In 1528, the Crown established the Royal Audiencia of Mexico, a council of royally appointed judges, hereby supplanting Cortés as chief magistrate and governor of New Spain (McAlister 188–91). In 1535—one year before Cabeza de Vaca's return to Spanish-controlled territory with the other survivors of the Narváez expedition—the first viceroy of New Spain, Antonio de Mendoza, arrived in Mexico, and the Crown promulgated laws that limited the grant of encomiendas to the conquerors and their descendants, which was originally made in perpetuity, to a duration of two or three lifetimes. In 1537—the year of Cabeza de Vaca's return to Spain—Pope Paul III issued the bull *Sublimis Deus* (*The Sublime God*), which asserted the capacities and rights of the American Indians as children of God, the implication being that they could not legally be held in personal servitude by the conquerors (Hanke 56; Adorno, *Polemics* 104–05). In 1542—the year of the first publication of the *Relación*—the Crown passed the so-called New Laws, which overwrote the earlier Laws of Burgos, renewing the prohibition on the enslavement of Indians and stipulating that all encomiendas were to revert to the Crown upon the death of their present incumbent. This was the most serious blow yet to the aristocratic pretensions of the conquistadores. "At one stroke," writes David Brading, the Crown "sought to terminate the institution which had been the foundation of the society established by the conquerors" (68).

Cabeza de Vaca's text was deeply invested in these intra-imperial political transformations leading up to the promulgation of the New Laws. Indeed, many of the events related in the first part of the text—leading up to the demise of the Narváez expedition—may be said to revolve around the underlying thematic conflict between an individualist and a corporatist idea of the imperial project. In the *Relación*, this conflict manifests itself for the first time even before the expedition's departure from its Caribbean base in Santo Domingo, when more than one hundred and forty men desert "because of the favors and promises" ("por los partidos y promessas"; 1: 23; 22; ch. 1) made to them by other conquerors on the island. The decision not to return to the ship due to individualist ambition threatens to disrupt the chain of command that linked the sovereign at the top with the common foot soldier at the bottom of the imperial order. This individualist ambition of the conqueror is personified by the character of the governor, Narváez, whose insolent insubordination to imperial goals betrays Spain's transcendent imperial mission in the New World. The corporate state is personified, of course, by Cabeza de Vaca himself, royal treasurer, loyal subject, and humble chronicler of the disasters that befell the Narváez expedition.

The conflict over leaving or returning to the ship soon evolves into a disagreement between two ways of proceeding once the North American mainland comes into sight. The governor favors leaving the ships behind and penetrating the interior on horseback. Others, such as Cabeza de Vaca and the imperial scribe who has come along on the expedition, firmly oppose leaving the ships without securing a safe port to protect them and the interest of the Crown; however, facing the governor's decision to go inland by horse, Cabeza de Vaca requests a notarized record of his opposition to Narvaez's ill-considered decision (Adorno and Pautz 1: 40–43; ch. 4). When writing his account, Cabeza de Vaca dwells on this incident because there is more at stake here than a disagreement over the best means of transportation in pre-Hispanic Florida. While the association of the horse with aristocratic individualism, autonomy, and cunning in Western culture is at least as old as Odysseus's famous feat at Troy, the literary trope of the ship stands for corporate enterprise in works from Apollonius Rhodius's *Argonautica*, in which the Argonauts hunt for the Golden Fleece, to the ship of state in Cicero's *De re Publica* (*On the Republic*) and Horace's *Odes*, and beyond.[3] Cabeza de Vaca's sixteenth-century Spanish reader, however, would have found a more current allegorical referent for the ship in Hapsburg official culture. As Mary Tanner has shown, the Hapsburgs were in the habit of fashioning themselves as the descendants of the Argonauts, the raiders of the Golden Fleece (9). Indeed, the year after the publication of Cabeza de Vaca's *Relación* at Valladolid, in 1556, Philip II had, upon his acceptance of the sovereignty of the Netherlands and Burgundy, even set out on a ship on which was built and painted a copy of the original *Argo*. That Cabeza de Vaca aimed to present his narrative in the context of Hapsburg imperial mythology and imagery is corroborated by the bibliographic history of his text, as both the 1542 and the 1555 editions appeared with a frontispiece that prominently features the double-headed eagle customarily displayed on the imperial banner of the Holy Roman Empire since the Middle Ages and later adopted in the Hapsburg coat of arms (*Relación que dio* and *Relación y comentarios*).

Significantly, in Cabeza de Vaca's *Relación*, the expedition's wreck follows in a straight plot line from the governor's decision to proceed by horse. It is not, however, the ship carrying Cabeza de Vaca that is wrecked in Florida—despite the running heads of the 1555 edition that say "Naufragios" ("Shipwrecks")— but rather the expedition that chose to abandon the ships. After the ships have left to meet up with the landed troops in another spot farther west and the penetration of the interior of Florida by horse has failed, the desperate men construct four rafts to reach Pánuco (in Veracruz). When Cabeza de Vaca and the men on his raft can no longer keep pace with the raft of the governor (who kept the healthiest men to himself), he begs his superior to tie the rafts together, but Narváez refuses. When Cabeza de Vaca asks Narváez what to do, he "answered me that it was no longer time for one man to rule another, that each one should do whatever seemed best to him in order to save his own life, [and] that he intended so to do it. And saying this he veered away with his raft" ("me respondió que ya no era tiempo de mandar unos a otros, que cada uno hiziesse lo que mejor le pareciese que era para salvar la vida, que él ansí lo entendía de hazer. Y diciendo esto se alargó con su barca"; Adorno and Pautz 1: 89, 91; 88, 90; ch. 10). The subsequent wreck of all the rafts and the death of Narváez's band (which the reader learns of only later in the narrative) are thus attributed to the breakdown of the corporate imperial body in the New World due to the individualist ambitions of autonomous hidalgos.

As Pier Luigi Crovetto points out in his analysis of the shipwreck motif in the literatures of the New World, the protagonist typically suffers shipwreck following "multiple [acts of] disobedience against paternal authority (the king)." The loss of contact with the paternal authority results "in an immediate and successive mutation characterized as a 'barbarization'" (40). In the *Relación*, this "barbarization" resulting from aristocratic insubordination against the authority of the monarch is realized by the gradual descent of Narváez's faction into chaos, anarchy, and even cannibalism.

> [B]eing disembarked, the governor had revoked the authority of the comptroller as his lieutenant, and he gave the command to a captain whom he had with him, named Pantoja. . . . Pantoja, who had remained as lieutenant, treated them very badly. And not being able to endure it, Sotomayor . . . who had come on the expedition as camp master, set against him and gave Pantoja such a blow that it killed him, and thus they went on dying. And the flesh of those who died was jerked by the others. (133, 135; ch. 17)

> [E]stando desembarcados, el governador avía revocado el poder que el contador tenía de lugarteniente suyo, y dio el cargo a un capitán que traía consigo que se dezía Pantoxa. . . . Allende desto, Pantoxa, que por teniente avía quedado, les hazía mal tratamiento. Y no poniéndolo sufrir, Sotomayor . . . , que en el armada avía venido por maestre de campo, se rebolvió con él y le dio un palo de que Pantoja quedó muerto, y así se fueron acabando. Y los que morían los otros los hazían tasajos. (132, 134)

The first half of Cabeza de Vaca's *Relación* thus articulates an ideological opposition between an older idea of empire—the feudal empire of "(re-) conquest," held together by the voluntary loyalty of largely autonomous neofeudal hidalgo conquerors—and a newer idea of empire—an empire of peace, based on a corporate, centralized Hapsburg state (Bauer 51).

Allegories of Transformation: Cabeza de Vaca's New World Epic

Because of its disenchanted account of the hardships suffered by the four survivors of the Narváez expedition in a barren landscape in North America where the fabulously rich cities they had sought to conquer remained elusive, Cabeza de Vaca's narrative has often been seen as more reliable and realistic by modern historians and literary critics than most other chronicles of discovery and conquest. And because of his detailed descriptions of the customs of indigenous groups that they encountered on their westward journey, Cabeza de Vaca has even been dubbed (somewhat anachronistically) North America's first ethnographer. However, this so-called modern proto-ethnographic rhetoric that emerges in Cabeza de Vaca's narrative is dependent on a dense literary signification that brings the persuasive power of time-honored motifs and tropes to bear on the reader. On the one hand, the *Relación* makes use, as Kun Jong Lee has argued, of the biblical source of the shipwreck motif, specifically of Pauline typology. Cabeza de Vaca "portray[s] himself as the Spanish Paul among American Gentiles" (245). But on the other hand, as many critics have also noted, the motives of shipwreck and wandering connect this text to the classical literary tradition, particularly the *Odyssey*. While some have therefore seen this New World narrative as a modern epic of sorts (e.g., Bishop), others have called it an anti-epic, arguing, in the words of Beatriz Pastor, that in its "cancellation of riches, glory, and power as fundamental motors of action," this text rejects "the previous model of epic action" (*Armature* 286, 288; see also González Acosta 167, 182–83).

To discern the close political connections between Cabeza de Vaca's arguments about conquest and empire on the one hand and the proto-ethnographic form of his text on the other, it is salient to revisit the relationship between this text and the epic tradition in more detail. In so doing, however, it must be observed at the outset that, despite many readers' strong sense of the epic qualities of this text, we find no explicit references to the *Odyssey* or the epic tradition anywhere in the *Relación*. What we do find is a curiously singular observation about one of his Indian captors in the 1555 edition of the *Relación* that was absent from the earlier, 1542 edition: "they gave me as a slave to an Indian with whom Dorantes was staying, who was blind in one eye, as was his wife and a son that he had as well as another person *who was in his company, to the effect that all of them were blind in one eye*" ("Con este concierto yo quedé allí y me dieron por esclavo a un indio con quien Dorantes estava, *el qual era tuerto, y su muger y un hijo que tenia y otro que estava en su compañia, de manera que todos eran tuertos*"; Adorno and Pautz 1: 129; 128; ch. 17; emphasis mine).

It is possible that Cabeza de Vaca added this curious passage after having encountered a summary of the joint report that three of the four survivors of the Narváez expedition filed upon their return to Mexico, which was written by the royal chronicler of the Indies, Gonzalo Fernández de Oviedo. In his summary Oviedo, who had received a humanist education in Italy as a young man, had repeatedly alluded to the "pilgrimage of Ulysses" ("peregrinación de Ulixes") in reference to Narváez's demise and commented upon his loss of an eye ("perdió un ojo"; *Historia general* [1853] 579) during his earlier confrontation with Cortés in order to elaborate the moral significance of his story:

> If Pánfilo de Narváez had not forgotten how he was treated in New Spain and could have seen how his intentions came out backward, he would not have looked for other reckless and fatiguing adventures. . . . Even after he got out of prison and out of Cortés' claws, he found his wife, María de Valenzuela, who had for some years been blessed with as good fame and reputation as Penelope may have had. . . . I advised him as a friend to remain peacefully at home in the company of his wife and children and to give thanks to God. . . . However, since his desires moved him to order others about, it must have seemed to him that what I was saying was not so fitting as what he was doing. And that's the end of it—like any bad business—owing to his death. (*Journey* 1–2)
>
> Si Pamphilo de Narvaez no perdiera la memoria de cómo fué tractatdo en la Nueva España, é mirára quán al revés le salieron sus pensamientos, no buscara otros torbellinos é fatigas. . . . É aun despues que salió de la prission é uñas de Cortés, halló á su mugger Maria de Valençuela, que avia algunos años que le atendia en tan Buena fama é reputaçionm como pudo estar Penélope. . . . é aconsejándole yo, como amigo, que se sosegasse ya en su casa é comañia de su muger é hijos, é diesse graçias á Dios. . . . como sus desseos guiaban á este mandar hijos agenos, debiérale de paresçer que lo que yo deçia no era tan á su propóssito como lo quél negoçiaba. É assi acabó como negoçios mal fundados é para su muerte. (580)

Also, it was Oviedo, not Cabeza de Vaca or one of his later editors, who first referred to the failure of the Narváez expedition as "naufragios" (*Historia general* [1853] 582) and to the subsequent travails of the four survivors as "peregrinaciones" ("pilgrimages" ; 582; my trans.).

As Rolena Adorno and Patrick Charles Pautz note, the sense in which Oviedo applied the term *naufragios* was "not with the literal meaning of 'shipwrecks' but rather the figurative one of 'disasters' or 'calamities,'" and this usage thus evidences the "moralizing purpose" to which Oviedo lent his account of the Narváez expedition (3: 42, 43). But what is the larger moral connection that Oviedo (and later Cabeza de Vaca) aimed to draw here for the sixteenth-century reader between one-eyed Narváez's demise and the *Odyssey*? After all, Narváez's one-eyedness would seem to associate him not with Ulysses but with his epic antagonist Polyphemus. However, already in the *Odyssey* the figure of one-eyed Polyphemus may be read, as Max Horkheimer and Theodor Adorno have pointed out in a celebrated reading, as representing Odysseus's older sense of identity as an Iliadic raider of cities who knew the world through conquest and whose behavior had "not yet become objectified in the form of 'character'" (66). Polyphemus's single eye, they argue, recalls the "nose and the mouth, more primitive than the symmetry of eyes and ears, which, with the security guaranteed by two unified perceptions, is the virtual prerequisite of identification, depth, and objectivity" (64). Odysseus's epic encounters with one-eyed Polyphemus—and with monsters more generally—thus demythify the notion of the human as demigod and the aristocratic value of *kleos*, a warrior's glory, that had prevailed in the mythic world of the *Iliad*. There, the boundary between mortals and immortals was entirely permeable and fluid, and the hero stood beyond the human categories of good and evil as well as beyond the moral bounds of duty and the subjection to temporal authority. By contrast, the *Odyssey* introduces a rift between the natural world of mortals and the supernatural world of immortals, thus initiating a long process of demythification in Western culture that Horkheimer and Adorno call the "dialectic of enlightenment," in which the individual asserts their self through self-denial (54). In other words, Odysseus "kills" his former Iliadic self by projecting it upon monsters in the first-person narrative that he relates to the Phaeacians, but only after he emerges naked and destitute on their island from a traumatic shipwreck and ritual cleansing—after spiritual death and rebirth—as an apparently better man.[4]

But when exploring the epic resonances in the literary record of the Narváez expedition, we must also remember that the early modern reader would have known the Greek hero not directly from the Homeric originals but only from their later classical and medieval mediations, mainly Virgil's rewriting of the two Homeric poems in the *Aeneid* and the medieval tradition that had culminated in Dante's *Divine Comedy* (see Bleicher 4–10). In this tradition, Ulysses (as Odysseus is named in Virgil's Latin) is a deeply problematic figure who meets a notoriously bad end. In the *Aeneid*, for example, it was precisely Homer's Odyssean cunning that became the object of Virgil's moral and metafictional critique when rewriting the Homeric epics for imperial Rome. As in the *Odyssey*, in the *Aeneid*, too, the motif of shipwreck was crucial in the elaboration of this new epic enterprise. As the reader may recall, however, it is not the epic hero himself, Aeneas, but rather his helmsman, Palinurus, who suffers and dies vicariously by falling into the sea after the Trojan party leaves Dido's Carthage. David Quint has argued that the substitution of Palinurus for the hero Aeneas as the sufferer of shipwreck represents Virgil's critique of the Homeric hero in a series of "repetitions with a difference" in which Virgil redefines the epic hero for a new age that demanded the individual's self-sacrifice for the community—the *pietas* ("piety") and *clementia* ("clemency") that Aeneas must acquire in the course of his own epic pilgrimage (91). The reason for this ethical transformation in the *Aeneid*, Quint argues, has to do with the different political structure of Roman (and especially Augustan) imperialism: whereas the Greek empire had been a colonial settler empire, a loose confederation of city-states spread across the Mediterranean, the Roman Empire was based on a centralized absolutist model. It is in Virgil's articulation of an ethos demanding the sacrifice of the individual's independent will in which Quint sees the profound influence of the *Aeneid* on the subsequent history of Western literature. The articulation of an ethical discourse of *pietas* and *clementia* in the *Aeneid* is accompanied by a metafictional commentary on the new epic poem's form. As Quint goes on to show, the poet's use of *letras* ("letters"), like his hero's use of *armas* ("weapons"), is self-consciously restrained in the *Aeneid*—plain, disciplined, passive, and, thus, subordinated to the higher truth of the imperial order. While Virgil generally upheld the value of rhetoric as the protector of virtue, he was also wary of the potential dangers that the aristocratic values espoused by the Homeric hero presented to imperial claims of universal truth (Quint 95).

If the Homeric epic hero was reinterpreted thus negatively in subsequent post-Hellenic epics, Ulysses was further demoted from pagan Hades to Christian hell during the Middle Ages, in Dante's Augustinian rereading in *Inferno*, where we find the Greek hero eternally engulfed in flames in the seventh circle of hell. It is in the context of this late medieval hagiographic substratum that Enrique Pupo-Walker, in a series of important essays, has seen the significance of the shipwreck motif in the *Relación*. According to Pupo-Walker, Cabeza de Vaca follows a hagiographic tradition of narrators who, after their experience of shipwreck, reflect back upon the *via non vera*, their aberrant lives before the pathbreaking disaster, and the subsequent pilgrimage of introspection, confession, conversion, and salvation. Like these literary predecessors, the narrator of the *Relación* portrays the shipwreck as an eye-cleansing experience with providential significance. As God's hand effecting a change of the pilgrim's *animo* (the rational apparatus of the mind), shipwreck confronts the individual with a new beginning and the opportunity for moral reevaluation. The literary motif of *naufragios* thus signals a general progression from loss to recovery, from perdition to salvation, from a state of sin to an awareness and rejection of the sin of Odyssean pride (Pupo-Walker, "Pesquisas," "Notas," and "Sobre el legado").

But there is yet another significance in the shipwreck motif, as well as in the oblique invocation of the *Odyssey* in the *Relación* and the explicit references in Oviedo. For, as Pupo-Walker notes, the transformation of the protagonist from conqueror to pilgrim in the *Relación* is accompanied by a "subtle rhetorical inversion" ("sutil inversión retórica"; my trans.; "Pesquisas" 535) that gradually transform the narrative from a *historia* ("history") to a spiritual autobiography following the relation of Cabeza de Vaca's shipwreck. Although Pupo-Walker does not pursue this line of inquiry, it is again instructive to see this rhetorical inversion in the context of Dante's *Divine Comedy* and its metafictional dialogue with the epic tradition. In other words, we must see this rhetorical inversion not only as the natural form following from the humble circumstances of Cabeza de Vaca's experience in the North American frontier but also as a deliberate narrative device that betrays a consciousness of the traditional connection between *armas* and *letras* and of the dual journey—fictional and metafictional—that has been an integral part of the epic genre from Homer's *Odyssey* to Derek

Walcott's *Omeros*. Thus, in the *Inferno*'s famous prologue scene, the poet compares himself, the imminent pilgrim before his return to "the path that does not stray" (Dante 1.3), to a man who, having been shipwrecked but now safely ashore, turns back to regard his former "life's way" (Dante 1.1) in the "shadowed forest" that almost led him to perdition (Dante 1.2). He "cannot clearly say how I had entered the wood" because he was "so full of sleep just at the point where I abandoned the true path" (1.10–12). But now he has been awakened.

> And just as he who, with exhausted breath,
> having escaped from sea to shore, turns back
> to watch the dangerous waters he has quit,
>
> so did my spirit, still a fugitive,
> turn back to look intently at the pass
> that never has let any man survive.
>
> E come quei che con lena affannata,
> uscito fuor del pelago a la riva,
> si volge a l'acqua perigliosa e guata,
>
> così l'animo mio, ch'ancor fuggiva,
> si volse a retro a rimirar lo passo
> che con lasciò già mai persona viva.   (1.22–27)

As Lansing has pointed out, nautical imagery was commonly applied in medieval and early modern literature not only to signify every man's journey through life but also a poet's experience in undertaking literary composition. Dante, for example, wrote his *Commedia* (*Divine Comedy*) in part as a palinode to his earlier works—*Convivio* (*The Banquet*) and the *Monarchia* (*Monarchy*)—which were "stained with a tincture of Aristotelian-Averroist philosophy" (Lansing 162n1). The "*selva oscura*," the forest trodden by the poet prior to his journey to hell, thus represents a period of Dante's life as a knower and a writer, "a spiritual slumber in which Dante followed the calling of Lady Philosophy" (Lansing 168). Other critics agree, arguing that the figure of Ulysses in the *Divine Comedy* personifies a presumptuous individualistic pride of philosophical independence and reflects "Dante's conscious concern with himself" as a poet (Barolini 116; see also Mazzotta). Thus, in canto 26, Dante's Ulysses laments, as Oviedo's Narváez may have, his fateful decision not to return home to his wife, his artful persuasion of his comrades to follow him, and his final shipwreck beyond the Pillars of Hercules, demarcating the circle of knowledge:

> I sailed away from Circe, who'd beguiled me
> to stay more than a year there, near Gaeta—
> before Aeneas gave that place a name—neither my fondness

> for my son nor pity
> for my old father nor the love I owed to
> Penelope, which would have gladdened her,
>
> was able to defeat in me the longing
> I had to gain experience of the world
> and of the vices and worth of men.
>
> [M]i departi' da Circe, che sottrasse
> me più d'un anno là presso a Gaeta,
> prima che sì Enëa la nomasse,
>
> né dolcezza di figlio, né la pieta
> del vecchio padre, né 'l debito amore
> lo qual dovea Penelopè far lieta,
>
> vincer potero dentro a me l'ardore
> ch'i' ebbi a divenir del mondo esperto
> e de li vizi umani e del valore . . .   (26.89–98)

Similar to St. Augustine's rejection of the Neoplatonic idea that the power of the individual's intellect was a sufficient vehicle for the attainment of Truth and the Absolute, Dante rejected the idea of natural philosophy as a means for the pursuit of truth by sending his Ulysses into shipwreck, death, and eternal damnation, which the poet himself was able to escape only by his pilgrimage through hell. For Dante, Ulysses's shipwrecked voyage beyond the Pillars of Hercules was an image of the "misguided philosophical Odyssey," the *via* ("life's path") that was revealed to the poet as *non vera* ("aberrant") only through the eye-opening experience of shipwreck (D. Thompson 53). Dante's *Divine Comedy* thus inflicts upon the classical epic tradition a "fundamental rupture between truth and a language which is caught up in the world of contingency. . . . The text gives a remarkable exemplification of the inadequacy of knowledge and rhetoric to reach truth." Whereas the ancients, such as Virgil and Cicero, had systematically linked rhetoric and history, Dante directed his critique "against Cicero's sense of history as the world of man's own construction" (Mazzotta 83, 69).

Thus, Cabeza de Vaca, after reading Oviedo's moralizing commentary, may have added in his 1555 edition of *Relación* a reference to a "one-eyed" ("tuerto") captor in order to evoke Ulysses's captivity in Polyphemus's cave at the very place that marks Cabeza de Vaca's narrative's rhetorical inversion from a chronicle of conquest to a spiritual autobiography and pilgrimage (Adorno and Pautz 1: 129; 128; ch. 17). This is not only an ethical commentary on his transformation from conqueror to pacifier but also a poetological and metahistorical commentary on his role as a historian in the writing of history of the New World. Thus, Cabeza de Vaca's oblique evocation of Odysseus is in striking rhetorical contrast to Oviedo's explicit invocation. In Oviedo's *Historia general y natural (General and Natural History)*, some of the prominent characters of classical literature—Ulysses, Jason, Hercules, and Medusa—recurrently function as rhetorical figures to convince the reader of Oviedo's moral interpretation of the demise of the Narváez expedition. In Cabeza de Vaca's text, by contrast, the story of Ulysses is evoked without ever being explicitly mentioned. Despite many readers' intuitive sense of the epic qualities of Cabeza de Vaca's narrative, there are no allusions to the Greek hero, his shipwreck and wanderings, or his alter ego Polyphemus anywhere in Cabeza de Vaca's narrative. This is significant because it sheds light on the role that the *Odyssey* and the classical tradition plays as a subtext for the *Relación* as a New World epic heralding the rise of a modern proto-ethnographic scientific rhetoric: whereas in Oviedo the evocation of the classical figure of Ulysses functions metaphorically to elaborate a certain moral lesson, in Cabeza de Vaca's narrative, the reference to Ulysses functions metonymically, never separating itself from the ethnographic realism of the narrative.[5] That is, Oviedo's metaphor apprehends the New World in terms of similitude, while Cabeza de Vaca's metonymy apprehends its subject matter by emphasizing difference and by reducing the general and the abstract to the concrete and particular. By effacing the author's awareness of the classical tradition, Cabeza de Vaca's *Relación* renounces his role as historian and active creator of meaning and instead emphasizes his role as a passive recorder of things experienced in a new world. It is through this modern rhetorical stance—the denial of classical rhetoric—that Cabeza de Vaca's account has persuaded his (early) modern readers, who have privileged this as a documentary source about early North American Native cultures and natural history that is more reliable than the chronicles of the conquest.

NOTES

1. That is to say, Echevarría's depiction engages with a teratological trope frequently seen in colonial narratives, where physical deformity or difference is used to symbolize moral or cultural otherness.

2. For a discussion of the theme of circularity in this film, see Gordon, "Exoticism"; see also Echevarría's own description of this scene in his introduction to the film's screenplay (Sheridan 18–19).

3. On the literary history of the ship of state, see N. Thompson. On the literary history of the shipwreck, see Blumenberg.

4. On the rhetoric of demythification in Cabeza de Vaca's *Relación*, see also Pastor, *Armature* 136–45.

5. On the "ethnographic allegoresis" of Cabeza de Vaca's *Relación*, see Rabasa 49–52; on metaphor and metonymy, see White, *Tropics* 5 and *Content* 115–19.

Naufragios and the Creation of a Latino Literary Canon

Lázaro Lima

Cabeza de Vaca's *Relación*, also known as *Naufragios* (*Shipwrecks*), is one of the most anthologized, studied, and representative texts from the Spanish colonial period in the Americas and holds the distinct honor of being canonized in the literary traditions of Spain, Latin America, and the United States. The processes through which these varied literary traditions have canonized Cabeza de Vaca's text provide a telling story about the nature of literary studies' three pillars—canonicity, periodicity, and critique—and how producing knowledge in the interpretive humanities is never a disinterested proposition. The designation of a text as valuable, representative, or great to any national literary tradition requires understanding that these designations are neither value-free nor neutral. *Naufragios* provides a case in point that allows students to evaluate how national literary canons are forged and renegotiated and how critique is central to these processes. In what follows, I focus on how teaching Cabeza de Vaca's *Naufragios* allows us to model an ethics of representation that is meaningful, beyond mastery of the text's rhetorical conceits, by allowing learners to parse knowledge production with more nuance than they would otherwise be accustomed to in the humanities classroom. It is in this sense that *Naufragios* becomes a text through which we can distinguish how our literary and cultural past—that is, how we periodize and canonize works in literary studies—is not a settled proposition but an ongoing negotiation between what we tell ourselves about that past. Questions regarding who gets to decide what we canonize, and to what ends, should be of signal importance not just to literary historians but also to students, who can extrapolate key lessons about how knowledge is produced: lessons that stand to serve them well beyond the classroom. In other words, when we decolonize texts such as *Naufragios*, we allow ourselves the freedom to pose interpretive problems about the nature of knowledge production, literary canon formation, and the ethics of representation. The recent removal from public spaces of statues of figures such as Christopher Columbus and Juan de Oñate, statues of Confederate generals, and Civil War monuments has shown that there is a new urgency in understanding how and why our historical, cultural, and literary forebears are being reinterpreted and to what ends.

A reckoning is taking place with the legacies of settler colonialism, exogenous domination, and the role of race, language, ethnic identity, and the politics of representation in the historical and literary imaginaries of the United States. *Naufragios* seems like a distant and unlikely player in these conversations, but its established canonical status, in both Spanish and Latin American literary studies, has allowed the text to serve as a malleable artifact in the more recent history of the Latino literary canon. This makes this text a fascinating case study that allows students to more clearly discern the role of the critic in reimagining literary history from the vantage point of the country's largest minority, and one of its most racially, ethnically and linguistically diverse groups: Latinos (over sixty million people). *Naufragios* has served critics interested in understanding how Latinos didn't simply appear overnight in what is today the United States or as merely the result of twentieth and twenty-first century migrations.

Once students have a clear grasp of the processes through which texts are deemed canonical in the creation of national literary histories, it becomes easier to contextualize how *Naufragios* either conforms to or deviates from the horizon of expectations we have about literary texts from the sixteenth-century Spanish colonial period in the Americas. What is more difficult to accomplish, however, is training students to discern how conflicts of interpretation over literary tradition are at the heart of literary canon formation; this difficulty arises whether we teach Cabeza de Vaca in English or in Spanish or in a survey course or a more advanced seminar. Teaching *Naufragios* through the lens of literary history allows us to more clearly demonstrate how conflicts of interpretation (critique) are central to producing new knowledge that builds on previous work. Secondary critical essays illustrate how conflicts of interpretation produce literary history that then beget canonized objects of study. As I show below, those essays' readings of *Naufragios* allow me to demonstrate how a seemingly temporally distant text can produce new understandings of how canon formation is intimately tied to questions of race, ethnic identity, and national belonging.

Teaching Naufragios *through Literary History*

The story of the founding of the Latino literary canon and how it intersects with American literary studies, as well as with Spanish and Latin American literary history, has not yet been written, but its genesis is the result of the indefatigable work undertaken by pioneering Chicano and Latino critics in the early 1970s (Lima 91–126). The late Mexican American literary critic Luis Leal was one of the first to argue for understanding Chicano literature, or Mexican American literature more broadly, as an extension of the literary canon of Spain and Latin America. Doing so, he hoped, would allow what today we call Latino literature to eventually be considered part of the literary tradition of the United States. In 1973 he provocatively wrote, "To consider Chicano literature as a part of American literature is an object too idealistic, at least for the time being, for socially Chicanos are considered a group apart" (19). In his now classic essay, "Mexican American Literature: A Historical Perspective," Leal went on to note that "we shall consider Chicano literature here to be that literature written by Mexicans and their descendants living or having lived in what is now the United States" (21). Despite acknowledging the idealistic nature of the project, Leal sets the geographic parameters for studying Chicano literature by suggesting that it begins with the literary-historiographical deconstruction of American literary culture. For Leal, this rewriting entails reenvisioning a Chicano past that begins with what he calls the "Hispanic Period," "characterized by prose writings of a historical or semi-historical nature including many descriptions left behind by explorers of the region where the majority of Chicanos now live" (22). Foremost among these, he avers, is "the *Relaciones* of Alvar Núñez Cabeza de Vaca" (22). Leal wrote his essay for the first issue of *Revista Chicano-Riqueña*, a journal that set the tone for Chicano, Puerto Rican, and, more broadly, Latino creative and scholarly writing. Leal's strategic positioning of Cabeza de Vaca's text as an example of early Chicano writing was clearly intended to situate Chicano, and more broadly, Latino literature within what is now the United States in order to problematize the nature of national belonging, literary affiliation, and America's relationship to Chicano writing. If Chicano literature could not "for the time being" be considered part of American literature because Chicanos were "a group apart," he set out to defamiliarize the United States as a stable cartographic unity by establishing the contingent and fluid nature of the United States, and its literary history, as an imagined community.

Leal was not the first to make this position tenable, but he was able to consolidate a literary project with very high social, cultural, and political stakes at a time when Chicano literature and Latino writing were virtually unknown in the academy. Leal was in essence echoing the critic Ray Padilla in asserting that "all work prior to 1848 can be treated as pre-Chicano Aztlanense materials" (Leal 19; Padilla 7). Padilla's assertion sought to remind literary critics that the end of the Mexican-American War did not mar the trajectory and continuity of Chicano culture. His invocation of Aztlán—the mythic homeland of the Aztecs (Mexica people) in the present-day southwest of the United States—sought to reinforce the ties between the region as a place of origin and as a place from which to legitimate a cultural enterprise, a place to stand and speak Chicano culture. For both Leal and Padilla, becoming Chicano is therefore part of a broader historical process determined by cause-effect relations between and among peoples of the United States. The historicist positions elaborated by these scholars, and the Spanish colonial narratives they included as examples of Chicano literature, coincided with the emergence of Chicano and ethnic studies departments and programs. The institutionalization of these academic units largely created the conditions under which the canon of Latino literary studies emerged, and, not inconsequentially, it also ushered in the reconfiguration of the canon of literature in the United States. With the institutionalization of Chicano literary studies in the West, and Latino literary studies in the East, there came the need to found and explicate the theoretical basis and justification for a field of inquiry that seemingly lacked the methodological apparatus to understand its modes of production and diffusion, silences, and apparent lack of temporal contiguity. If a Chicano and Latino presence existed in the United States before the identity projects of the 1960s, then how could the apparent absence of cultural, historical, and literary forebears be explained?

Juan Bruce-Novoa provides the answer to this question in a foundational 1990 essay, "Naufragios en los mares de la significación: De la relación de Cabeza de Vaca a la literatura chicana," translated into English as "Shipwrecked in the Seas of

Signification: Cabeza de Vaca's *La relación* and Chicano Literature." Bruce-Novoa boldly asserts that Cabeza de Vaca's *Naufragios* founds Chicano literature, thereby renewing the investment begun by Leal and Padilla in a genealogy of Chicano writing as the necessary strategic starting point for its inclusion in American literature as a decidedly American object of study: "those of us who toil in the malleable field of Chicano criticism have utilized Leal's position to our advantage because it provides us with a historical base for what many consider to be a phenomenon too recent to be taken seriously at the level of national literature, or even established regional literatures" ("Shipwrecked" 3). For Bruce-Novoa, "one of the strategies that literary criticism incorporates to privilege certain canons is the theory of genealogical origins—the tracing of literary heritages to a remote antiquarian lineage" (3). His strategic rereading of *Naufragios* posits that Cabeza de Vaca's peregrinations are analogous to the struggles that Chicanos and other Latinos face in the United States:

> Those initiated into Chicano culture will now recognize the similarity with ANCdV [Cabeza de Vaca]. In fact, the similarities are astounding: leaving a native land in search of riches in a territory mostly unknown except for the hyperbolic legends surrounding it; the disillusionment felt upon facing the harsh and humiliating truth of the reality encountered; the loss of original cultural context in exchange for a new one which is hostile and alienating, capable of reducing the immigrant to slavery. Through a slow apprenticeship, great hardships, and mimesis, immigrants begin to improve their social position . . . frequently immigrants must take jobs the local citizens do not care to engage in because they are difficult, dangerous, or even illegal. Oftentimes the jobs require the workers to travel from one place to another. . . . In addition immigrants are forced to learn a new language. . . . In moments of crisis the immigrants seek refuge in the memories of their native land. (20–21)

Other critics, however, were not convinced by Bruce-Novoa's rewriting of literary history. Héctor Calderón and José Saldívar were quick to note that a "Spanish chronicler of the area which was later to form the northern regions of the viceroyalty of New Spain, like Cabeza de Vaca or Coronado writing in the sixteenth century, regardless of whatever sympathies he may have had for Native Americans, is not a Chicano but a Spaniard" (2). Their assertion raises the logical question, What does a sixteenth-century Spaniard have to do with Chicano or Latino writing? The literary historian Francisco Lomelí attempted to come to terms with these two conflicting positions. For Lomelí, "Cabeza de Vaca feels himself oscillating between two worlds after his extensive contact with various Indian groups, as if he were a transformed person, no longer only Spanish" (227). Lomelí distinguishes between Bruce-Novoa's and Leal's periodizing projects:

> To Juan Bruce-Novoa, this explorer intimates what a third culture would become, and by extension, what a Chicano would be. To Luis Leal, the

psychological impact had less importance within the extant sociohistorical forces as defined by the geopolitical interplay between Mexico and Anglo America. Instead, regionality and consciousness of race played primary roles in determining Chicano literary history. Therefore, the only requirement for a work to be considered under this rubric was for it to be written by a person of Mexican descent, no matter how remote or recent. (227–28)

Lomelí asks a crucial question: "In the process of erecting demarcations and parameters, one pivotal concern has emerged: How to grapple with the politics and poetics of reconstructing and/or appropriating a literary past. In doing so, is there in fact a danger of historical imperialism by adopting a work or author that supposedly pertained to another set tradition, or to no tradition at all?" (228). Yet despite his own caveat, Lomelí concludes that rereading this literary past is viable and necessary "even if it involves appropriating it," since "it seems obvious that Chicanos did not spring up like mushrooms in the 1960s nor from the ashes of nothingness, by extension of that logic neither have their writings" (230, 231). Lomelí points out that "there is ample evidence of literature produced by peoples of Mexican descent even before the term Chicano—or for that matter, Mexican American—existed." He concludes that "[a]ppropriation, consequently, becomes an indispensable methodology of revisionism and a medium for reconstructing origins, antecedents and background, all within a framework focusing on regional expression in the shadows of memory" (231). Lomelí convincingly argues that "[f]ew would quibble today about the classification of Alonso de Ercilla's *La araucana* as a foundational work of Chile—and by extension Latin America—, although it was always claimed by Spain until modern times" (230). Yet a Latino Cabeza de Vaca seems to find many detractors.

Lomelí's contribution to the debate has affirmed Leal and Bruce-Novoa's position. Lomelí's essay was written for the important Recovering the United States Hispanic Literary Heritage Project, and his conclusions have had clear repercussions insofar as they have legitimated the genealogical search for origins "in the shadows of memory" (231). Discussing with students just what versions of American cultural memories are to be salvaged, reconfigured, created, or re-created from the "shadows" provides a dynamic opportunity to demonstrate how these critics, and their work, have attempted to decolonize the academy and the canon of literary studies in the United States. From a distance it is now clear that Lomelí's position has attained de facto legitimacy in Latino literary studies. For example, *The Latino Reader*, by Harold Augenbraum and Margarita Fernández-Olmos—one of the earliest anthologies of pan-Latino literature of the United States—from its jacket purports to be "the first anthology to present the full history of this important *American literary tradition*" (my emphasis) and situates the beginnings of Latino literature precisely with *Naufragios*. The editors' introduction states:

[O]ne can say that Latinos are linked, directly or indirectly, to their precursors, the early Hispanic explorers in the southeastern and southwestern United States, in having to chart a course through a treacherous and often bewildering landscape. For contemporary Latino authors, however, the frontier is the literary culture of the United States, where they have been struggling to gain their rightful place. (xi)

It would appear that the "rightful place" Augenbraum and Fernández-Olmos refer to is both literal and metaphoric, as it implies a literal place (America) as well as a cognitive space (identity) from which to speak as Latinos and as Americans in the context of American literature. Augenbraum and Fernández-Olmos assert that Cabeza de Vaca serves an important function since his

> metamorphosis into a being neither European nor Indian, a cultural hybrid created by the American experience, converts the explorer into a symbolic precursor of the Chicano/a. Not entirely identified with either Mexican or Anglo society, the Chicano/a, like Cabeza de Vaca, undergoes a cultural adaptation and transformation that makes him or her the ideal New World American. S/he can change her/himself to fit the situation and celebrate that change—in other words, s/he can make a virtue of necessity. (xv)

For Augenbraum and Fernández-Olmos, the displacement of Latinos from the American literary culture and landscape necessarily involves remembering that they came from the place now called America. However, I am troubled by their notion that "[t]he Chicano/a, like Cabeza de Vaca, undergoes a cultural adaptation and transformation that makes him or her the ideal New World American," and I find it useful to explain my discomfort to students. First, the assertion assumes that becoming an American is not reciprocal but rather a process of accommodating to majoritarian ideology, hardly an ideal alternative in the face of cultural erasure and national subjection. Second, the argument comes dangerously close to assimilationist paradigms that do not question whether it is possible, or even plausible, for individuals to assimilate and make a virtue of necessity. Quite simply, irrespective of necessity, some bodies cannot assimilate, because of their corporeal markers of difference. Augenbraum and Fernández-Olmos echo what Bruce-Novoa considers to be Cabeza de Vaca's greatest asset: the "alterity . . . that permits [Cabeza de Vaca] to be the intermediary between two exclusive codes" (Augenbraum and Fernández-Olmos 13).

Bruce-Novoa's sacking of the literary-historiographical archive and Augenbraum and Fernández-Olmos's acceptance of the critical legacy of *Naufragios* are significant because they established the parameters from which to legitimate a literary project at a moment when the inroads made by the early 1970s civil rights movement to decolonize academic curricula were eroding as attacks on Latinos were being carried out in the courts of law and public opinion. The crisis surrounding the Latino disenfranchisement from American civic life was related to initiatives attempting to limit Latino political power by attacking the most vulnerable: immigrants. These initiatives gained a stronghold of support first in California and later throughout the country and consisted of legal assaults against Latino health care, education, and entry into civic life. The most notable legal actions in California were Proposition 187, introduced in 1994 to deny medical and public services to undocumented immigrants; Proposition 209, a referendum passed in 1996 outlawing "preferential" treatment based on race, color, ethnicity, or national origin (see California); and Proposition 227, introduced in 1998 to eliminate bilingual education, to name a few. In this cultural climate of crisis for Latinos in the 1990s, hiding or passing (neither possible in most cases nor ethically desirable) became pronounced strategies precisely when the curriculum was diversifying to reflect the historical realities of the populations the country had exploited as labor but barred from civic life through educational roadblocks. While Chicano and Latino studies programs were busy legitimizing their fields and areas of inquiry, the work that the Latino community craved was largely in the hands of those with the fewest resources: community advocates and Latino groups and organizations (San Miguel). At a time when diversity was gaining a stronghold in the academy and the nuances of race, ethnicity, and language were complicating the Manichean concept of race in the United States as an exclusively Black and white problem, these legal reactionary assaults against Latinos ultimately demanded that they should continue to be represented as the "forever foreigners" they were always assumed to be in the nation's official historical and cultural imaginary.

Not surprisingly, texts like *Naufragios* were embraced by many Chicano and Latino scholars because they offered proof to students and readers that Latinos were not a recent phenomenon in the United States, even though new waves of Latino immigration gave that impression. In the process, a text like this could assure Latino students that they too could be embraced by the state much the same way as Cabeza de Vaca had been assimilated into the emerging Latino literary canon, which—purportedly—was part of American literature. As Lisa Lowe notes, the institutionalization of ethnic studies and literature "provides a material base within the university for transformative critique," but "any field or curriculum that establishes orthodox objects and methods submits in part to the demands of the university and its educative function of socializing subjects into the state" (40, 41). Lowe's caveat is instructive. Literary critics could refer to colonial texts that made the theoretical inclusion of Latinos in the American literary canon plausible, often at the expense of foregoing the practical dirty work that cultural politics demands of committed cultural producers. This is not to suggest that academics working with endangered knowledge projects or their communities have to assume roles they are unwilling or unable to fulfill. It does mean that, when engaged with such projects, we need a clear understanding of what is at stake and who stands to benefit from disseminating the complex stories endangered knowledge projects are dying to tell.

Cabeza de Vaca's purported metamorphosis, his ability to serve as a cultural mediator—which presumably enabled him to pass for an Amerindian—helps to foreground problematic identity practices that posit assimilation as a paradigmatic solution to subaltern cultural displacements. Notable is the multicultural celebration of Cabeza de Vaca's ability as an outsider in the New World to become an other, in and through discourse, by virtue of the tales he weaves to his explicit reader (Charles V) about what led Amerindians to believe that he was a trader, shaman, leader, and demiurge. Thus, we begin to question *Naufragios*'s function as a foundational text in Latino literary studies, especially as it relates to the interpretive positions espoused by Leal, Bruce-Novoa, and Lomelí: critics who were deeply invested in reading Cabeza de Vaca as a Latino forefather. I do this to foreground an ethics of reading that would help instructors understand how serving as cultural brokers of Cabeza de Vaca's form of multiculturalism stands to reproduce what we presumably seek to undermine. Many sections in *Naufragios* illustrate different aspects related to these concerns regarding Chicano and Latino identity. Here, I offer some examples that allow for stimulating conversations in the classroom.

Teaching Cabeza de Vaca's Embodied Experience and Identity as a Latino

First, it is important to establish for students how *Naufragios* rhetorically establishes a type of self-fashioning that allows Cabeza de Vaca to be seen in a sympathetic light. *Naufragios*'s theme of loss of home, or migrancy, partakes of a long tradition of the wanderer that I often reiterate to students—from Odysseus to Moses and more recently to texts of migrant displacements—where a protagonist fights the odds to return home or find a sense of home in a diaspora. This metaphoric and literal homeward quest is essential for Cabeza de Vaca, since it will signal the restoration of order, unity, and status, the opposite of his naked ruminations through the American environment. His eventual return to Spain and the longed for accoutrements of monarchical favor mean that he will no longer be a foreigner, enslaved person, or guest at the mercy of his host's will. Cabeza de Vaca's narrative imbues his quest with meaning by relating what his body endured through the American territories that marked him. The story in *Naufragios* conjures his absent body for his explicit reader: what his eyes have seen, what his body has ingested, what his hands have touched, and what his heart has felt—the mortifications of a penitent in the service of the king of Spain. However, it is worth noting to students that unlike other conquistadores' narratives, Cabeza de Vaca's story recounts not how many bodies he subjected to imperial rule but how his own body was altered and marked by his American experience. His failure to "to conquer and govern the provinces that are found from the Rio de las Palrnas to the cape of Florida" ("para conquistar y governar las provincias que están desde el Río de las Palmas hasta el cabo de la Florida"; Adorno and Pautz 1: 23; 22; ch. 1) puts him in a precarious position where he must refashion his loss as a triumph and vest his testimony with authority. To this end, Cabeza de Vaca's corporeality will take center stage as he weaves a narrative of misfortunes reminiscent of biblical suffering and eventual redemption (Glantz, "Cuerpo" 420). The corporeal cost of his survival, however, in the scene in *Naufragios* where he and his companions encounter other Spaniards, reinforces the extent to which his body has been defamiliarized by his New World experience. I turn to this scene now as it is emblematic of many other instances in *Naufragios* where he passes through various registers of identity as shaman, healer, cultural go-between, or linguistic mediator.

Cabeza de Vaca relates how at the end of his eight-year quest he and the other survivors finally saw "traces of Christians" ("rastro claro de xhristianos"), and realizing "we understood that we were near them, we gave many thanks to God our Lord for wanting to take us out of so sad and wretched captivity" ("entendimos que tan çerca estavamos dellos, dimos muchas graçias a Dios nuestro Señor por querernos sacar de tan triste y miserable captiverio"; Adorno and Pautz 1: 245; 244; ch. 33). He appealed to his companions to go ahead and search for the Spaniards, but they refused because of fatigue. Then he walked ten leagues in a day, with Esteban and eleven Indians, in search of the Christians. The eventual meeting was fraught with corporeal misreadings. The Spanish "experienced great shock upon seeing me so strangely dressed and in the company of Indians. They remained looking at me a long time, so astonished that they neither spoke to me nor managed to ask me anything" ("recibieron gran alteración de verme tan extrañamente vestido y en compañía de indios. Estuviéronme mirando mucho espacio de tiempo, tan atónitos que ni me hablavan ni acertavan a preguntarme nada"; 1: 245; 244; ch. 33).

I point out to students how Cabeza de Vaca's corporeal markers of difference, his dress and sun-bronzed skin, prevent the Spaniards from recognizing one of their own (or so he says). The Spaniards have to recover from their astonishment in order to speak to their fellow Christian, who looks like the "Indians" with whom he has arrived. The Spaniards must recognize familiar linguistic utterances that mark Cabeza de Vaca as a fellow Christian. The Christian-Indian binary is resemanticized, and the encounter serves as the framing scene of the text, since it plays out the reiterative conflict around Cabeza de Vaca's becoming an other so convincingly that he risks losing any stable reference marker to his Spanish identity: he could not have survived without successfully passing as something other than a Spaniard.

After Cabeza de Vaca unsuccessfully attempted to prompt Narváez to fulfill his duty as a commander, there was a power vacuum that allowed Cabeza de Vaca to become the leader. On or near the mouth of the Mississippi river, Governor Narváez decided to separate the makeshift barges they had been using in the hope of reaching land. Narváez ordered that each barge attempt to reach land by whatever means necessary and began to row away from Cabeza de Vaca's makeshift raft. Narávez's barge had the "healthiest and most robust men," and Cabeza de Vaca and the men with him could not keep up. Cabeza de Vaca asked for a rope to attach his raft, which Narvaez refused. Then, he asked the governor for orders: "He answered me that it was no longer time for one man to rule another, [and] that each one should do whatever seemed best to him in order to save his own life" ("Él me respondió que ya no era tiempo de mandar unos a otros, que cada uno hiziesse lo que mejor le pareciesse, que era para salvar la vida"; Adorno and Pautz 1: 89, 91; 88, 90; ch. 10). The governor's leadership collapsed when he abandoned his post and men to save himself. In contrast, Cabeza de Vaca's call for unity in adversity casts a heroic aura over his actions (Molloy 431).

Cabeza de Vaca's hunger also serves as both a literal quest for food and a metaphoric search for home: home conceived as both a place to be (Spain) and a condition of being (as a Spanish subject). His metaphoric hunger for home is constantly threatened by his literal hunger for food. Indeed, food and the search for food become central metaphors for cultural interaction, identity formation, and passing. What he consumes affects both his survival and the more nuanced commodity exchanges that ensure his body's integrity through commerce. His dependency on the environment and his captors for food demonstrates that Spanish autonomy and mastery over the American environment is a myth. Cabeza de Vaca's recounting of how he was forced to become a medicine man makes the association between hunger, food, commerce, and identity clear:

> On that island . . . they tried to make us physicians without examining us or asking us for our titles. . . . And they demanded that . . . [we] make ourselves useful. We laugh at this. . . . And because of this, they took away our food until we did as they told us . . . ; and on account of this they treated us well, and refrained from eating in order to give their food to us, and they gave us skins and other things.   (Adorno and Pautz 1: 113; ch. 15)

> En aquella isla . . . nos quisieron hazer físicos sin esaminarnos ni pedirnos los títulos. . . . Y mandáronnos que hiziéssemos lo mismo y sirviéssemos en algo. Y nosotros nos reíamos dello. . . . Y por esto nos quitavan la comida hasta que hiziéssemos lo que ellos nos dezían . . . ; y por este respecto nos hazían buen tratamiento, y dexavan ellos de comer por dárnoslo a nosotros, y nos davan cueros y otras cosillas."   (1: 112; ch. 15)

Cabeza de Vaca's uncredentialed entry into Amerindian culture as a medicine man garners him a great reputation. Despite the misfortune and suffering of the Spaniards, "God our Lord" favors them with healing powers and the reciprocal favors of hospitable treatment and food from the indigenous peoples.

Once his identity is established as a healer, Cabeza de Vaca's "trade" as a medicine man allows him easier access to and coexistence with other Amerindian communities as well (1: 153; ch. 20). God's will, then, is posited as that which keeps Cabeza de Vaca alive. The association he establishes between his being favored by God and his success as a healer could not be more evident than in his story about the raising of a Susola Indian who seems dead and who functions in *Naufragios* as an Amerindian Lazarus figure. Cabeza de Vaca made the sign of the cross over the body, and that night "our Indians, to whom I had given prickly pears, . . . returned . . . and said that that one who had been dead and whom I had cured in their presence had arisen revived and walked about and eaten and spoken with them" ("nuestros indios a quien di las tunas . . . , se volvieron . . . y dixeron que aquél que estava muerto y yo avía curado en presencia dellos se avía levantado bueno y se avía passeado y comido y hablado con ellos"; 1: 163; 162; ch. 22).

It is useful for instructors to remind students of the biblical narrative of Lazarus of Bethany and how because of his resurrection Jesus's authority threatened to displace the Pharisees's control over the Jews who were coming to believe in Jesus. The point of contact between the biblical story and its appearance in *Naufragios* is the implicit association Cabeza de Vaca makes between himself and Jesus. The verisimilitude of Cabeza de Vaca's miraculous raising of a dead man, as told to him by the Amerindians, is achieved by his stating, in no uncertain terms, that "in all the land no one talked of anything else" ("en toda la tierra no se hablava en otra cosa"; 1: 165; 164). Cabeza de Vaca's miracle legitimates his position among the Amerindians to his explicit reader by demonstrating how they came to believe in him. Furthermore, in the economy of survival, he suggests that he is able to eat and survive by exploiting the role of healer that he says he has been thrust into. Before the apparent resurrection of the Amerindian, after all, he is rewarded with both an Amerindian's "bow . . . and a bag of crushed prickly pears" ("arco . . . yuna sera de tunas molidas"; 1: 165; 164).

It is worth noting that if food is the reward for the healings, which thus assure Cabeza de Vaca's survival, then it is not surprising that prickly pears—so essential to his subsistence—are the one alimentary constant that he alludes to. He is a connoisseur of these fruits, which he describes as being "the size of an egg, . . . vermilion and black and of very good flavor" ("del tamaño de huevo, . . . y son bermejas y negras y de muy buen gusto"; 1: 129; 128). They become a metaphor for his incorporation into the American natural environment and the identity negotiations that assure his transition from captive to healer in his economy of survival:

> During the entire time we ate the prickly pears we suffered thirst, and to remedy this we drank the juice of the prickly pears . . . until we were satisfied. It is sweet and the color of boiled must. . . . There are many kinds of prickly pears, and among them some are very good, although all of them seemed to me to be so, and my hunger never permitted me to choose among them or to consider which were the best . . .   (1: 149, 151; ch. 19)
>
> [E]n todo el tiempo que comíamos las tunas teníamos sed, y para remedio desto bevíamos el çumo de las tunas, y . . . hasta que nos hartávamos. Es dulçe y es de color de arrope. . . . Ay muchas maneras de tunas y entre ellas ay unas muy buenas, aunque a mi todas me paresçían ansí y nunca la hambre me dió espacio para escogerlas ni parar mientes en quáles eran mejores . . .   (1: 148, 150)

Cabeza de Vaca can distinguish the "kinds of prickly pears" that "are very good" from those he has to ingest for basic subsistence. He takes pleasure in relating the taste and color of their juice insofar as they serve not only as food and drink but also as satisfaction to his palate. His description of the prickly pears bears a direct relation to his faith, which he constructs discursively by echoing the promise made in the Gospel of John for those who have faith in God's word: "He who comes to Me shall never hunger, and he who believes in Me shall never thirst" (*Bible*, John 6.35). The prickly pears become a metaphor for Cabeza de Vaca's identity negotiations as a Christian subjected to the American environment. As he delivers his *relación* ("account") to the king of Spain, he also recounts how his enterprise is sanctioned by God. As a distinctly American food, the prickly pear becomes a symbol for going native through the incorporation of an other's foodstuff: his statement that "my hunger never permitted me to choose" ultimately signals how subsistence determines social relations and how outsiders must assimilate if they are to survive the local environment.

If going native means for the Spaniards identifying in important ways with the environment and the people who inhabit it by relinquishing the markers of their Spanish identities, then the inverse process of disidentification with the local people and their surroundings is underscored by the other apparent foreigner in *Naufragios*, Mala Cosa (Evil Being). Yet the similarities between the devilish being and the penitent Cabeza de Vaca are striking. They are both outsiders, medicine men who interact with the Amerindians enough to inspire awe and fear (Jáuregui, *Espectros* 89–122). The Amerindians relate to Cabeza de Vaca that fifteen or sixteen years earlier appeared a man they called Mala Cosa who took them and performed cuts and extractions, "pulled out their entrails" ("sacávales las tripas"; Adorno and Pautz 1: 167; 166; ch. 22), dislocated their arms, and later healed them. Like Cabeza de Vaca, this bearded outsider who seems to have come out of nowhere is capable of healing, but unlike the Christian healer, Mala Cosa performed surgery on those who did not need surgery. Cabeza de Vaca's surgical prowess is posited as a benefit to Amerindian bodies since his patients are understood to be ill, as when he opened the chest of an Amerindian man and extracted the point of an bone arrow from near the man's heart (ch. 29).

This incident, which takes place after he has had considerable practice healing, refers to the first and only time that Cabeza de Vaca performs surgery. This afflicted Amerindian's body is vested with the language of suffering and the arrow in his body is presented as the outward sign of an inter-Amerindian conflict that *Naufragios* remains silent about. We are left to assume that this Amerindian, lacking name and rank, is a casualty of the tribal wars Cabeza de Vaca refers to occasionally. His body is at once deficient and dependent on Cabeza de Vaca's ability to cure. So it is not coincidental that Cabeza de Vaca's one attempt at surgery is so fraught with danger. The danger of losing his authority as a medicine man if he fails, coupled with the danger of operating so near the heart, imbues his reportage with both sentimentality and courage. His acceptance of his role as surgeon makes his success all the greater. Perhaps deriving confidence from his prior successes, Cabeza de Vaca seemingly outperforms Mala Cosa's diabolical ability to heal.

By relating the story, Cabeza de Vaca creates for himself an identity that relies on the emerging self-sufficient subject: the conqueror who can aspire to monarchical favor even when returning home empty-handed except for his knowledge of the environment and people he has come in contact with. Through writing he can authorize both his competency and his subjectivity through the fiction of absolute mastery over the bodies of Amerindians.

This visible display of Cabeza de Vaca's goodness stands in stark contrast to Mala Cosa's evilness. Cabeza de Vaca exhorts the Amerindians "to believe in God and serve him because he was Lord of all things in the world, and that he blessed and rewarded the good, and punished the bad with perpetual fire" ("que creyessen en Dios y lo sierviessen por que era Señor de todas quantas cosas avía en el mundo, y que él dava galardón, y pagava a los buenos, pena perpetua de fuego a los malos"; Adorno and Pautz 1: 257; 256; ch. 35). Having established trust with the Amerindians, he describes how they rejoiced and began to lose their fear, an episode that reinforces his mastery over them. His words, like his hands, can appease and heal them.

Cabeza de Vaca's embrace of Amerindian food also allows him to distance himself from an earlier scene in the text where he mentions the anthropophagy and savagery of some of the Spaniards, which represents the epitome of social disorganization. A group of five survivors of the Narváez expedition arrived at Malhado Island, refused to be rescued by the Indians, and ended up being tested by hunger and cold weather: they "came to such dire need that they ate one another until only one remained" ("llegaron a tal estremo que se comieron los unos a los otros hasta que quedó uno"; 1: 105, 107; 104, 106; ch. 13). He goes on to relate how these actions produced a great scandal among the Indians, who—had they known the Spaniards would resort to cannibalism—"would have killed them, and all of us would have been in grave danger" ("los mataran, y todos nos diéramos en grande trabajo"; 1: 107; 106). Indeed, the traditional colonial analysis of cannibalism as a metaphor for savagery cannot account for its appearance in *Naufragios*. In analyzing this scene, I suggest to students that the inversion of stereotypical roles (Christians as cannibals, Amerindians as admonishers of cannibalism) is another example of Cabeza de Vaca's disidentification from other Spaniards. A second case of cannibalism occurred in the Narváez party on the coast of Texas, after a mutiny among the Spaniards, and that tale is passed from hand to hand until it reaches Cabeza de Vaca several years after the fact (ch. 17). This infamous incident further indemnifies him from complicity with the Narváez expedition; any culpability for its failure is the result of Narváez's leadership, or lack thereof. The Spaniards' cannibalism signals degeneration and the complete collapse of the civilizing mission and empire (see Jáuregui, "Going Native").

What I call Cabeza de Vaca's disidentifications from the Spanish cannibals, Narváez, and his party do not mean that Cabeza de Vaca identifies with the

Amerindians to the degree that readings of *Naufragios* by Bruce-Novoa, Lomelí, or Augenbraum and Fernández-Olmos would suggest. As I often remind students, Cabeza de Vaca's identifications with the Amerindians serve the interests of the empire. He disassociates himself from some Spaniards but never from the prerogatives of Spanish conquest and colonization.

Let's not forget that *Naufragios* has a colonial teleology and that Cabeza de Vaca states that he is informing the Spanish king about lands, peoples, and customs not just to cater to curiosity but because this information would be crucial in confrontations with the Indians during future expeditions (Adorno and Pautz 1: 187; ch. 25). This is a reiteration, in fact, of the purpose for his narration provided in his prologue to Charles V: "the account of it all is, in my opinion, information not trivial for those who in your name might go to conquer those lands" ("aviso, a mi parescer no liviano, para los que en su nombre fueren a conquistar aquellas tierras"; 1: 19; 18).

The Afterlives of Naufragios

When the passages referenced above are understood as opportunities for interrogating identity formation, they allow us to see how the type of assimilative and complete identification that Bruce-Novoa wishes to read into *Naufragios* is an overt literalization of the events related by Cabeza de Vaca. The events narrated in these passages foreground how Cabeza de Vaca's various identity negotiations were fashioned discursively and—it is important to restate this point, which may not be obvious to students—retrospectively in *Naufragios*. No matter how successful he was in fashioning his identities through *ingenio* ("wit"), Cabeza de Vaca did so rhetorically, and his success should be measured in relation to the identity performances he creates and not a true or immutable identity that may have existed outside the text. The myth of identification with the Amerindians that was to become a stand-in for Chicano and Latino identity projects positions *Naufragios* dangerously close to a unidirectional cultural capitulation that reifies assimilation, even if unwittingly. Equally unsatisfactory are the essentializing notions of subjectivity, characterized by Calderón and Saldívar, that permanently bracket Cabeza de Vaca as a foreigner in the land of Aztlán.

The legitimation crisis that beset Chicano and Latino studies and literature programs in the academy—and the endangered knowledge projects they were entrusted to document and represent—allows us to better understand the limits and possibilities of canon formation. Reading the crisis of legitimation in Latino literary studies along with *Naufragios* as the field's foundational text allows us to model for students how literary studies can intervene in the world and turn literary histories of exclusion to different ends. And if we are fortunate, students will be in a position to make better and more exacting demands of the literary forebears they have inherited.

From the Desert to the Digital World: Adapting Cabeza de Vaca

Luis Fernando Restrepo

As public and institutional support for literary studies and the humanities erodes, new opportunities for critical work are opening at the crossroads of new media and computing innovations that are revolutionizing approaches to cultural objects. In this context, as educators, we should incorporate into the curriculum the literacies and cultural competencies of our students in a digitally mediated world. With this goal in mind, I would like to propose a two-step approach to teaching the work of Álvar Núñez Cabeza de Vaca that starts, in one unit of the course, by examining the literary and multimedia adaptations of the sixteenth-century *Relación* (*Account*) and then proceeds, in a second course unit, with student-led multimedia public humanities projects such as podcasts, art interventions, and virtual exhibits, among other possibilities.

Unit 1: Adaptation as Engagement with the Colonial Archive

Among the iconic images of the North American West produced by Fredric Remington is the painting *Cabeza de Vaca in the Desert*. Remington's work is stamped on T-shirts and baby apparel sold online. Someone is profiting from the conquistadores' bad rap! This is just one of multiple adaptations of the *Relación*. For Rolena Adorno, the opaqueness and ambiguities of the *Relación* have kept alive the mystery and invited multiple reinventions of Cabeza de Vaca's story ("Cabeza de Vaca Phenomenon" 20). What other factors make this colonial text so attractive to audiences from different times and places? The fact is that the novels, films, children's books, artwork, and musical compositions that Cabeza de Vaca and his companions have inspired are a valuable resource to examine critically how Iberian colonialism and the *Relación* have been understood by different generations and how adapters have projected their aspirations and idiosyncrasies onto the sixteenth-century historical figures that survived Narvaez's disastrous expedition. In other words, these adaptations allow us to examine the aesthetics, politics, and even the marketing of memory. With so many options for video streaming, our students come to college with a developed taste for visual narratives, including many films and television series adapted from literary texts. However, students' command of a critical vocabulary for analyzing film adaptations is quite uneven and often limited to the novel-to-film paradigm that focuses on an adaptation's fidelity to the original text. Adaptations, however, are much more than copies. Therefore, starting with an introduction to adaptation theory is important, either with a lecture summarizing key points or with a selection of assigned readings. There is an ample bibliography on adaptation (Cutchins et al.; Leitch; Hutcheon). Linda Hutcheon presents adaptation as a creative mining of texts, a telling and retelling of tales in intentional variations, transcoding into different media, in a complex interplay of the familiar and the new that brings new meanings without canceling the adapted text (9). Thus, briefly stated, adaptation is a critical and creative appropriation that goes beyond the common concerns for fidelity and proximity to a fixed original. With this theoretical foundation, I assign selections of the different adaptations of Cabeza de Vaca's *Relación*, asking students to consider the following questions: What does each adaptation borrow from the original? Does it project the present into the past or bring the past to the present? What new perspectives on the past are offered? What is added in the transcoding process, from account to novel, music, or painting? What is gained and lost in these adaptations?

Since I generally teach Cabeza de Vaca in time-constrained survey courses that cover the colonial period in one semester, I assign selections of contemporary adaptations instead of whole works. I include passages that provide information about the adaptation criteria employed (see examples below). Alternatively, students may be asked to select one adaptation and report to the class. Examining the point of view of the different adaptations allows students to decenter the *Relación* and invites them to conceive different perspectives of (and thus politics about) the past. If the past is the result of critical readings and is open to multiple interpretations, interventions, and assessments, is every take or version of it valid or useful? Further analysis is necessary to unravel the ethical and political implications of the adaptation process. With this goal in mind, I focus the discussion on two pivotal topics in the *Relación* and its subsequent adaptations: the narrative of suffering and the humanitarian hero. Both mediate the representation of colonial violence.

The Naked Conquistador

Addressing Emperor Charles V in the prologue of the *Relación*, Cabeza de Vaca stresses the multiple hardships he endured, "naked through many and very strange lands" ("Por muchas y muy extrañas tierras que anduve perdido y en cueros"; Cabeza de Vaca, *Narrative* 46, 45) in the service of the Crown and the church. This nakedness has been read metaphorically as a tale of going native or of man against nature.[1] The naked-man narrative displaces the image of the cruel conquistador, offering the story of a suffering and exceptional individual with whom the reader can identify. We find this suffering figure in the expressionist watercolors of Ettore DeGrazia. The Arizona artist retells Cabeza de Vaca's story in brief first-person narrative vignettes accompanying each painting. For example, "We were kept as prisoners and made slaves of the Indians" (22). The text frames an expressionistic depiction of Cabeza de Vaca in a cage with a striking red background that suggests the hardships he endured (24). We also find a distressed Cabeza de Vaca carrying a large, heavy bundle on his back and another painting depicting the four survivors under a scorching sun (27, 39). DeGrazia's book is short and can be assigned for a single class activity. Students can contrast DeGrazia's empathic narrative with Andres Serrano's installation *Cabeza de Vaca*, in which a dead cow's head looks back at the spectator, disrupting the compassionate gaze.

In Nicolás Echevarría's film *Cabeza de Vaca*, we also encounter a narrative framework that inspires the compassion of the viewer for the shipwrecked conquistadores (see Restrepo; Juan-Navarro; Mayers). Echevarría's film starts when the four survivors reached a Spanish frontier camp in northwestern Mexico in 1536 (ch. 33). The camera pans over their ragged hides and emaciated bodies, visually telling their story before it is narrated, and cementing the viewer's empathy for the ailing survivors coming out of the wilderness. In the next sequence, the narrative goes back to November 1528, when the expedition collapsed and the conquistadores ventured into the Gulf of Mexico in five makeshift rafts that were swept by currents and washed ashore on or near Galveston Island, Texas (Cabeza de Vaca, *Narrative* 83; chs. 10–11). The film omits most of the expedition's first inland incursion (the first nine chapters in the 1555 edition), in which Cabeza de Vaca and the other conquistadores raided Native villages across Florida, taking hostages and ransacking their maize crops (*Narrative* 64–72; chs. 6–8). Thus, in the film narrative, empathy for the survivors depends on the suppression of Cabeza de Vaca's and the other conquistadores' actions as agents of colonial violence. In a similar way, Michael Wood's documentary series *Conquistadors* highlights the suffering of Cabeza de Vaca and the other survivors in a film narrative that accompanies the narrator (Wood) from Florida to northwestern Mexico, reconstructing the survivors' route. As in Rick Steve's television travel series, the camera of *Conquistadors* follows the narrator, who, with a backpack on his shoulders, travels from the Florida swamps to the southwestern desert. In the opening scenes, a crocodile emerges from the swamps, reproducing the colonial narrative of a hostile environment endured by the survivors. Like in Echevarría's film, the violence against Amerindian villages in the first parts of the *Relación* is erased in Wood's series.

Three novels rewrite the expedition survivors' experiences from the point of view of the enslaved Black African Esteban. These adaptations imaginatively offer the point of view of the conquest not recorded in the official records—the voices of the enslaved Africans. The scholar Helen Rand Parish's *Estebanico* recreates his story in well-documented historical prose followed by a rigorous appendix of the historical sources consulted (111–18). Daniel Panger's later novel *Black Ulysses* elaborates the story without problematizing ethnicity or subalternity and concentrates on the strong bond developed among the survivors from the hardships endured. The narrator draws from his Christian faith to make sense of their suffering (but never questioning the colonial venture). When the expedition raids a Native village and pillages its corn, Esteban thanks God for the maize "encountered" (59). He regards Cabeza de Vaca with reverence, noting that the treasurer of the Narváez expedition prays for the well-being of the camp and makes sound decisions seeking the common good of the troop (17). Schematically, Cabeza de Vaca is portrayed as a humane conquistador compared to a cruel Narváez (58). The novel leaves out the encounter with Spanish slavers in Culiacán narrated in the *Relación* (chs. 33–34). In the end, *Black Ulysses* taps into and magnifies the allegorical elements of the *Relación*, presenting the naked experience in the desert as a spiritually transformative journey. *The Moor's Account*, written by the Moroccan American writer Laila Lalami, takes the tale in another direction. Esteban is given a Muslim name: Mustafa ibn Muhammad ibin Abdussalam al-Zamori. Mustafa endures hardships: he is sold into slavery in Seville and wounded by Indians in Florida, and he nearly starves with the Avavares (99, 114, 221). The narrative, however, is not centered on his victimhood. Rather the novel seeks to restore Esteban's personhood and freedom, creatively retelling his life story from his childhood in Azemmour to his apocryphal defection from Marcos de Niza's expedition at the end of the novel and his return to the land of his Avavare wife (320). Mustafa endures his ordeals with great stoicism, assuming a moral stance that distances him from the Spaniards and the injustices he witnesses. He seems like a Lascasian figure, albeit one with a more tempered voice.

The enslaved person's autobiographical narrative in Lalami's novel projects onto the sixteenth-century subaltern subject a set of contemporary cosmopolitan sensitivities, and the character's individual ethos, racial difference, and Muslim identity seem to address a sympathetic liberal contemporary reader. Thus the narrative ideologically aligns the reader with the assumed moral superiority that distances Esteban from colonial violence witnessed. This narrative scheme eludes the colonial implications of writing and reading that from the conquest to the nineteenth-century genocidal campaigns of the new nation states have pitted the civilized against the barbarian. Consequently, the novel does not pay much attention to the colonial writing practices that produced texts such as the *Relación*. The materiality of the story of Esteban is conspicuously absent from the novel, except for a short description of historical sources in the acknowledgments. That is, the novel itself does not have metacritical comments explaining how Esteban/Mustafa's account got to us in perfect English (as it could have been written in Arabic, Spanish, or the language of his indigenous wife). Found manuscripts are a staple in historical novels that not only explains the origin of the work at hand but also offers valuable reflections on the writing of history.

In contrast, critical reflections on history can be found in new Latin American historical novels like Abel Posse's *El largo atardecer del caminante* (*Walking into the Setting Sun*). In this novel, a nostalgic Cabeza de Vaca reflects on his experience in the Indies decades after his return to Spain.[2] Cabeza de Vaca narrates what he left out of his *Relación*. He views the experience of the desert as a liberating event in which he was "naked and without Spain" ("desnudo y sin España"; my trans.; 65). The tension between the narratives of going native and going home is evident in the protagonist's relationship with his apocryphal Native wife, Amaria. He does not teach her any words of Spanish and seeks to leave her and her children, "savage as they were" ("en estado salvaje"; my trans.; 140). Soon after leaving Amaria, Alvar Núñez, the character, asks the other survivors to bury all their Spanish possessions, including a Bible, in order to separate themselves from Narváez and Spanish colonialism before starting their journey westward. They begin the maize route "completely naked" ("desnudos de todo"; my trans.; 141–42). Between these two passages, there is a jump forward to the time when Alvar Núñez is in Seville ruminating on the past, and he sees an apparition of his younger self in the Indies. The old conquistador affirms, "[W]ithout me and my papers, he would not exist" ("sin mi y sin mis cuartillas, no existiría"; my trans.; 140). In the end the nostalgic, egocentric conquistador is trapped in his own writing—where he attempts to come to terms with his traumatic experiences in the Indies (262). The novel appeals to the reader's empathy, more at the intellectual than the emotional level, for the existential nakedness of the human condition. However, such philosophical reflections are not extended to his Native wife and her people, who are described as "natural beings" ("seres de la tierra"; my trans.; 137). This division of the world into so-called civilized and natural societies reproduces colonial epistemic violence.

In José Sanchis Sinisterra's play *Alvar Núñez Cabeza de Vaca o la herida del otro* (*Alvar Nuñez Cabeza de Vaca; or, The Other's Wound*), a naked man runs across the stage at several points during the performance.[3] The play is set in a bedroom where a modern-day Cabeza de Vaca sits on the edge of the bed, sleepless. He hears the voices of Sheila, the apocryphal Native wife that he left behind, and of other members of the Narváez expedition, who confront him about the things he left out of the *Relación*. Sheila speaks to Cabeza de Vaca, where the adapted text borrows passages from the *Relación*: "When you say . . . , 'and during that time I had a very bad life, feeling hungry and being mistreated by the Indians' . . . , remember me, and how in the middle of the night I looked for you and pressed my body against yours to keep you warm . . ." ("Cuando digas . . . 'y en este tiempo yo pasé muy mala vida, así por la mucha hambre como por el mal tratamiento que de los indios recibía' . . . , acuérdate de mí, y de cómo en mitad e la noche yo te buscaba y apretaba mi cuerpo contra el tuyo para darte calor . . ."; my trans.; 93; ellipsis in original). The narrative of suffering is displaced from Cabeza de Vaca to Sheila, who reproaches the conquistador for leaving her. She carries a plastic bag with the remnants of their dead infant son (133). The pathos of the play is thus the imagined suffering of the other (Juan-Navarro 78). This appeal for solidarity for the vulnerable is ideologically progressive in its openness to the other. However, it is also subject to ideological traps, as discussed below in the humanitarianism section.

The spiritual awakening derived from Cabeza de Vaca's extreme experiences (shipwreck, captivity, hunger, desert) is also the main theme of George Antheil's cantata *Cabeza de Vaca*.[4] The lyrics, by Allan Dowling, are brief and can be analyzed in one class session. I asked Juan Luis Restrepo-Viana, an expert in colonial Latin American music, to guide me in interpreting the musical component of the cantata. Briefly described, *Cabeza de Vaca* is written for a mixed choir, with various voices including Cabeza de Vaca (baritone), King Philip II (tenor),[5] a mystical voice of a boy (soprano), the Indians, and the Spaniards of the expedition. The Spanish king asks, "Where are my Cities, where are my slaves?" (Antheil, *Cabeza de Vaca: A Cantata* 14). Cabeza de Vaca narrates the ordeal: "Nothing, nothing did we find, but four dark angels who seemed to hover over this dead land of sickness, hunger, poverty, and pain" (33). The narrator adds that he found something more valuable, the voice of God, whom he also heard long before the expedition, in the Battle of Ravenna, where the artillery destroyed thousands of people in one day. The boy sings, "[F]orget the worldly riches, find the power within," and this phrase is emphatically repeated and musically underscored in the grand finale of the cantata, according to Restrepo-Viana.

The shipwreck theme that aligns the audience with the conquistador's perspective can be found in Colin Matthews's *The Great Journey*, a composition for baritone and eight-member chamber ensemble. The baritone voice narrates passages of the *Relación* in English. Four musical movements follow the journey of the expedition survivors: shipwreck, landing, flight, and return. Matthews incorporates the music of the early modern Spanish composer Hernando Franco, who spent the last three decades of his life in Mexico and Guatemala. Restrepo-Viana noted that Matthews paraphrases Franco's music in the section "Wee gave God heartie thanks," in the third movement, using the small ensemble to recreate the music of *ministriles* ("minstrels") that was present in Spanish and Spanish American cathedral chapels along with vocal polyphony in Cabeza de Vaca's time. In the fourth-movement section "We went Westward," long, sustained drones and doubling of the voice and the instruments in unison evoke the arid desert. The Spanish soldiers encountered by Cabeza de Vaca's party are represented by the horn and percussion effects. The grave voice of the baritone narrating the events underscores the disastrous end of the expedition, lamenting the misfortunes. In his description of the project, Matthews presents Cabeza de Vaca as an exceptional figure who was transformed by immense hardships, including storms, inhospitable lands, and hostile Native peoples. Both Antheil's cantata and Matthews's *Journey* can be approached in a unit that includes other musical compositions inspired by the conquest of America, including operas such as Antonio Vivaldi's *Motezuma*, Aniceto Ortega de Villar's *Guatimozin*, and Carlo Enrico Pasta's *Atahualpa*.

The Humanitarian Conquistador

Another theme of Cabeza de Vaca's account that has drawn much attention is his peaceful approach to conquest and his care for ailing Native peoples that he reportedly cured miraculously.[6] The adaptations described above allow us to propose a critical approach to humanitarianism, past and present. I suggest starting with the students' view of humanitarianism and engaging them next in a critical discussion on the images of distant suffering others. I ask students to comment on the representation of suffering in Michelangelo's sculpture *Pietà* and in social media depictions of Angelina Jolie, Bono, Mother Teresa, and other celebrities holding destitute children in their arms or participating in other relief efforts (Mitchell). I explain how humanitarian efforts might be well intended but tend to affirm the geopolitical status quo rather than question its structural inequities (Fassin). Humanitarianism tends to view vulnerable populations paternalistically as needing to be saved. In this context, the celebrity figure becomes a problematic go-between for the metropolitan audience and the vulnerable populations. Humanitarian narratives frame representations of suffering, leading the reader or spectator to identify with the international aid figure more than the destitute other. With this basic critical perspective, we can examine Christian compassion in early modern Spanish culture. The Spanish humanist Juan Luis Vives provides a useful description of compassion in *De Anima et Vita* (*On the Soul and Life*; 289–94; bk. 3, ch. 7). In general terms, Vives follows Aristotle's view in the *Poetics*, reframed in the Christian humanist perspective, in which emotions are means by which individuals can strive for the good through *libre arbitrio* ("free will") (Aristotle 238–41; chs. 13–14). In this moral view of emotions, *misericordia* ("compassion") is a gift from God to human beings to help each other (Vives 292). For Vives, life without compassion would be cruel, hard, atrocious, and inhuman. One Aristotelian element of compassion that the Spanish humanist highlights is that it is felt for someone who is similar to the reader or spectator. Consequently, the suffering of distant others does not seem to generate much compassion without a mediating figure (Nussbaum, *Upheavals* 321).

In the *Relación*, the narrator is a benevolent figure mediating colonial violence, attending to vulnerable indigenous groups, much like the narratives of Doctors without Borders today. Cabeza de Vaca's humanitarian aura grew when he was able to cure an Amerindian wounded by an arrow (Cabeza de Vaca, *Narrative* 141; ch. 29). As a result of these healings, in which the other Spanish survivors also participated, Cabeza de Vaca narrates that they were welcomed in many villages and followed by hundreds of Indians. In this way, Cabeza de Vaca presents himself as a peaceful conquistador. This is shown in one widely cited passage at the end of the *Relación* where the surviving party encounters slave-raiding Spaniards (Molloy 448; Glantz, "Nakedness" 109). In the end, the account presents Cabeza de Vaca as an exemplary apostolic Christian figure that is peacefully spreading the faith and curing the sick (cf. Jesus's actions in Mark 16.15–18). This compassionate conquistador will reappear in many of the adaptations.

The poet Haniel Long's novella *The Marvelous Adventures of Cabeza de Vaca* reproduces and amplifies the peaceful conquistador narrative.[7] In his introduction, Long outlines the plan for his adaptation, seeking to go beyond historical facts: "I try to show what, quite plainly, was happening to the spirit of the man. That is, I allow him to speak as though unafraid of his King and his times." For Long, Cabeza de Vaca is a generous and courageous individual, a symbol for the modern world: "He helped when he had no means of helping, and gave when he had nothing to give" (viii). Long's idealized view is hardly sustainable. There is, however, a strong denunciation of violence in the novella. The first-person narrator remembers the great loss of lives he witnessed at the Battle of Ravenna. He also denounces the brutality of his slave-trading grandfather (1, 13). Still, Long's Cabeza de Vaca is a problematic figure that narrates how he cured the "miserable

Indians" and ends his narrative by presenting Amerindian poverty as a state of bliss where everyone helps everyone else and by comparing it to the power-hungry people in his homeland: "But where plenty abounds, we surrender our generosity" (35). Long also problematically recycles stereotypical images: he uses the derogatory name *Estevanico* and describes the character as "carrying a copper rattle in his hand, and on his shoulder a green and orange parrot" (22).

The humanitarian narrative reappears in DeGrazia's recreation of the cure of the arrow-wounded Amerindian (51; see also "From *DeGrazia*"). The careful composition of the picture is worth exploring with students to identify the different gazes framing the representation of suffering. Surrounded by a crowd of faceless Indians, Cabeza de Vaca tends to the wounded Amerindian. Next to him, Esteban kneels and holds a cross. Extended in the front part of the canvas is the wounded Amerindian, held by the other two conquistadores. The scene seems like Renaissance depictions of Christ's deposition from the cross, such as those by Rogier van der Weyden and Raphael. Comparing these images, especially the interplay of gazes in each of them, helps to bring students' critical attention to how visual representation mediates the experience of suffering. Cabeza de Vaca and his companions appear truly as doctors without borders.

In Echevarría's film, the same passage takes a melodramatic turn. The wounded man cured by Cabeza de Vaca is the young Native chief Ariano. After he recuperates, Ariano follows Cabeza de Vaca on his journey westward. They form a tacit homoerotic bond, as John Kraniauskas has suggested (120–21). When the conquistadores encountered by Cabeza de Vaca's party in northwestern Mexico kill Ariano, the film narrative focuses on the pain felt by Cabeza de Vaca. In this egotistical-melodramatic moment, a strong emotional rapture diverts the attention from the dead Indian toward the naked conquistador narrative, leaving aside the tears of the Indians for those of the white man.

Unit 2: *Digital Humanities Work*

Broadly defined, digital humanities encompass the intersecting work in the humanities and in computing technologies and disciplines, allowing scholars to mine large archival data for textual analysis, produce multimedia narratives, and generate critical understandings of the epistemological, aesthetic, and political implications of technology in human experience at the individual and collective levels. Students may be quite tech savvy from gaming and using smartphones, social media, and the like. However, they may not develop an understanding of digital humanities merely from being consumers of the latest gadgets. So, for instructors, there is much work to be done. An excellent place to start is a class discussion on the relevance of the humanities today and the new opportunities that digital humanities bring. A selection from Martha Nussbaum's *Not for Profit* would help students understand the issues at play (1–46). This can be complemented with concrete digital humanities examples from the recent MLA collection *Digital Pedagogy in the Humanities*, edited by Rebecca Frost

Davis and colleagues. This collection offers an ample variety of replicable digital humanities projects such as the text encoding initiative by Domingo Ledezma and Scott Hamlin, titled "Exploring New Worlds in Old Texts."[8]

A good introductory reading is the Massachusetts Institute of Technology open-source book *Digital Humanities* (Burdick et al. 121–35). The book describes five digital humanities projects, including one on maps and the conquest of America that challenges Western perspectives, epistemologies, and coordinate systems as normative (63). Although the case portfolios and "Short Guide" included in *Digital Humanities* are proper undergraduate reading, for graduate students the whole book provides a more critical assessment of the opportunities and challenges that digital humanities pose. *Digital Humanities* offers a cautionary stance regarding the emancipatory, democratizing, and decolonizing potential of technological advances, since these same technologies are also being used for surveillance and repression (81).

A practical challenge to approaching Cabeza de Vaca's *Relación* and similar texts through digital humanities is that the field draws on multiple competencies and usually encompasses collaborative projects that cannot be easily developed in a semester and following the traditional model for individual research projects. A strategic approach is necessary. I learned that the hard way. Years ago, I was invited to participate in a National Endowment for the Humanities project called Teaching with Technology with my colleagues George Sabo III in archaeology and Linda Jones in French studies to produce the multilingual CD *First Encounters: Native Americans and Europeans in the Mississippi Valley* (Sabo et al.). My part was to design the Spanish modules, including selections from Cabeza de Vaca's *Relación*. Learning to use the software (*Dreamweaver*) without much graphic design experience and having to resolve multiple time-consuming copyright permissions requests while working in a tenure-track position was stressful. I have since managed to find other ways to create the conditions for collaborative multimedia student projects that explore alternatives to the traditional research paper and seek to broaden the impact of intellectual work beyond academia.

Recently, I have benefited immensely from a couple of colleagues in English studies (Lissette Lopez Szwydky) and education studies (Sean Connors) who put together a summer institute for K–12 educators called Remaking Monsters and Heroines: Adapting Classic Literature for Contemporary Audiences, sponsored by the National Endowment for the Humanities.[9] Lopez Szwydky suggests that we do not have to worry about teaching students the technical know-how to develop their projects. There are plenty of resources online for developing multimedia projects such as podcasts, blogs, and videos, and most campuses have technology centers that can also assist students in these projects.[10] So, building on the multiple perspectives of the past that the adaptation unit illustrated, I have been able to assign doable multimedia collaborative projects I call *memoria abierta* ("open memory"). These projects invite students to engage critically with a cultural text, object, or topic of the past (not limited to Cabeza de Vaca). The key is to have clear expectations of what the students can achieve in a semester. Students should focus on, first, the conceptual development of the project; second, background research; third, a critical reflection on the use of technology, and fourth, a reflection on the multiple tasks and competencies that the project requires. I ask the students to submit a beta version of the project and a one-thousand-word rationale explaining the above mentioned four points. This is more than technical know-how. I stress the importance of the conceptual development of the project and its value: what it is and what it is for. I invite students to engage in their projects as conceptual artists whose primary goal is to articulate a rationale and give directions for the development of the artwork or project. I use the example of Maya Lin's entry for the Vietnam Veterans Memorial design competition, which she won as an undergraduate student. I saw the National Building Museum exhibition of the submissions for the design competition. Most entries were traditional military heroes' statues. In contrast, Lin's project was illustrated by a simple hand drawing depicting a crevice in the ground that seemed like an open wound. It honored the loss of American lives without celebrating war. So, with this inspiring example, I invite students to think beyond the technological challenges to develop public art projects, exhibitions, podcasts, presentations, and so on. Since they are asked to engage with an object or topic from the colonial past, it is necessary for the class to discuss the politics of memory. Studying the social uses of cultural heritage, Nestor García-Canclini provides valuable reflections on how the state, the market, and different social groups compete for the use and control of cultural heritage. Also useful for students is a brief look at UNESCO's definition of the cultural heritage of humanity as part of the economic, social, and cultural rights (General Conference). Moreover, the definition of intangible cultural heritage raises good discussion questions regarding the uses of the past ("What"). Who owns the past? Who determines what it means, and who decides what to preserve and what to discard?

In the end, by learning about Cabeza de Vaca and Spanish colonialism and engaging in creative readings of the sixteenth-century archive, students become aware that, as privileged university-educated individuals, they are cultural brokers of a violent colonial past and bear the ethical responsibility to address its unsettled accounts.

NOTES

1. For an examination of nakedness as a transculturation metaphor in the *Relación*, see Molloy; Glantz, "Nakedness." Nakedness is also a theme in Posse's *Atardecer* and the public art sculpture *Cabeza de Vaca*, by Raúl Ayala Arellano, in Ciudad Juárez.

2. The novel is part of a trilogy on the conquest of the Americas, including *Daimón*, about Lope de Aguirre, and *Los perros del paraíso*, about Christopher Columbus. Verdesio notes the reproduction of stereotypical colonial images by Posse. For the new historical novel, see Menton.

3. This play is part of Sinisterra's *Trilogía americana* (*American Trilogy*), as are the plays *Lope de Aguirre, traidor* (*Lope de Aguirre, Traitor*) and *El retablo de Eldorado*

(*Altarpiece of El Dorado*). *La herida* premiered in Madrid's Teatro María Guerrero in 2020 and was directed by Magüi Mira.

4. For a recording of the cantata, see Antheil, *Cabeza de Vaca: Cantata*; for the score, see Antheil, *Cabeza de Vaca: A Cantata*.

5. Since Cabeza de Vaca's sovereign and correspondent was Charles V, the name *Philip II* is not historically accurate for this character.

6. For a critical discussion on the benevolent conquistador figure and his program of peaceful conquest, see Ahern; Juan-Navarro 75–77; Rabasa 37; and Jáuregui, "Going Native" 176.

7. Long's novella—a first-person narrative—is based on Fanny Bandelier's English translation of the *Relación* (Cabeza de Vaca, *Journey*). The novella presents Cabeza de Vaca as an idealized compassionate conquistador critical of the violence of war, slavery, and the Inquisition.

8. Other early modern digital humanities projects include J. Silva et al.; Alpert-Abrams and McCarl; and Morrás and Castro.

9. Students can consult the institute's final projects; see "2018 Final Projects."

10. See the digital tools collection at the University of Minnesota, Duluth, library (libguides.d.umn.edu/DH/dh_tools).

NOTES ON CONTRIBUTORS

Rolena Adorno is Sterling Professor Emerita of Spanish at Yale University. Her cowritten, three-volume work *Álvar Núñez Cabeza de Vaca: His Account, His Life, and the Expedition of Pánfilo de Narváez* (1999) won prizes from the American Historical Association, the Western History Association, and the New England Council of Latin American Studies. Her *Polemics of Possession in Spanish American Narrative* (2007) was awarded the Modern Language Association's Katherine Singer Kovacs Prize, and in 2014 she received the MLA Award for Lifetime Scholarly Achievement. An honorary professor at Pontificia Universidad Católica del Perú, Adorno is a member of the American Academy of Arts and Sciences.

Ralph Bauer is professor of English and comparative literature at the University of Maryland focusing on the literatures and cultures of the early modern Americas. His most recent monograph, *The Alchemy of Conquest: Science, Religion, and the Secrets of the New World* (2019), was awarded the Modern Language Association's 2020 Aldo and Jeanne Scaglione Prize for Comparative Literary Studies.

René Carrasco is assistant professor of Spanish in the world languages and cultures department at California Polytechnic State University, San Luis Obispo. He is the author of *Grammar of Redemption: Logics and Paradoxes of Indigenista Discourse in México* (forthcoming), and his work has appeared in journals such as *Revista Iberoamericana*, *A Contracorriente*, and *Revista de Crítica Literaria Latinoamericana*.

Loreley El Jaber is associate professor of Latin American literature at the University of Buenos Aires and a researcher at the National Scientific and Technical Research Council. Her work focuses on colonial Río de la Plata discourses, voices, and narratives, with a special interest in the sixteenth century. She is the author of *Un país malsano: La conquista del espacio en las crónicas del Río de la Plata* (2011), editor of the critical edition of the chronicle of Ulrich Schmidl, *Derrotero y viaje a España y las Indias* (2016), and coeditor of *Fronteras escritas: Cruces, desvíos y pasajes en la literatura argentina* (2008), volume 1 of *Historia crítica de la literatura argentina* (2014), and *Modernidad, colonialidad y escritura en América Latina* (2020). Her articles have appeared in journals such as *Latin American Literary Review*, *Revista de Crítica Literaria Latinoamericana*, *Bibliographica Americana*, *Anales de Literatura Hispanoamericana*, and *Letterature d'America*, among others.

Carlos A. Jáuregui teaches Latin American literature and anthropology at the University of Notre Dame. He is the author of *Bartolomé de las Casas y el paradigma biopolítico de la modernidad colonial* (2024; with David Solodkow), *Espectros y conjuras: Asedios a la cuestión colonial* (2020), *Canibalia: Canibalismo, calibanismo, antropofagia cultural y consumo en America Latina*, which received the Casa de las Américas Award (2005; rev. ed. 2008), and *Theatre of Conquest: Carvajal's Complaint of the Indians in the "Court of Death"* (2008) and the coeditor of, among other volumes, *Coloniality at Large: Latin America and the Postcolonial Debate* (2008; with Enrique Dussel and Mabel Moraña), *Of Rage and Redemption: The Art of Oswaldo Guayasamín* (2008;

with Joseph Mella and Edward Fischer), and *Emiliano Zapata: 100 años, 100 fotos* (2020; with David Solodkow and Karina Herazo).

Lázaro Lima is chair and professor in the Department of Africana, Puerto Rican, and Latino Studies at Hunter College, City University of New York. Lima's books include *The Latino Body: Crisis Identities in American Literary and Cultural Memory* (2007), *Ambientes: New Queer Latino Writing* (2011; with Felice Picano), and *Being Brown: Sonia Sotomayor and the Latino Question* (2019). His documentary film work, in partnership with Carrie Brown, focuses on the Latina educational equity gap and includes the films *Las Mujeres: Latina Lives, American Dreams* (2016) and the award-winning *Rubí: A DACA Dreamer in Trump's America* (2019).

Kathryn Joy McKnight is professor of Spanish at the University of New Mexico. She coedited *Afro-Latino Voices: Narratives from the Early Modern Ibero-Atlantic World, 1550–1812* (2009) with Leo J. Garofalo and the OER textbook *Para vivir con salud: Leyendo la salud y la literatura* (2021) with Jill S. Kuhnheim. Her book *The Mystic of Tunja: The Writings of Madre Castillo, 1671–1742* (1997) won the Modern Language Association's Katherine Singer Kovacs Prize. Her work on African-descent narratives and health humanities appears in edited volumes, the ADE and ADFL bulletins, *Colonial Latin American Review*, *Colonial Latin American Historical Review*, *Journal of Colonialism and Colonial History*, and *Revista de Estudios Hispánicos*.

Mariselle Meléndez is professor of colonial Spanish American literatures and cultures at the University of Illinois, Urbana-Champaign. She is the author of *Deviant and Useful Citizens: The Cultural Production of the Female Body in Eighteenth-Century Peru* (2011) and *Raza, género e hibridez en* El lazarillo de ciegos caminantes (1999) and is coeditor of *Mapping Colonial Spanish America: Places and Commonplaces of Identity, Culture, and Experience* (2002) and *The Enlightenment in Colonial Spanish America*, a special issue of *Colonial Latin American Review* (2015). Her articles have appeared in journals such as *Latin American Research Review*, *Colonial Latin American Review*, *Hispanic Review*, and *Revista Iberoamericana*, among others.

Jeffrey M. Mitchem is emeritus station archeologist for the Arkansas Archeological Survey and emeritus research associate professor in the Department of Anthropology, University of Arkansas. For nearly thirty-two years, he directed research at the Parkin Research Station at Parkin Archeological State Park. His research focus is on the archaeology of Mississippian and Woodland Native American cultures in the southeastern United States. He also does research on sixteenth- and seventeenth-century Spanish–Native American contact in the southern United States. He has carried out field and museum research domestically in Arkansas, Florida, Georgia, Alabama, Louisiana, and Idaho and internationally in Spain and Jordan.

José Rabasa is professor emeritus in Latin American literature at the University of California, Berkeley, and retired long-term visiting professor in Romance languages and literatures at Harvard University. He is the author of *Without History: Subaltern Studies, The Zapatista Insurgency, and the Specter of History* (2010), *Tell Me the Story of How I Conquered You: Elsewheres and Ethnosuicide in the Colonial Mesoamerican World* (2011), *Writing Violence on the Northern Frontier: The Historiography of Sixteenth-Century New Mexico and Florida and the Legacy of Conques*t (2000), and

Inventing America: Spanish Historiography and the Formation of Eurocentrism (1993).

Luis Fernando Restrepo is university professor at the University of Arkansas, Fayetteville, where he has also served as director of the graduate program in comparative literature and cultural studies. His areas of research are colonial Latin America and literature and human rights. Among his publications and editions are *Un nuevo reino de imaginado* (2nd ed., 2020); *Antología crítica de Juan de Castellanos* (2004); *El estado impostor* (2014), which received the Roggiano Award for Latin American Criticism; *Narrativas en vilo entre la estética y la política* (2016), coedited with Clemencia Ardila and Sergio Villalobos; and *El malestar del posconflicto* (2018), coedited with Sophie von Werder and Violeta Lorenzo Feliciano. He is currently working on a book project on early modern humanitarianism.

George Sabo III directed the Arkansas Archeological Survey from 2013 until 2021. He also taught in the Department of Anthropology at the University of Arkansas, Fayetteville, for more than forty years. He is coauthor of *Arkansas: A Narrative History* (2002) and *Arkansas: A Concise History* (2019).

Vanina M. Teglia teaches Latin American literature at the University of Buenos Aires and is a researcher at Argentina's Consejo Nacional de Investigaciones Científicas y Técnicas (National Scientific and Technical Research Council). She has published several articles in colonial studies and prepared critical editions of works by Álvar Núñez Cabeza de Vaca, Christopher Columbus, and Bartolomé de las Casas. She is currently preparing a book on utopian thought in the works of Las Casas and Gonzalo Fernández de Oviedo y Valdés.

Paola Uparela is assistant professor at the University of Florida. She specializes in colonial studies; gender, sexuality and queer studies; cultural studies; history of art and medicine; visual culture; and biopolitics. Her first book, *Invaginaciones coloniales: Mirada, genitalidad y (de)generación en la Modernidad Temprana* (2024), which received the 2023 Klaus D. Vervuert Hispanic Essay Award, examines the early modern gyneco-scopic regime in art, literature, anatomy, and medicine that reduced the female body to sexual and reproductive functions. Her research has been recognized with the Eli J. and Helen Shaheen Award in Humanities; the Victoria Urbano Essay Award; the Feministas Unidas Essay Prize; the Latin American Studies Association's Culture, Power, and Politics Section Award and José María Arguedas Essay Award; the Sturgis Leavitt Award from the Southeastern Council of Latin American Studies; and the Best Collaborative Project Award from Grupo de Estudios sobre la Mujer en España y las Américas (pre-1800), among others.

SURVEY RESPONDENTS

William Arighi, *Springfield College*
David Blackmore, *Chatham University*
Luis C.deBaca, *University of Michigan*
Benjamin Crawford, *University of Alabama*
Monica Diaz, *University of Kentucky*
John Tabb DuVal, *University of Arkansas*
Karen Graubart, *University of Notre Dame*
Faith Harden, *University of Arizona*
Tamara Harvey, *George Mason University*
John Havard, *Kennesaw State University*
Nicole Legnani, *Princeton University*
Danna A. Levin Rojo, *Universidad Autónoma Metropolitana*
Daniel O. Mosquera, *Union College*
Rachel Norman, *Linfield University*
Rubén Sánchez-Godoy, *Southern Methodist University*
Vanina M. Teglia, *Universidad de Buenos Aires*
George Anthony Thomas, *California State University, San Bernardino*
Paola Uparela, *University of Florida*

WORKS CITED

Adorno, Rolena. "The Cabeza de Vaca Phenomenon: Confounding the Prestigious Lie of Exactitude." *Remembering the Past, Retrieving the Future: New Interdisciplinary Contributions to the Study of Colonial Latin America*, edited by Verónica Salles-Reese, Universidad Javeriana, 2005, pp. 4–23.

———. *Colonial Latin American Literature: A Very Short Introduction*. Oxford UP, 2011.

———. *De Guancane a Macondo: Estudios de literatura hispanoamericana*. Renacimiento, 2008.

———. "The Discursive Encounter of Spain and America: The Authority of Eyewitness Testimony in the Writing of History." *William and Mary Quarterly*, vol. 49, no. 2, 1992, pp. 210–28.

———. "The Negotiation of Fear in Álvar Núñez Cabeza de Vaca's *Naufragios*." *Representations*, no. 33, 1991, pp. 163–99.

———. "Peaceful Conquest and Law in the *Relación* (Account) of Alvar Nunez Cabeza de Vaca." *Coded Encounters: Writing, Gender, and Ethnicity in Colonial Latin America*, edited by Francisco Javier Cevallos-Candau et al., U of Massachusetts P, 1994, pp. 75–86.

———. *The Polemics of Possession in Spanish American Narrative*. Yale UP, 2007.

Adorno, Rolena, and Patrick Charles Pautz. *Álvar Núñez Cabeza de Vaca: His Account, His Life, and the Expedition of Pánfilo de Narváez*. U of Nebraska P, 1999. 3 vols.

Ahern, Maureen. "The Cross and the Gourd: The Appropriation of Ritual Signs in the *Relaciones* of Álvar Núñez Cabeza de Vaca and Fray Marcos de Niza." *Early Images of the Americas: Transfer and Invention*, edited by Jerry Williams and Robert Lewis, U of Arizona P, 1993, pp. 215–44.

———. "Cruz y calabaza: La apropiación del signo en las relaciones de Álvar Núñez Cabeza de Vaca y de fray Marcos de Niza." Glantz, *Notas*, pp. 351–77.

Alegría, Ricardo E. *Juan Garrido, el Conquistador Negro en las Antillas, Florida, México y California c. 1503–1540*. Centro de Estudios Avanzados de Puerto Rico y el Caribe, 1990.

A. L. I. [Kalyan Balaven]. *Carbon Cycle Diaries*. 12 Recordz, 2011.

———. "Who Is Black Steven?" *A. L. I. Waxes Poetic*, 18 July 2010, aliwaxespoetic.blogspot.com/2010/07/who-is-black-steven.html.

Alpert-Abrams, Hannah, and Clayton McCarl, editors. *Digital Humanities and Colonial Latin American Studies*. Special issue of *Digital Humanities Quarterly*. Vol. 14, no. 4, 2020, www.digitalhumanities.org/dhq/vol/14/4/000531/000531.html.

Anderson, E. N. *Everyone Eats: Understanding Food and Culture*. New York UP, 2014.

Anghiera, Pietro Martire d' [Peter Martyr of Anglería]. *Décadas del Nuevo Mundo.* Edited by Edmundo O'Gorman, Sociedad Dominicana de Bibliófilos, 1989. 2 vols.

Antheil, George. *Cabeza de Vaca: A Cantata Based on the Experience and Letters of Alvar Nuñez, "Cabeza de Vaca."* Libretto by Allan Dowling, Templeton Publishing / Shawnee Press, 1961.

———. *Cabeza de Vaca, Cantata. Internet Archive,* 29 July 2019, archive.org/details/cd_antheil-benson-compositions_george-antheil-warren-benson.

Arano-Lean, Milagros. "¡Juicio a los rebeldes! La configuración del enemigo en los Comentarios de Álvar Núñez Cabeza de Vaca." *Nuevas de Indias: Anuario del CEAC,* vol. 2, 2017, pp. 1–29.

Aristotle. *The Rhetoric and the Poetics of Aristotle.* The Modern Library, 1984.

Atwood, Margaret. *The Handmaid's Tale.* McClelland and Stewart, 1985.

Augenbraum, Harold, and Margarita Fernández-Olmos, editors. *The Latino Reader: An American Literary Tradition from 1542 to the Present.* Houghton Mifflin, 1997.

Austin, Shawn. *Colonial Kinship: Guaraní, Spaniards, and Africans in Paraguay.* U of New Mexico P, 2020.

Ayala Arellano, Raúl. *Cabeza de Vaca.* 2001, Ciudad Juárez, Mexico.

Badiou, Alain. *Ethics: An Essay on the Understanding of Evil.* Verso Books, 2002.

Bane, Teresa. *Encyclopedia of Imaginary and Mythical Places.* McFarland, 2014.

Barolini, Teodolinda. "Dante's Ulysses: Narrative and Transgression." *Dante: Contemporary Perspectives,* edited by Amilcare Iannucci, U of Toronto P, 1997, pp. 113–32.

Barrera López, Trinidad. Introduction. Cabeza de Vaca, *Naufragios* [Barrera], 1985, pp. 7–55.

Barrera López, Trinidad, and Carmen de Mora Valcárcel. "Los Naufragios de Alvar Núñez Cabeza de Vaca: Entre la crónica y la novela." *Actas de las Jornadas de Andalucía y América,* vol. 2, 1983, pp. 331–64.

Bartra, Roger. *El salvaje artificial.* Ediciones Era, 1997.

Bauer, Ralph. *The Cultural Geography of Colonial American Literatures: Empire, Travel, Modernity.* Cambridge UP, 2003.

Benjamin, Walter. *Illuminations: Essays and Reflections.* Houghton Mifflin Harcourt, 2019.

Bentham, Abby. "Art or Science? Formulating Empathy." *Exploring Empathy: Its Propagations, Perimeters and Potentialities,* edited by Rebecca J. Nelems and L. J. Theo, Brill, 2017, pp. 161–92.

Beverley, John. *Against Literature.* U of Minnesota P, 1993.

The Bible. New King James Version, Thomas Nelson, 1982.

Bishop, Morris. *The Odyssey of Cabeza de Vaca.* The Century, 1933.

Blanton, Dennis. "Tracking an Entrada by Comparative Analysis of Sixteenth-Century Archaeological Assemblages from the Southeast." Boudreaux et al., *Contact,* pp. 73–101.

Bleicher, Thomas. *Homer in der deutschen Literatur, 1450–1740: Zur Rezeption der Antike und zur Poetologie der Neuzeit.* Metzlersche Verlagsbuchhandlungen, 1972.

The Blue Lagoon. Directed by Randal Kleiser, Columbia Pictures, 1980.

Blumenberg, Hans. *Shipwreck with Spectator: Paradigm of a Metaphor for Existence.* Translated by Steven Rendall, MIT Press, 1997.

Borges, Jorge Luis. "The Ethnographer." *Collected Fictions,* by Borges, translated by Andrew Hurley, Viking Press, 1998, pp. 334–35.

———. *Ficciones; El Aleph; El Informe de Brodie.* Biblioteca Ayacucho, 1986.

Boudreaux, Edmond, III, et al., editors. *Contact, Colonialism, and Native Communities in the Southeastern United States.* U of Florida P, 2020.

Boudreaux, Edmond, III, et al. "The Early Contact Period in the Black Prairie of Northeast Mississippi." Boudreaux et al., *Contact,* pp. 35–56.

Bourdieu, Pierre. *Distinction: A Social Critique of the Judgement of Taste.* Harvard UP, 1984.

Boxer, Charles Ralph. *The Portuguese Seaborne Empire, 1415–1825.* Carcanet, 1991.

Bradbury, Ray. *Fahrenheit 451.* Ballantine Books, 1953.

Brading, David. *The First America: The Spanish Monarchy, Creole Patriots, and the Liberal State, 1492–1867.* Cambridge UP, 1991.

Brain, Jeffrey. "Artifacts of the Adelantado." *Conference on Historic Site Archaeology Papers,* vol. 8, 1975, pp. 129–38.

Brown, Ian. "Bells." *Tunica Treasure,* edited by Jeffrey Brain, Peabody Museum of Archaeology and Ethnology, Harvard U, 1979, pp. 197–205.

———. "Historic Trade Bells." *Conference on Historic Site Archaeology Papers,* vol. 10, 1977, pp. 69–82.

Brown, Michael. "Dark Side of the Shaman." Narby and Huxley, pp. 251–56.

Bruce-Novoa, Juan. "Naufragios en los mares de la significación: De la relación de Cabeza de Vaca a la literatura chicana." Glantz, *Notas,* pp. 291–308.

———. "Shipwrecked in the Seas of Signification: Cabeza de Vaca's *La relación* and Chicano Literature." *Reconstructing a Chicano/a Literary Heritage: Hispanic Colonial Literature of the Southwest,* edited by María Herrera-Sobek, U of Arizona P, 1993, pp. 3–23.

Burdick, Anne, et al. *Digital Humanities.* MIT Press, 2012. *MIT Press Direct,* direct.mit.edu/books/oa-monograph/5346/Digital-Humanities.

"Bury My Art at Wounded Knee." *Tumblr,* uploaded by burymyart, 13 Feb. 2019, burymyart.tumblr.com/post/182795435223/burymyart-high-resolution-18-x-24-poster-of-an.

Butler, Judith. *Undoing Gender.* Routledge, 2009.

Cabeza de Vaca. Directed by Nicolás Echevarría, Producciones Iguana / Instituto Mexicano de Cinematografía y Televisión Española, 1991.

Cabeza de Vaca, Álvar Núñez. *The Account: Alvar Núñez Cabeza de Vaca's Relación.* Translated by Martín Favata and Jose Fernández, Arte Publico Press, 1993.

———. *Castaways.* Edited by Enrique Pupo-Walker, translated by Frances López-Morillas, U of California P, 1993.

———. *Chronicle of the Narváez Expedition.* Translated by Fanny Bandelier, edited by Harold Augenbraum, Penguin Books, 2002.

———. *The Journey of Alvar Núñez Cabeza de Vaca and His Companions from Florida to the Pacific, 1528–1536.* Translated by Fanny Bandelier, A. S. Barnes, 1905.

———. *The Narrative of Cabeza de Vaca.* Translated and edited by Rolena Adorno and Patrick Charles Pautz, U of Nebraska P, 2003.

———. *Naufragios.* Edited by Trinidad Barrera López, Alianza Editorial, 1985.

———. *Naufragios.* Edited by Eloísa Gómez-Lucena and Rubén Caba, Cátedra, 2018.

———. *Los naufragios.* Edited by Enrique Pupo-Walker, Castalia, 1992.

———. *Naufragios.* Edited by Vanina M. Teglia, Corregidor, 2016.

———. *Naufragios de Álvar Núñez Cabeza de Vaca, y relación de la jornada que hizo a la Floria con el adelantado Pánfilo de Narváez.* Historiadores primitivos de las Indias Occidentales, edited by Andrés González de Barcía Carballido y Zúñiga, vol. 1, no. 7, Madrid, 1749, pp. 1–43. *Library of Congress*, www.loc.gov/item/04008076/.

———. *Naufragios y comentarios.* Editorial Porrúa, 1998.

———. *Naufragios y comentarios.* Espasa-Calpe España, 1985.

———. *Naufragios y comentarios.* Edited by Roberto Ferrando, Historia 16, 1984.

———. *Relación de las cosas sucedidas en el Río de la Plata, por Pero Hernández: Año 1545.* Cabeza de Vaca, *Relación de los naufragios*, vol. 2, pp. 307–58.

———. *Relación de los naufragios y comentarios de Alvar Núñez Cabeza de Vaca: Ilustrado con varios documentos inéditos.* Edited by Manuel Serrano y Sanz, Librería General de Victoriano Suárez, 1906. 2 vols.

———. *Relación general que yo Álvar Núñez Cabeça de Baca Adelantado y Gouernador y Capitán general de la provincia del rrío de la Plata, por merced de Su Majestad, hago para le ynformar, y á los señores de su Rreal Consejo de Indias, de las cosas subcedidas en la dicha provincia . . . .* 1545. Cabeza de Vaca, *Relación de los naufragios*, vol. 2, pp. 1–98.

———. *La relación que dio Álvar Núñez Cabeça de Vaca de lo acaescido en las Indias en la armada donde iva por gobernador Pánphilo de Narbáez, desde el año de veinte y siete hasta el año de treinta y seis que bolvió a Sevilla con tres de su compañía.* Agustín de Paz y Juan Picardo, 1542.

———. *La relación y comentarios del governador Álvar Núñez Cabeça de Vaca, de lo acaescido en las dos jornadas que hizo a las Indias.* Francisco Fernández de Córdova, 1555.

———. *The South American Expeditions, 1540–1545.* Translated by Baker Morrow, U of New Mexico P, 2011.

Calderón, Héctor, and José David Saldívar, editors. *Criticism in the Borderlands: Studies in Chicano Literature, Culture, and Ideology.* Duke UP, 1991.

California, Secretary of State. "Proposition 209: Prohibition against Discrimination or Preferential Treatment by State and Other Public Entities." *California Ballot Pamphlet, General Election*, 5 Nov. 1996, vigarchive.sos.ca.gov/1996/general/pamphlet/209text.htm.

Cañizares-Esguerra, Jorge. *Puritan Conquistadors: Iberianizing the Atlantic, 1550–1700.* Stanford UP, 2006.

Carpenter, Roger. "Womanish Men and Manlike Women: The Native American Two-Spirit as Warrior." Slater and Yarbrough, pp. 146–64.

Castañeda, Pedro de. "Relación de la jornada de Cíbola." Winship, pp. 413–69.

———. *Translation of the Narrative of Castañeda*. Winship, pp. 470–546.

Castañeda-Delgado, Paulino. *La teocracia pontifical en las controversias sobre el Nuevo Mundo*. Universidad Nacional Autónoma de México, 1996.

Cast Away. Directed by Robert Zemeckis, 20th Century Fox / DreamWorks Pictures / ImageMovers, 2000.

CDI [*Colección de documentos inéditos relativos al descubrimiento, conquista y organización de las antiguas posesiones en América y Oceanía*]. Edited by Joaquín Pacheco et al., Ministerio de Ultramar Imprenta de José María Pérez, 1864–84. 42 vols.

Chira, Adriana. "Atlantic Creoles." *Oxford Bibliographies: Latin American Studies*, Oxford UP, 2013, https://doi.org/10.1093/OBO/9780199766581-0217.

Claramonte y Corroy, Andrés de, et al. *The Valiant Black Man in Flanders*. Edited by Baltasar Fra Molinero and Manuel Olmedo Gobante, translated by Nelson López, Liverpool UP, 2023.

Clifford, James. "On Ethnographic Allegory." *Writing Culture: The Poetics and Politics of Writing Ethnography*, edited by James Clifford and George Marcus, U of California P, 1986, pp. 98–121.

Colombi, Beatriz. "El viaje, de la práctica al género." *Viaje y relato en Latinoamérica*, edited by Mónica Marinone and Gabriela Tineo, Katatay, 2010, pp. 287–308.

Conquistadors. Written and presented by Michael Wood, MayaVision, 2000.

Cook, Sherburne F., and Woodrow Borah. *Essays in Population History: Mexico and the Caribbean*. U of California P, 1979. Vol. 1 of *Essays in Population History*, 3 vols.

Cortés, Hernán. *Letters from Mexico*. Yale UP, 1986.

Counihan, Carole, and Penny Van Esterik. "Why Food? Why Culture?" *Food and Culture: A Reader*, edited by Counihan and Van Esterik, Routledge, 2013, pp. 1–15.

Covarrubias, Sebastián de. *Tesoro de la lengua castellana o española*. 1611. Edited by Martín de Riquer, S. A. Horta de Impresiones y Ediciones, 1943.

Crovetto, Pier Luigi. "El naufragio en el Nuevo Mundo: De la escritura formulizada a la prefiguración de lo novelesco." *Palinure*, 1985–86, pp. 30–41.

Cutchins, Dennis, et al. *The Pedagogy of Adaptation*. Scarecrow Press, 2010.

Dante Alighieri. *Inferno*. Translated by Allen Mandelbaum, Bantam Books, 1982.

Davis, Rebecca Frost, et al. *Digital Pedagogy in the Humanities*. Modern Language Association of America, 2020, digitalpedagogy.hcommons.org.

Deagan, Kathleen. *Ceramics, Glassware, and Beads*. Smithsonian Institution Press, 1987. Vol. 1 of *Artifacts of the Spanish Colonies of Florida and the Caribbean, 1500–1800*.

De Bry, Theodor, and Thomas Hariot. *A Briefe and True Report of the New Found Land of Virginia*. Frankfurt, 1590.

DeGrazia, Ettore. *DeGrazia Paints Cabeza de Vaca: The First Non-Indian in Texas, New Mexico, and Arizona, 1527–1536*. De Grazia Gallery in the Sun, 1973.

Derrida, Jacques. *Of Grammatology*. Translated by Gayatri Chakravorty Spivak, fortieth anniversary ed., Johns Hopkins UP, 2016.

Dinshaw, Carolyn. *Getting Medieval: Sexualities and Communities, Pre- and Postmodern*. Duke UP, 1999.

Domínguez, Luis, et al. *The Conquest of the River Plate, 1535–1555*. Routledge, 2016.

Dowling, Lee. "Story vs. Discourse in the Chronicle of the Indies: Álvar Núñez Cabeza de Vaca's *Relacion*." *Hispanic Journal*, vol. 5, no. 2, 1984, pp. 89–99.

Durán, Diego. *Historia de las Indias de Nueva España e islas de la tierra firme*. 1579. *Biblioteca Digital Hispánica*, Biblioteca Nacional de España, bdh.bne.es/bnesearch/detalle/bdh0000169486.

Dwight, Ed. *Texas African American History Memorial*. 2016, Austin, Texas.

El Hamel, Chouki. *Black Morocco: A History of Slavery, Race, and Islam*. Cambridge UP, 2013.

Eliade, Mircea. *Shamanism: Archaic Techniques of Ecstasy*. Princeton UP, 1972.

El Jaber, Loreley. "Álvar Núñez Cabeza de Vaca: Gustos y olvidos: Legalidad, viaje y escritura." *Cuadernos del CILHA*, vol. 13, no. 2, 2012, pp. 57–74.

———. *Un país malsano: La escritura del espacio en las crónicas del Río de la Plata*. Beatriz Viterbo / U Nacional de Rosario, 2011.

Ethridge, Robbie. "Differential Responses across the Southeast to European Incursions: A Conclusion." Boudreaux et al., *Contact*, pp. 216–28.

———. *From Chicaza to Chickasaw: The European Invasion and the Transformation of the Mississippian World, 1540–1715*. U of North Carolina P, 2010.

Ethridge, Robbie, and Charles Hudson, editors. *The Transformation of the Southeastern Indians, 1540–1760*. U of Mississippi P, 2002.

Ewen, Charles, and John Hann. *Hernando de Soto among the Apalachee: The Archaeology of the First Winter Encampment*. UP of Florida, 1998.

Fassin, Didier. *Humanitarian Reason: A Moral History of the Present*. U of California P, 2012.

Fikes, Robert, Jr. "Juan de Pareja and Sebastián Gómez: Masters of Spanish Baroque Painting." *The Crisis*, vol. 87, no. 2, 1980. NAACP, pp. 49–54.

Flores, Ángel. "Magical Realism in Spanish American Fiction." *Hispania*, vol. 38, no. 2, 1955, pp. 187–92.

Frank, Lois Ellen. *Foods of the Southwest Indian Nations*. Ten Speed Press, 2002.

———. *Native American Cooking: Foods of the Southwest Indian Nations*. C. N. Potter, 1991.

Freud, Sigmund. *The Standard Edition of the Complete Psychological Works of Sigmund Freud*. Translated by James Strachey, vol. 17, Hogarth Press, 1955.

"From *DeGrazia Paints Cabeza De Vaca* by Ted DeGrazia." *Cabeza de Vaca*, Texas State U, exhibits.library.txstate.edu/cabeza/items/show/35.

Gadamer, Hans Georg. "The Hermeneutics of Suspicion." *Man and World*, vol. 17, no. 3, 1984, pp. 313–23.

Gandía, Enrique de. *Historia de la conquista del Río de la Plata y del Paraguay; los gobiernos de don Pedro de Mendoza, Alvar Núñez y Domingo de Irala, 1535–1556*. A. García-Santos, 1932.

———. *Indios y conquistadores en el Paraguay*. Librería García Santos, 1931.

Gandini, María Juliana. "Experiencias desde los márgenes: Armas, letras y alteridad en los Comentarios de Álvar Núñez Cabeza de Vaca (1555)." *Anuario del Centro de Estudios Históricos*, vol. 12, no. 12, 2012, pp. 81–96.

Ganson, Barbara. *The Guaraní under Spanish Rule in the Río de la Plata*. Stanford UP, 2003.

García-Canclini, Nestor. "Los usos sociales del patrimonio cultural." *El patrimonio cultural de México*, edited by Enrique Florescano, Fondo de Cultura Económica, 1993, pp. 41–60.

García Márquez, Gabriel. *Relato de un náufrago*. Periódico el Espectador, 1955.

Garofalo, Leo. "The Shape of a Diaspora: The Movement of Afro-Iberians to Colonial Spanish America." *Africans to Spanish America: Expanding the Diaspora*, edited by Sherwin Bryant et al., U of Illinois P, 2012, pp. 27–49.

Geertz, Clifford. *Works and Lives: The Anthropologist as Author*. Stanford UP, 1988.

General Conference of the United Nations Educational, Scientific and Cultural Organization. "Convention Concerning the Protection of the World Cultural and Natural Heritage." *UNESCO*, November 1972, whc.unesco.org/en/documents/170665.

Gibson, Charles. *Spain in America*. Harper and Row, 1966.

Glantz, Margo. "El cuerpo inscrito y el texto escrito o la desnudez como naufragio." Glantz, *Notas*, pp. 403–34.

———. "Nakedness as Shipwreck: Alvar Núñez Cabeza de Vaca." *Travesía*, vol. 1, no. 2, 1992, pp. 86–112.

———, editor. *Notas y comentarios sobre Alvar Núñez Cabeza de Vaca*. Consejo Nacional para la Cultura y las Artes, 1993.

Gómez-Galisteo, Carmen. "Subverting Gender Roles in the Sixteenth Century: Cabeza de Vaca, the Conquistador Who Became a Native American Woman." Slater and Yarbrough, pp. 11–29.

González Acosta, Alejandro. "Álvar Núñez Cabeza de Vaca: Náufrago y Huérfano." *Cuadernos Americanos*, new series, vol. 1, no. 49, 1995, pp. 165–99.

González-Echevarría, Roberto. *Alejo Carpentier, the Pilgrim at Home*. Cornell UP, 1977.

Goodwin, Robert T. C. *Crossing the Continent, 1527–1540: The Story of the First African-American Explorer of the American South*. HarperCollins Publishers, 2008.

———. "'De lo que sucedió a los demás que entraron en las Indias': Álvar Núñez Cabeza de Vaca and the Other Survivors of Pánfilo Narváez's Expedition." *Bulletin of Spanish Studies*, vol. 84, no. 2, 2007, pp. 147–73.

———. "Texts and Miracles in the New and Old Worlds: Alvar Núñez Cabeza de Vaca." *Early Modern Spain*, 13 Dec. 2005, www.ems.kcl.ac.uk/content/pub/b035.html.

Gordon, Richard. "Exoticism and National Identity in *Cabeza de Vaca* and *Como Era Gostoso o Meu Francés*." *Torre de Papel*, vol. 10, no. 1, 2000, pp. 77–119.

———. "Following Estevanico: The Influential Presence of an African Slave in Sixteenth-Century New World Historiography." *Colonial Latin American Review*, vol. 15, no. 2, 2006, pp. 183–206.

Gougeon, Ramey A. "New Frontier, Old Frontier." Boudreaux et al., *Contact*, pp. 114–25.

Greenblatt, Stephen, editor. *New World Encounters*. U of California P, 1993.

Greer, Margaret R., et al. *Rereading the Black Legend: The Discourses of Religious and Racial Difference in the Renaissance Empires*. U of Chicago P, 2008.

Hammond, George, and Agapito Rey, editors. *Narratives of the Coronado Expedition, 1540–1542*. U of New Mexico P, 1940. 12 vols.

Hanke, Lewis. *Aristotle and the American Indians*. Indiana UP, 1970.

Haring, Clarence Henry. *The Spanish Empire in America*. Oxford UP, 1947.

Harner, Michael. "Magic Darts, Bewitching Shamans, and Curing Shamans." Narby and Huxley, pp. 195–99.

Hayes, Merdies. "Estevanico: The Man, the Myth, the Legend." *Our Weekly*, 15 Feb. 2019, ourweekly.com/news/2019/feb/14/estevanico-man-myth-legend/.

Heidegger, Martin. *Being and Time*. State U of New York P, 1966.

Herrero-Massari, José Manuel. "El naufragio en la literatura de viajes peninsular de los siglos XVI y XVII." *Revista de Filología Románica*, vol. 2, no. 14, 1997, pp. 205–13.

Herrick, Dennis. *Esteban: The African Slave Who Explored America*. U of New Mexico P, 2018.

Horkheimer, Max, and Theodor Adorno. *Dialectic of Enlightenment*. Translated by John Cumming, Herder and Herder, 1972.

Horswell, Michael. *Decolonizing the Sodomite: Queer Tropes of Sexuality in Colonial Andean Culture*. U of Texas P, 2005.

Hudson, Charles, Jr. *The Juan Pardo Expeditions: Exploration of the Carolinas and Tennessee, 1566–1568*. Smithsonian Institution Press, 1990.

———. *Knights of Spain, Warriors of the Sun: Hernando de Soto and the South's Ancient Chiefdoms*. U of Georgia P, 1997.

Hudson, Charles M., and Carmen Chaves-Tesser, editors. *The Forgotten Centuries: Indians and Europeans in the American South, 1521–1704*. U of Georgia P, 1994.

Hutcheon, Linda. *A Theory of Adaptation*. Routledge, 2013.

I Am Legend. Directed by Francis Lawrence, Warner Bros. Pictures / Village Roadshow Pictures / Weed Road Pictures, 2007.

Iglesia, Cristina. "Conquista y mito blanco." *Cautivas y misioneros: Mitos blancos de la conquista*, edited by Iglesia et al., Catálogos, 1987, pp. 11–88.

The Impossible. Directed by Juan Antonio Bayona, Apaches Entertainment / Telecinco Cinema, 2012.

"The Incredible Journey of Cabeza de Vaca, 1527–1536." *YouTube*, uploaded by History Time, 5 Sept. 2017, www.youtube.com/watch?v=P_ozbidkNZo.

Irala Solano, Ramón, and Roberto Quevedo. "Sentencia definitiva contra Alvar Núñez Cabeza de Vaca." *Historia Paraguaya*, vol. 46, 2006, pp. 365–82.

Jansen, Silke. "Spanish Anthropology under an Ecolinguistic View: The Antillean Society in the Early Sixteenth Century." *Language Ecology and Language Contact*, edited by Ralph Ludwig et al., Cambridge UP, 2019, pp. 147–76.

Jáuregui, Carlos A. "Cabeza de Vaca, Mala Cosa y las vicisitudes de la extrañeza." *Revista de Estudios Hispánicos*, vol. 48, no. 3, 2014, pp. 421–47.

———. *Canibalia: Canibalismo, calibanismo, antropofagia cultural y consumo en América Latina*. Iberoamericana/Vervuert, 2008.

———. *Espectros y conjuras: Asedios a la cuestión colonial*. Iberoamericana/Vervuert, 2020.

———. "Going Native, Going Home: Ethnographic Empathy and the Artifice of Return in Cabeza de Vaca's *Relación*." *Colonial Latin American Review*, vol. 25, no. 2, 2016, pp. 175–99.

Jáuregui, Carlos A., and David Solodkow. "Utopia, Biopolitics, and the Farming (of) Life in Bartolomé de las Casas." *Bartolomé de Las Casas, O. P. History, Philosophy, and Theology in the Age of European Expansion*, edited by David Orique and Rady Roldán-Figueroa, Brill, 2018, pp. 127–66.

Jáuregui, Carlos A., and Paola Uparela. "La vagina-ojo y otros monstruos ginecoescópicos." *Freakish Encounters*, special issue of *Hispanic Issues*, edited by Sara Muñoz-Muriana and Analola Santana, vol. 20, 2018, pp. 97–141.

Jones, Nicholas R. *Staging Habla de Negros: Radical Performances of the African Diaspora in Early Modern Spain*. Pennsylvania State UP, 2019.

Jordan, Mark D. *The Invention of Sodomy in Christian Theology*. U of Chicago P, 1997.

Juan-Navarro, Santiago. "Constructing Cultural Myths: Cabeza de Vaca in Contemporary Hispanic Criticism, Theatre, and Film." *A Twice-Told Tale: Reinventing the Encounter in Iberian/Iberian American Literature and Film*, edited by Juan-Navarro et al., U of Delaware P, 2001, pp. 67–79.

Klein, Herbert, and Ben Vinson. *African Slavery in Latin America and the Caribbean*. Oxford UP, 2007.

Knight, Vernon, Jr., editor. *The Search for Mabila*. U of Alabama P, 2009.

Kraniauskas, John. "Cabeza de Vaca." *Travesia*, vol. 1, no. 2, 1992, pp. 113–22.

Krieger, Alex D. *We Came Naked and Barefoot: The Journey of Cabeza de Vaca across North America*. Edited by Margery H. Krieger, U of Texas P, 2002. *ProQuest Ebook Central*, www.proquest.com/docview/2131431715.

Lafaye, Jacques. "Los 'milagros' de Alvar Núñez Cabeza de Vaca (1527–1536)." Glantz, *Notas*, pp. 17–35.

Lagmanovich, David. "Los *Naufragios* de Álvar Núñez como construcción narrativa." *Kentucky Romance Quarterly*, vol. 25, no. 1, 1978, pp. 23–37.

Lalami, Laila. *The Moor's Account*. Vintage Books, 2015.

Lang, Sabine. *Men as Women, Women as Men: Changing Gender in Native American Cultures*. U of Texas P, 1998.

Lansing, Richard. "Two Similes in Dante's *Commedia*: The Shipwrecked Swimmer and Elijah's Ascent." *Romance Philology*, vol. 28, no. 2, 1974, pp. 161–77.

Las Casas, Bartolomé de. *Apologética historia sumaria*. Universidad Nacional Autónoma de México, 1967.

———. *Historia de las Indias*. 3 vols. Ayacucho, 1986.

———. *The Only Way*. Edited by Helen Rand Parish, translated by Francis Sullivan, Paulist Press, 1992.

———. *A Short Account of the Destruction of the Indies*. Penguin Classics, 1999.

———. *Tratados*. Fondo de Cultura Económica, 1997. 2 vols.

Leal, Luis. "Mexican American Literature: A Historical Perspective." *Modern Chicano Writers: A Collection of Essays*, edited by Joseph Sommers and Tomás Ybarra-Frausto, Prentice-Hall, 1979, pp. 18–30.

Lee, Kun Jong. "Pauline Typology in Cabeza de Vaca's *Naufragios*." *Early American Literature*, vol. 34, no. 3, 1999, pp. 241–62.

Legg, James, et al. "The Stark Farm Enigma: Evidence of the Chicasa (Chickasha)-Soto Encounter in Mississippi?" Mathers, pp. 43–67.

Le Goff, Jacques. *La civilización del Occidente medieval*. Juventud, 1969.

———. "Lo maravilloso en el Occidente medieval." *Historia y literatura: Maravillas, magia y milagros en el Occidente medieval*, edited by Israel Álvarez Moctezuma and Daniel Gutiérrez Trápaga, Universidad Nacional Autónoma de México, 2015.

Leitch, Thomas. *The Oxford Handbook of Adaptation Studies*. Oxford UP, 2017.

Levi-Strauss, Claude. *The Savage Mind*. U of Chicago P, 1966.

Lewis, Robert. "Los *Naufragios* de Álvar Núñez: Historia y ficción." *Revista Iberoamericana*, vol. 48, no. 120, 1982, pp. 681–94.

Life of Pi. Directed by Ang Lee, Fox 2000 Pictures / Dune Entertainment, 2012.

Lima, Lázaro. *The Latino Body: Crisis Identities in American Literary and Cultural Memory*. New York UP, 2007.

Little, Keith. "Sixteenth-Century Glass Bead Chronology in Southeastern North America." *Southeastern Archaeology*, vol. 29, no. 1, 2010, pp. 222–32.

Lomelí, Francisco. "Po(l)etics of Reconstructing and/or Appropriating a Literary Past: The Regional Case Model." *Recovering the U.S. Hispanic Literary Heritage*, edited by Ramón Gutiérrez and Genaro Padilla, vol. 1, Arte Público Press, 1993, pp. 221–40.

Long, Haniel. *The Marvelous Adventures of Cabeza de Vaca*. Ballantine Books, 1973.

López de Hinojosos, Alonso. *Summa y recopilacion de cirugia, con un arte para sangrar, y examen de barberos*. Casa de Pedro Balli, 1595.

Lowe, Lisa. *Immigrant Acts*. Duke UP, 1996.

Marrinan, Rochelle, et al. "Prelude to de Soto: The Expedition of Pánfilo de Narváez." D. Thomas, pp. 71–82.

Marsh, Lexi Jamieson, and Ellen Currano. *The Bearded Lady Project: Challenging the Face of Science*. Columbia UP, 2020.

Marshall, Daniel, et al. Introduction. *Queering Archives: Historical Unravelings*, special issue of *Radical History Review*, edited by Marshall et al., vol. 120, 2014, pp. 1–11.

Martínez-Carrión, José Miguel, and Javier Puche-Gil. "The Evolution of Height in France and Spain, 1770–2000: Historiographic Background and New Evidence." *Dynamis*, vol. 31, no. 2, 2011, pp. 429–52.

Martínez–San Miguel, Yolanda. *From Lack to Excess: "Minor" Readings of Latin American Colonial Discourse*. Bucknell UP, 2008.

Martínez–San Miguel, Yolanda, and Santa Arias, editors. *The Routledge Hispanic Studies Companion to Colonial Latin America and the Caribbean, 1492–1898.* Routledge, 2021.

Mathers, Clay, editor. *Modeling Entradas: Sixteenth-Century Assemblages in North America.* U of Florida P, 2020.

Mathers, Clay, et al., editors. *Native and Spanish New Worlds: Sixteenth-Century Entradas in the American Southwest and Southeast.* U of Arizona P, 2013.

The Matrix. Written and directed by Lana and Lilly Wachowski, Warner Bros. Pictures, 1999.

Matthews, Colin. *The Great Journey.* NMC Recordings, 1997. CD.

Maura, Juan Francisco. *El gran burlador de América: Alvar Núñez Cabeza de Vaca.* Universidad de Valencia / Parmaseo-Lemir, 2008.

Mayers, Kathryn. "Of Third Spaces and (Re)Localization: Critique and Counterknowledge in Nicolas Echeverria's *Cabeza De Vaca*." *Confluencia*, vol. 24, no. 1, 2008, pp. 2–16.

Mazzotta, Giuseppe. *Dante, Poet of the Desert: History and Allegory in the Divine Comedy.* Princeton UP, 1979.

McAlister, Lyle. *Spain and Portugal in the New World, 1492–1700.* U of Minnesota P, 1984.

Melville, Herman. *Moby-Dick.* Harper and Brothers, 1851.

Menton, Seymour. *Latin America's New Historical Novel.* U of Texas P, 2011.

Mignolo, Walter. *The Darker Side of the Renaissance: Literacy, Territoriality, and Colonization.* U of Michigan P, 2003.

———. "La lengua, la letra, el territorio (o la crisis de los estudios literarios coloniales)." *Dispositio*, vol. 11, nos. 28–29, 1986, pp. 137–60.

Milanich, Jerald, and Susan Milbrath, editors. *First Encounters: Spanish Explorations in the Caribbean and the United States, 1492–1570.* U of Florida P, 1989.

Mitchell, Katharyne. "Celebrity Humanitarianism, Transnational Emotion and the Rise of Neoliberal Citizenship." *Global Networks*, vol. 16, no. 3, 2016, pp. 288–306.

Mitchem, Jeffrey. "Artifacts of Exploration: Archaeological Evidence from Florida." Milanich and Milbrath, pp. 99–109.

———. "Initial Spanish-Indian Contact in West Peninsular Florida: The Archaeological Evidence." D. Thomas, pp. 49–59.

Molloy, Sylvia. "Alteridad y reconocimiento en los 'Naufragios' de Alvar Núñez Cabeza de Vaca." *Nueva Revista de Filología Hispánica*, vol. 35, no. 2, 1987, pp. 425–50.

Montaigne, Michel de. *Des cannibales; Des coches (essais).* Hatier, 2019.

Montanari, Massimo. *Food Is Culture.* Columbia UP, 2004.

Moore, Jason. *Capitalism in the Web of Life: Ecology and the Accumulation of Capital.* Verso Books, 2015.

Morales Padrón, Francisco. *Teoría y leyes de la Conquista.* U de Sevilla, Secretariado de Publicaciones, 2008.

Morrás, Maria, and Antonio Rojas Castro, editors. *Humanidades digitales y literaturas hispánicas*. Special issue of *Ínsula: Revista de Letras y Ciencias Humanas*. No. 822, June 2015, www.insula.es/ver-revista/71693.

Narby, Jeremy, and Francis Huxley, editors. *Shamans through Time: Five Hundred Years on the Path to Knowledge*. Tarcher/Putnam, 2001.

"New Texas African American Monument." *Legislative Reference Library of Texas*, 14 Feb. 2017, lrl.texas.gov/whatsNew/client/index.cfm/2017/2/14/New-Texas-African-American-Monument.

Niza, Marcos de. *Descubrimiento de las siete ciudades por el P. Fr. Marcos de Niza*. Biblioteca Virtual Miguel de Cervantes, 2005, www.cervantesvirtual.com/obra-visor/descubrimiento-de-las-siete-ciudades-por-el-p-fr-marcos-de-niza--0/html/4b095958-ec1e-4033-9eeb-8563450eb3cf_2.html.

———. "Relation." Translated by Percy Baldwin. *The New Mexico Historical Review*, vol. 1, no. 2, 1926, pp. 193–223.

"North American Tribal Regions." *Tribal Directory*, 2018, tribaldirectory.com/north-american-tribal-regions.html.

Nussbaum, Martha. *Not for Profit: Why Democracy Needs the Humanities*. Princeton UP, 2010.

———. *Upheavals of Thought: The Intelligence of Emotions*. Cambridge UP, 2001.

Oldstone-Moore, Christopher. *Of Beards and Men: The Revealing History of Facial Hair*. U of Chicago P, 2016.

"The Original Americans." *Taste the Nation*, hosted by Padma Lakshmi, directed by Sarina Roma, season 1, episode 7, *Hulu*, 18 June 2020.

Ortega de Villar, Aniceto. *Guatimozin*. 1871. Biblioteca Nacional de Mexico, Mexico City. Manuscript.

Orwell, George. *1984*. Secker and Warburg, 1949.

Oviedo, José Miguel. *Historia de la Literatura Hispanoamericana I. De los orígenes a la Emancipación*. Alianza Editorial, 1995.

Oviedo y Valdés, Gonzalo Fernández de. *Historia general y natural de las Indias, islas y tierra firme del mar océano: Tomo segundo de la segunda parte, tercero de la obra*. Edited by José Amador de los Ríos, Real Academia de la Historia, 1853. Vol. 3 of *Historia general y natural de las Indias, islas y tierra firme del mar océano*, 5 vols.

———. "Joint Report." Translated by Catherine Johnston, *Digital Commons@ University of South Florida*, 2021, digitalcommons.usf.edu/early_visions_bucket/7.

———. *The Journey of the Vaca Party: The Account of the Narváez Expedition, 1528–1536*. Translated by Basil Hedrick and Carroll Riley, Southern Illinois University Museum, 1974.

———. *Sumario de la natural historia de las Indias*. Fondo de Cultura Económica, 1950.

Padilla, Ray. "Apuntes para la documentación de la cultura chicana." *El Grito*, vol. 5, no. 2, 1971, pp. 3–36.

Padrón, Ricardo. *Cartography, Literature, and Empire in Early Modern Spain*. U of Chicago P, 2004.

Pagden, Anthony. *The Burdens of Empire: 1539 to the Present*. Cambridge UP, 2015.

———. *The Fall of Natural Man: The American Indian and the Origins of Comparative Ethnology.* Cambridge UP, 1982.

Panger, Daniel. *Black Ulysses.* Ohio UP, 1982.

Paniagua-Pérez, Jesús. "Los mirabilia medievales y los conquistadores y exploradores de América." *Estudios Humanísticos Historia,* no. 7, 2008, pp. 139–59.

Pan y Agua, Juan Carlos. *Black Bride of Christ: Chicaba, an African Nun in Eighteenth-Century Spain.* Edited by Sue E. Houchins and Baltasar Fra Molinero, Vanderbilt UP, 2018.

Parish, Helen Rand. *Estebanico.* Viking Press, 1974.

Pasta, Carlo Enrico. *Atahualpa.* Universal, 2015. CD.

Pastor, Beatriz. *The Armature of Conquest: Spanish Accounts of the Discovery of America, 1492–1589.* Stanford UP, 1992.

———. *Discursos narrativos de la conquista: mitificación y emergencia.* Ediciones del Norte, 1988.

Pérez, Miguel. "Cabeza de Vaca's Journey: Gay Marriage's American History Started in Spanish." *HiddenHispanicHeritage.com,* 2014, www.hiddenhispanicheritage.com/44-cabeza-de-vacas-journey-8203gay-marriages-american-history-started-in-spanish.html.

Phillips, William, Jr. *Slavery in Medieval and Early Modern Iberia.* U of Pennsylvania P, 2013.

Popol Vuh: The Mayan Book of the Dawn of Life. Translated by Dennis Tedlock, rev. ed., Simon and Schuster, 1996.

Posse, Abel. *Daimón.* Argos, 1978.

———. *El largo atardecer del caminante.* Emecé, 1992.

———. *Los perros del paraíso.* Argos Vergara, 1983.

Pranzetti, Luisa. "El naufragio como metáfora." Glantz, *Notas,* pp. 57–73.

Pratesi, Gwen. "Indigenous Foods of the Southwest—Original Native American Cuisine." *Pratesi Living,* 31 Dec. 2013, www.pratesiliving.com/indigenous-foods-of-the-southwest-original-native-american-cuisine/.

Pupo-Walker, Enrique. "Los *Naufragios* de A. Núñez Cabeza de Vaca: Notas sobre la relevancia antropológica del texto." *Revista de Indias,* vol. 47, no. 181, 1987, pp. 755–66.

———. "Notas para la caracterización de un texto seminal: Los *Naufragios* de Álvar Núñez Cabeza de Vaca." *Nueva Revista de Filología Hispánica,* vol. 38, no. 1, 1990, pp. 163–96.

———. "Pesquisas para una nueva lectura de los *Naufragios,* de Álvar Núñez Cabeza de Vaca." *Revista Iberoamericana,* vol. 53, no. 140, 1987, pp. 517–39.

———. "Sobre el legado retórico en los *Naufragios* de Álvar Núñez Cabeza de Vaca." *Revista de Estudios Hispánicos,* no. 19, 1992, pp. 179–88.

Quint, David. *Epic and Empire: Politics and Generic Form from Virgil to Milton.* Princeton UP, 1993.

Quintilian. *The* Institutio oratoria *of Quintilian.* Translated by H. E. Butler, vol. 3, Harvard UP, 1976.

Rabasa, José. *Writing Violence on the Northern Frontier: The Historiography of Sixteenth-Century New Mexico and Florida and the Legacy of Conquest*. Duke UP, 2000.

Radin, Paul. *The Trickster: A Study in American Indian Mythology*. 1956. Schocken Books, 1972.

Rama, Ángel. *La ciudad letrada*. Arca, 1998.

Ramenofsky, Ann, and Patricia Galloway. "Disease and the Soto Entrada." *The Hernando de Soto Expedition: History, Historiography, and "Discovery" in the Southeast*, edited by Patricia Galloway, U of Nebraska P, 1997, pp. 259–79.

Raphael. *The Deposition*. 1507. *Borghese Gallery*, 2024, borghese.gallery/paintings/deposition-by-raphael.html.

Reff, Daniel. "Text and Context: Cures, Miracles, and Fear in the *Relación* of Álvar Núñez Cabeza de Vaca." *Journal of the Southwest*, vol. 38, no. 2, 1996, pp. 115–38.

Restall, Matthew, editor. *Beyond Black and Red: African-Native Relations in Colonial Latin America*. U of New Mexico P, 2005.

———. "Black Conquistadors: Armed Africans in Early Spanish America." *The Americas*, vol. 57, no. 2, Oct. 2000, pp. 171–205.

———. *Seven Myths of the Spanish Conquest*. Oxford UP, 2003.

Restall, Matthew, and Felipe Fernández-Armesto. *The Conquistadors: A Very Short Introduction*. Oxford UP, 2012.

Restall, Matthew, and Kris Lane. *Latin America in Colonial Times*. Cambridge UP, 2011.

Restrepo, Luis F. "Primitive Bodies in Latin American Cinema: Nicolás Echevarría's *Cabeza de Vaca*." *Primitivism and Identity in Latin America: Essays on Art, Literature, and Culture*, edited by Eric Camayd-Freixas and José Eduardo González, U of Arizona P, 2000, pp. 189–208.

Ricœur, Paul. *Freud and Philosophy: An Essay on Interpretation*. Yale UP, 1970.

———. *The Symbolism of Evil*. Translated by Emerson Buchanan, Beacon Press, 1969.

Rodning, Christopher. "From the Coast to the Mountains: Marine Shell Artifacts at Cherokee Towns in the Southern Appalachians." Boudreaux et al., *Contact*, pp. 156–72.

Rodríguez Carrión, José. *Apuntes para una biografía del jerezano Alvar Núñez Cabeza de Vaca: Primer hombre blanco en Norteamérica*. Centro de Estudios Históricos Jerezanos, 1985.

Rojinsky, David. "Found in Translation: Writing beyond Hybridity in Alvar Núñez Cabeza de Vaca's *Naufragios*." *Hofstra Hispanic Review*, vol. 3, no. 1, 2006, pp. 11–25.

Roscoe, Will. *Changing Ones: Third and Fourth Genders in Native North America*. St. Martin's Griffin, 2000.

"Route of Cabeza de Vaca." *Portal of Texas History*, 16 Apr. 2024, texashistory.unt.edu/ark:/67531/metapth492978/m1/1/.

Sabo, George, et al. *First Encounters: Native Americans and Europeans in the Mississippi Valley*. Archeological Survey, 2000.

Sahagún, Bernardino de. *Historia general de las cosas de Nueva España*. 1569–82. Edited by Ángel María Garibay K., Porrúa, 1979.

Saldarriaga, Gregorio. "Taste and Taxonomy of Native Food in Hispanic America: 1492–1640." *Food, Texts, and Cultures in Latin America and Spain*, edited by Rafael Climent-Espino and Ana M. Gómez-Bravo, Vanderbilt UP, 2020, pp. 76–98.

Salmón, Enrique. *Eating the Landscape: American Indian Stories of Food, Identity, and Resilience*. U of Arizona P, 2012.

Sanchis Sinisterra, José. *Alvar Núñez Cabeza de Vaca o la herida del otro. Trilogía americana*, by Sanchis Sinisterra, edited by Virtudes Serrano, Cátedra, 1996, pp. 91–176.

San Miguel, Guadalupe. "Actors Not Victims: Chicanas/os in the Struggle for Educational Equality." *Chicanas/Chicanos at the Crossroads: Social, Economic, and Political Change*, edited by David Maciel and Isidro D. Ortiz, U of Arizona P, 1996, 159–80.

Schmidl, Ulrich. *The Conquest of the River Plate, 1535–1555*. 1567. Hakluyt Society, 1891.

———. *Derrotero y viaje a España y las Indias*. Edited by Loreley El Jaber, Editorial de la Universidad Nacional de Entre Rios, 2016.

Schwartz, John. "The Great Food Migration: Pasta without Tomato Sauce?" *Newsweek*, vol. 118, no. 1, 1991, pp. 58–62.

Serrano, Andrés. *Cabeza de Vaca*. 1984. New Museum, archive.newmuseum.org/images/3728.

Serrano y Sanz, Manuel, editor. *Colección de libros y documentos referentes a la historia de América*. Librería General de Victoriano Suárez, 1906. 20 vols.

Sheridan, Guillermo. *Cabeza de Vaca: Inspirada libremente en el libro* Naufragios, *de Álvar Núñez Cabeza de Vaca*. Ediciones El Milagro, 1994.

Shreve, Nathan K., et al. "An Arc of Interaction, a Flow of People, and Emergent Identity: Early Contact Period Archaeology and Early European Interactions in the Middle Nolichucky Valley of Upper East Tennessee." Boudreaux et al., *Contact*, pp. 140–55.

Sigal, Peter. *Infamous Desire: Male Homosexuality in Colonial Latin America*. U of Chicago P, 2003.

Silva, Alan. "Conquest, Conversion, and the Hybrid Self in Cabeza de Vaca's *Relación*." *Post Identity*, vol. 2, no. 1, winter 1999, pp. 123–46.

Silva, Jennifer Mara de, et al., editors. *Early Modern Classroom*. Special issue of *The Sixteenth-Century Journal*. Vol. 51, supp. 1, 2020, www.journals.uchicago.edu/toc/scj/2020/51/S1.

Slater, Sandra. "'Nought but Women': Constructions of Masculinities and Modes of Emasculation in the New Word." Slater and Yarbrough, pp. 30–53.

Slater, Sandra, and Fay A. Yarbrough, editors. *Gender and Sexuality in Indigenous North America, 1400–1850*. U of South Carolina P, 2011.

Smith, Buckingham. *Relation of Alvar Núñez Cabeça de Vaca*. Printed by J. Munsell for H. C. Murphy, 1971.

Smith, Marvin. "Chronology from Glass Beads: The Spanish Period in the Southeast, 1513–1670." *Proceedings of the 1982 Glass Trade Bead Conference*, Rochester Museum and Science Center, 1983. Research Records 16.

———. "European Materials from the King Site." *Southeastern Archaeological Conference Bulletin*, no. 18, 1975, pp. 63–66.

Smith, Marvin, and Mary Elizabeth Good. *Early Sixteenth Century Glass Beads in the Spanish Colonial Trade*. Cottonlandia Museum Publications, 1982.

Smith, Marvin, and David J. Hally. "The Acquisition of Sixteenth-Century European Objects by Native Americans in the Southeastern United States." *Modeling Entradas: Sixteenth-Century Assemblages in North America*, edited by Clay Mathers, U of Florida P, 2020, pp. 203–46.

Spitta, Silvia. *Between Two Waters: Narratives of Transculturation in Latin America*. Rice UP, 1995.

———. "Chamanismo y cristiandad: Una lectura de la lógica intercultural de los *Naufragios* de Cabeza de Vaca." *Revista de Crítica Literaria Latinoamericana*, vol. 19, no. 38, 1993, pp. 317–30.

Star Wars. Directed by George Lucas, Lucasfilm Ltd., 1977.

Strang, Cameron. *Frontiers of Science: Imperialism and Natural Knowledge in the Gulf South Borderlands, 1500–1850*. Omohundro Institute / U of North Carolina P, 2018.

Streit, Lizzie. "Prickly Pear: Nutrition, Benefits, Recipes, and More." *Healthline*, 25 Aug. 2021, www.healthline.com/nutrition/prickly-pear-benefits#benefits.

Surviving Columbus. 1992. Directed by Diana Reyna, Public Broadcasting Service, 1 Aug. 2020.

Swanton, John, editor. *Final Report of the United States de Soto Expedition Commission*. 1937. Smithsonian Institution Press, 1985.

Tanner, Marie. *The Last Descendant of Aeneas: The Hapsburgs and the Mythic Image of the Emperor*. Yale UP, 1993.

Tats Cru. *Estevanico*. *Flickr*, uploaded by tatscruinc, 2 June 2013, www.flickr.com/photos/tatscru/8924195209.

Taussig, Michael. *Shamanism, Colonialism, and the Wild Man: A Study in Terror and Healing*. U of Chicago P, 1987.

Terminator. Directed by James Cameron, Hemdale Film Corporation, 1984.

Thomas, David Hurst, editor. *Archaeological and Historical Perspectives on the Spanish Borderlands East*. Smithsonian Institution Press, 1990. Vol. 2 of *Columbian Consequences*.

Thomas, Hugh. "The Rivers Plate and Paraguay." *World without End: Spain, Philip II, and the First Global Empire*. Random House, 2015, pp. 165–76.

Thompson, David. *Dante's Epic Journey*. Johns Hopkins UP, 1974.

Thompson, Norma. *Ship of State: Statecraft and Politics from Ancient Greece to Democratic America*. Yale UP, 2001.

Titanic. Directed by James Cameron, Paramount Pictures / 20th Century Fox / Lightstorm Entertainment, 1997.

Todorov, Tzvetan. *The Conquest of America: The Question of the Other.* U of Oklahoma P, 1999.

———. *The Fantastic: A Structural Approach to a Literary Genre.* Cornell UP, 1975.

Torres Cendales, Leidy Jazmín. "Polvo y cenizas: Bestialidad y transgresión sexual en Antioquia colonial." *Microhistorias de la Transgresión,* edited by Max Sebastián Hering Torres and Nelson A. Rojas, U del Rosario / U Cooperativa de Colombia / U Nacional de Colombia, 2015, pp. 45–84.

Tortorici, Zeb, et al., editors. *Ethnopornography: Sexuality, Colonialism, and Archival Knowledge.* Duke UP, 2020.

"2018 Final Projects." *Remaking Monsters and Heroines,* U of Arkansas, 2024, wordpressua.uark.edu/monstersandheroines-archive/2018-final-projects/.

Tyler, Steven. "Post-modern Ethnography: From Document of the Occult to Occult Document." *Writing Culture,* edited by James Clifford and George Marcus, U California P, 1986, 122–40.

Uparela, Paola. "Guaman Poma y la güergüenza colonial." *Revista de Estudios de Género y Sexualidades / Journal of Gender and Sexuality Studies,* vol. 44, no. 2, 2018, pp. 17–36.

———. *Invaginaciones coloniales: Mirada, genitalidad y (de)generación en la modernidad temprana.* Iberoamericana/Vervuert, 2024.

———. "'Multiplicarse ha la tierra de gente y de fruto': Gender and Re-production in Las Casas's and Guaman Poma's Biopolitical Projects (1516, 1615)." *The Transatlantic Las Casas: Historical Trajectories, Indigenous Cultures, Scholastic Thought, and Reception in History,* edited by David T. Orique and Rady Roldán-Figueroa, Brill, 2022, pp. 35–60.

———. "'Yo llana estoy' o el despliegue de una virginidad queer." *Revista de Estudios de Género y Sexualidades / Journal of Gender and Sexuality Studies,* vol. 48, no. 1, 2022, p. 53–74.

Uparela, Paola, and Carlos Jáuregui. "The Vagina and the Eye of Power (Essay on Genitalia and Visual Sovereignty)." *H-ART,* vol. 3, 2018, pp. 79–114.

Valdez, Luis, and Stan Steiner, editors. *Aztlán: An Anthology of Mexican American Literature.* Vintage Books, 1972.

Vargas, Claret. "'De muchas y muy bárbaras naciones con quien conversé y viví': Alvar Núñez Cabeza de Vaca's *Naufragios* as War Tactics Manual." *Hispanic Review,* vol. 75, no. 1, 2007, pp. 1–22.

Vas Mingo, Milagros del. *Las capitulaciones de Indias en el siglo XVI.* Instituto de Cooperación Iberoamericano, 1986.

Venkat Narayan, K. M. "Diabetes Mellitus in Native Americans: The Problem and Its Implications." *Changing Numbers, Changing Needs: American Indian Demography and Public Health,* edited by Gary D. Sandefur et al., National Academies Press, 1996, pp. 262–88. *National Library of Medicine,* www.ncbi.nlm.nih.gov/books/NBK233089/.

Verdesio, Gustavo. "Cabeza de Vaca: Una visión paródica de la épica colonial." *Nuevo Texto Crítico,* vol. 10, no. 1, 1997, pp. 195–204.

Verne, Jules. *Vingt mille lieues sous les mers.* Pierre-Jules Hetzel, 1869–70.

Villagrá, Gaspar Pérez de. *Historia de La Nueva México*. 1610. U of New Mexico P, 1992.

Vinson, Ben, and Greg Graves III. "The Black Experience in Colonial Latin America." *Oxford Bibliographies: Latin American Studies*, 26 Apr. 2018, https://www.doi.org/10.1093/OBO/9780199766581-0038.

Vivaldi, Antonio. *Motezuma*. Archiv Produktion, 2006.

Vives, Juan Luis. *De anima et vita: El alma y la vida*. Ajuntament de València, 1992.

Wade, Mariah. "Go-Between: The Roles of Native American Women and Alvar Núñez Cabeza de Vaca in Southern Texas in the Sixteenth Century." *The Journal of American Folklore*, vol. 112, no. 445, 1999, pp. 332–42.

Weddle, Robert. *The Gulf of Mexico in North American Discovery, 1500–1685*. Texas A&M UP, 1985.

Weyden, Rogier van der. *El descendimiento*. Before 1443. *Museo del Prado*, www.museodelprado.es/coleccion/obra-de-arte/el-descendimiento/856d822a-dd22-4425-bebd-920a1d416aa7?searchid=a8a5da82-bd63-802a-a4ee-0e955e847f5d.

"What Is Intangible Cultural Heritage?" *UNESCO*, ich.unesco.org/en/what-is-intangible-heritage-00003.

White, Hayden. *The Content of the Form: Narrative Discourse and Historical Representation*. Johns Hopkins UP, 1987.

———. *Tropics of Discourse: Essays in Critical Criticism*. Johns Hopkins UP, 1978.

Winship, George Parker, editor. *Annual Report of the Bureau of Ethnology to the Secretary of the Smithsonian Institution*. Smithsonian Institution, 1892–93.

Wood, Michael. *Conquistadors*. U of California P, 2000.

Worth, John. "Spanish Florida and the Southeastern Indians, 1513–1650." Boudreaux et al., *Contact*, pp. 102–13.

Wright, Elizabeth. *The Epic of Juan Latino: Dilemmas of Race and Religion in Renaissance Spain*. U of Toronto P, 2016.

Yang, Jeffrey. "Estevanico." *Poetry*, July 2017, www.poetryfoundation.org/poetrymagazine/poems/142851/estevanico.

Zavala, Silvio. *Orígenes de la colonización en el Río de la Plata*. Editorial de El Colegio Nacional, 1978, pp. 25–116.